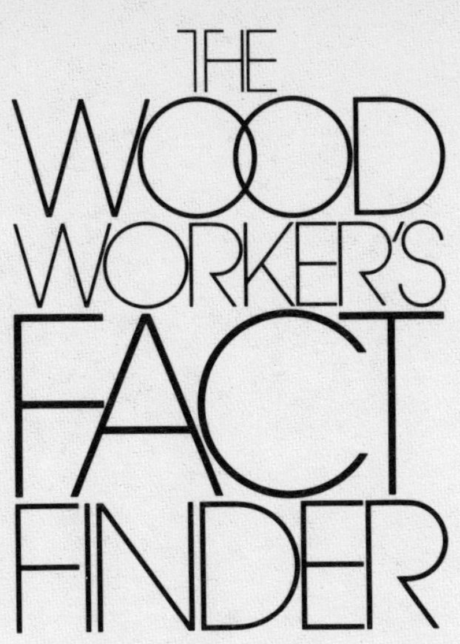

The essential reference for all who work in wood

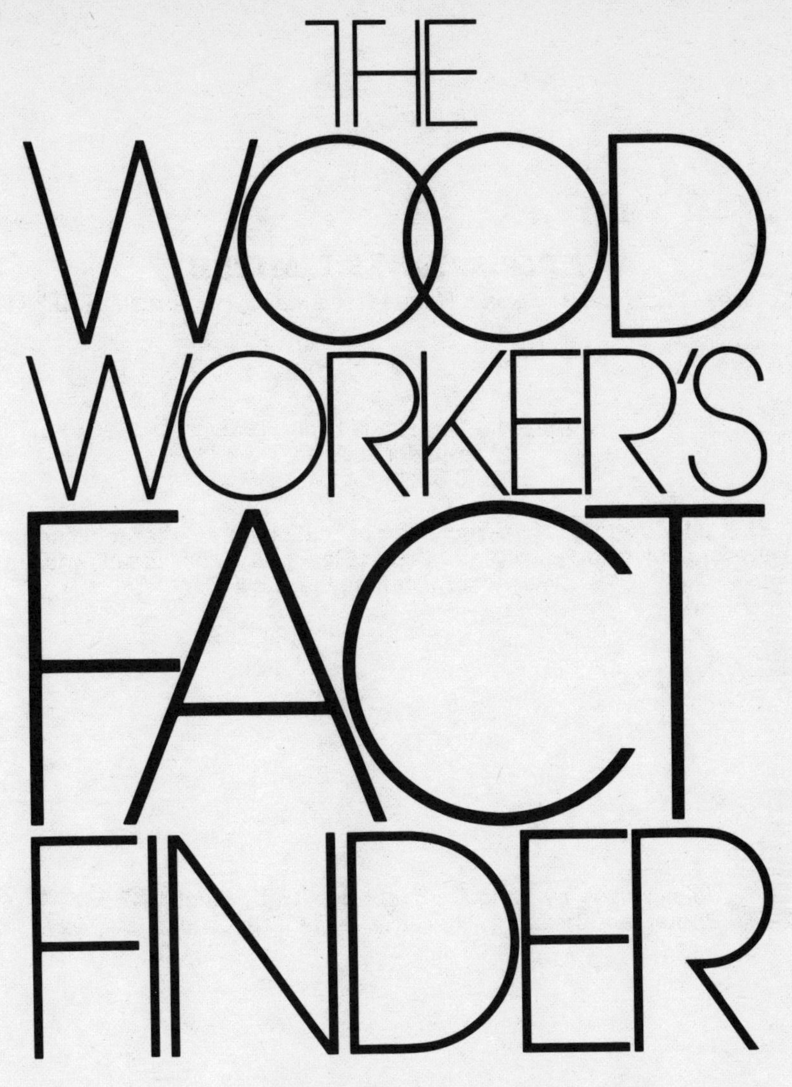

The essential reference for all who work in wood

VIC TAYLOR

ARGUS BOOKS

ARGUS BOOKS LIMITED
Wolsey House, Wolsey Road, Hemel Hempstead, Hertfordshire HP2 4SS

First published by Argus Books 1988

ISBN 0 85242 935 5

Photosetting by En to En, Tunbridge Wells, Kent, TN2 3XD
Printed and bound by Richard Clay Ltd, Chichester, Sussex

CONTENTS

INTRODUCTION

DESPITE the many woodworking books on sale today, we are confident that this one will prove particularly valuable to amateur and professional woodworkers alike.

Why? – because it contains facts and figures covering all the main subjects of interest presented in a practical, concise and easy-to-find way – and in so doing, it will save you consulting perhaps a dozen books to find the information you want.

The subjects have been carefully selected to help the modern woodworker, and the emphasis is away from hand methods and tools in favour of machine and power tool techniques. Similarly, contemporary materials such as man-made boards and the fittings designed to be used with them have received exhaustive treatment and should be immensely helpful. Some of the text has been re-printed from various numbers of 'Woodworker' magazine, but most of it has been researched and compiled specially for this book.

To give you an idea of the range of the contents, here is a list of the main chapters: how to select timber and recognise its defects; types of mouldings available; specifications of man-made boards; machine speeds and data with particular attention paid to routers; workshop geometry and basic furniture design; modern methods of polishing; upholstering, including the use of plastic foam, resilient rubber webbing and different forms of springing; details of today's adhesives; how to sharpen all kinds of tools; and up-to-date methods of joining timber parts.

It's definitely a book for the workshop bookshelf of the serious woodworker, and one which will repay its cost time and time again.

CHAPTER ONE

Choosing, measuring and buying timber

CHOOSING, measuring, and buying timber is an area of woodworking which is fraught with problems for beginners and experts alike. There are so many factors involved, such as seasoning, strength, ease of working and polishing and possible defects, that the whole procedure can become a massive headache. The information in this section will enable you to avoid the pitfalls.

Classification
Timber is divided into two classes, hardwoods and softwoods. Hardwoods come from deciduous, broad-leaved trees which, in temperate climates, shed their leaves in winter. More scientifically, hardwoods are porous in that they have open cells (as distinct from self-contained cells) which carry moisture throughout the tree; the cells are therefore moisture-conducting rather than moisture-absorbing. The term 'hard' has no bearing on the actual hardness of the wood; thus, obeche is softer than most softwoods but is nevertheless classed as hardwood.

Softwoods come from coniferous (cone-bearing) trees with needle-pointed leaves. They are non-porous woods, in that the cells are not open-ended as in hardwoods, and the sap passes from cell to cell through fragile party walls.

Methods of conversion
The way in which the log (the tree trunk with all branches cut off and the ends sawn square) is sawn is determined by (a) the need to obtain as much sawn timber as possible and (b), in the case of hardwoods, the further requirement that the sawn planks (or 'boards') should exhibit a specified type of grain pattern.

Dealing with softwoods first, Fig 1.1 shows the principal forms into which they are converted and Fig 1.2 gives the main types of machined timbers and mouldings.

Hardwood conversion is more complicated. Fig 1.3 shows how a log would be converted if the grain pattern is immaterial, as in the case of beech which is never used in large widths but for rails, legs etc. The plank shown is

Fig 1.1

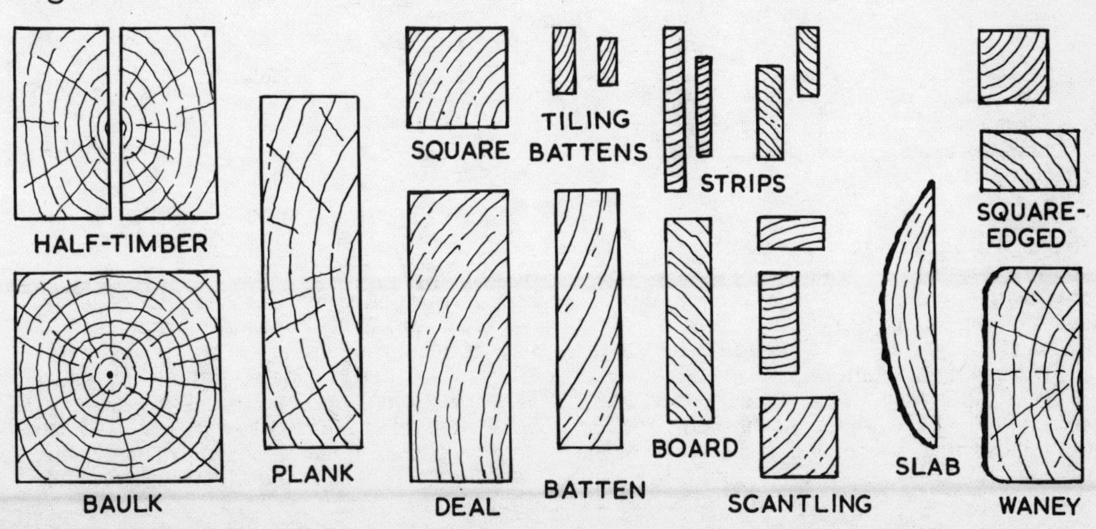

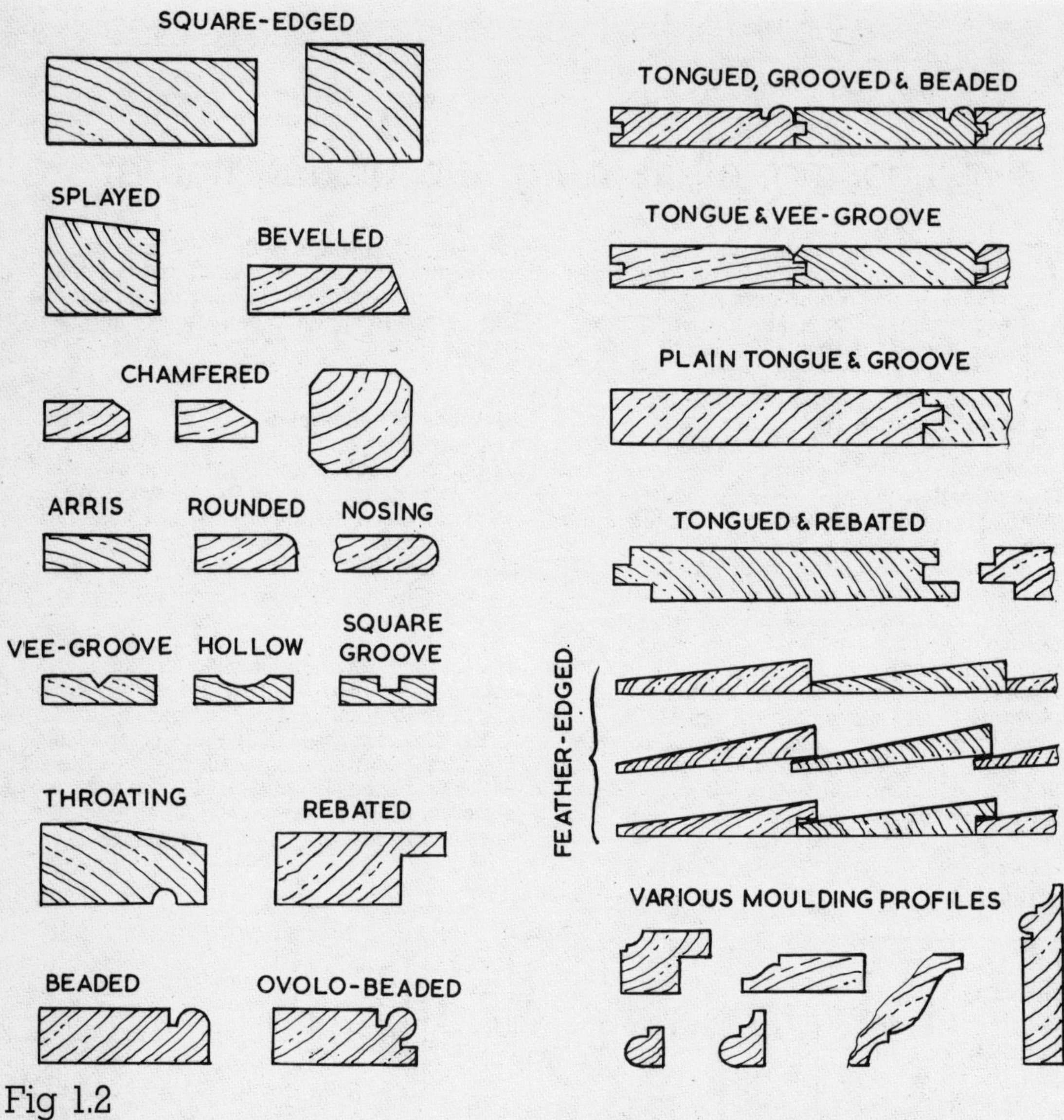

Fig 1.2

75mm (3in) thick in all examples, and (A) shows it cut into five 12mm (½in) boards; (B) cut down the centre to form two pieces; (C) cut into four 16mm (⅝in) or (not shown) three 22mm (⅞in) boards; and (D) cut into two, and (E) cut into thick quartering.

Some other ways to convert hardwood are shown in Fig 1.4, where (A) is 'through-and-through' sawing, also called 'slash sawn'; (B) is billet-sawn; (C) plain sawn; (D) modern quarter-sawn; and (E) true quarter-sawn. The way in which the log is cut has a marked effect on the grain pattern of the resulting boards, depending on whether it is tangential (Fig 1.5A) or radial (Fig 1.5B). The point is further developed in Fig 1.6, where the tangential cut (A) yields no figure; (B), which is half tangential and half radial, reveals a small amount of figure; while (C) and (D) are both parallel with the medullary rays and are therefore both radial cuts which give the full figure.

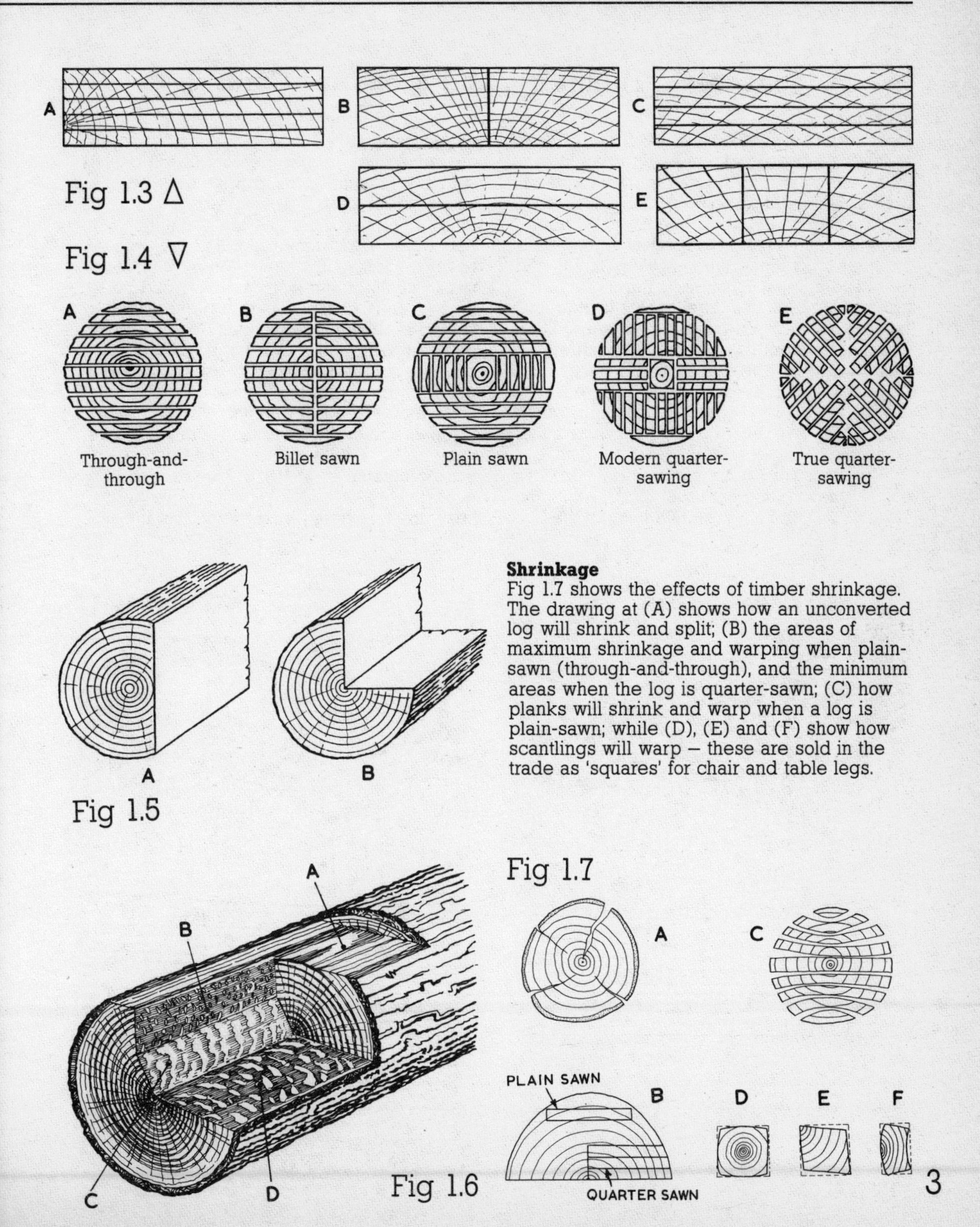

Shrinkage

Fig 1.7 shows the effects of timber shrinkage. The drawing at (A) shows how an unconverted log will shrink and split; (B) the areas of maximum shrinkage and warping when plain-sawn (through-and-through), and the minimum areas when the log is quarter-sawn; (C) how planks will shrink and warp when a log is plain-sawn; while (D), (E) and (F) show how scantlings will warp – these are sold in the trade as 'squares' for chair and table legs.

Seasoning, Humidity, and Moisture Control

Seasoning

Most, if not all, shrinking and warping problems can be overcome by correct storage in the open air or by a programme of kiln-drying. The latter is, however, an industrial process and so is outside the scope of this book. Fig 1.8 (A) and (B) show two good methods of stacking. The lowest plank should be raised at least 150mm (6in) from the ground. At (A), this is effected by using timber bearers, while in (B) piles of bricks are used. The latter method is preferable as timber bearers can be affected by timber pests if left *in situ* for several years. In any case, it is always advisable to spray around them with a proprietary insecticide every year during the summer.

The skids (or sticks) are important. In section they should be about 25mm by 19mm (1in by ¾in) and long enough to span the width of the widest board with 25mm (1in) or so protruding at each side. They must all be the same thickness or the boards will bend as shown at (D); they should preferably be of the same timber as that being stacked so that the effect of any staining due to the timber becoming wet is minimised; and they should never be softwood which often exudes resin in strong sunlight and will stain the wood badly. Illustration (C) emphasises that the skids should be placed above each other to avoid distorted boards. A covering of corrugated iron or waste timber to keep off the rain is also a good idea – a plastic sheet is not, as it will tend to create condensation.

The ends of the boards are the parts most vulnerable to splitting. To prevent this, they can be cleated as at (E), or coated with paraffin wax, or painted. All three methods keep the rain from being driven into the end grain.

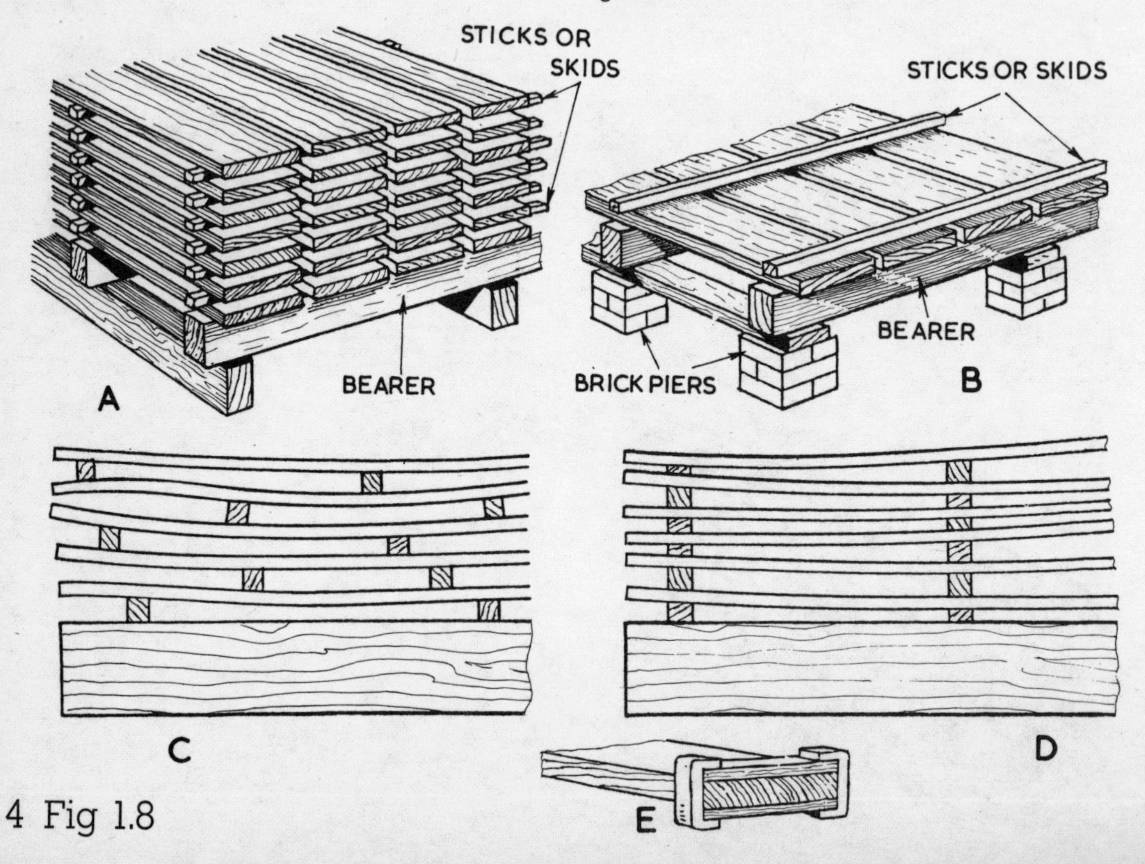

 Fig 1.8

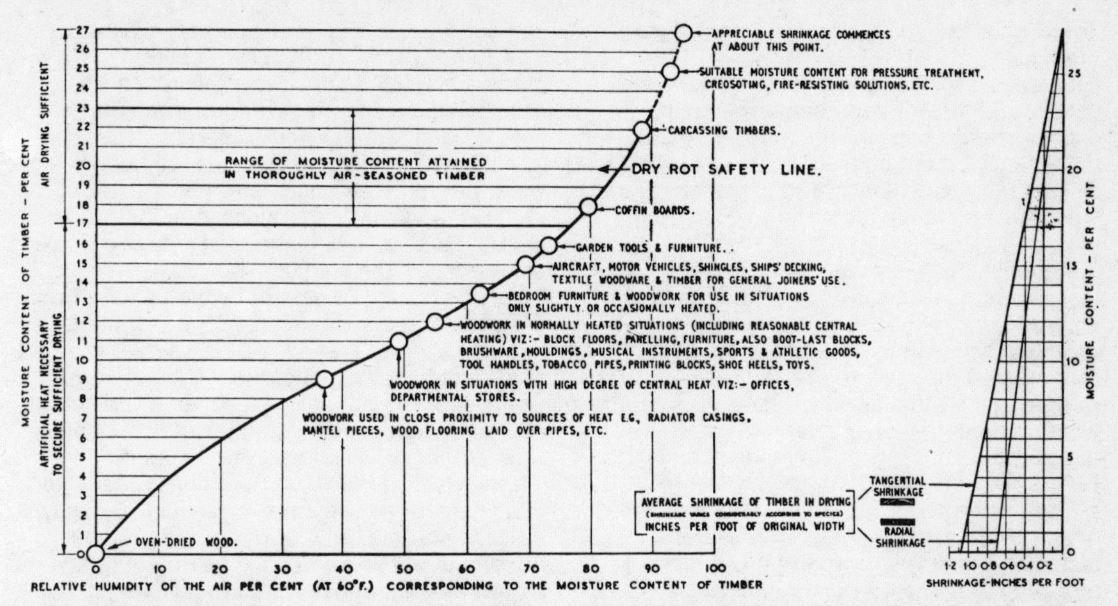

The moisture content of timber for building purposes ranges from about 8 per cent for joinery such as panelling and skirting boards near to radiators and hot pipes, to about 22 per cent for rough carpentry such as roofing timbers which can dry fairly rapidly after fixing.

The chart, above, prepared by the Forest Products Research Laboratory and reproduced by kind permission of the Controller of Her Majesty's Stationery Office shows typical values for moisture content of timber for various purposes. The figures for different species vary, and the chart shows only average values.

Fig 1.9

Moisture content

This must be correct for any timber you are using in relation to its final situation. The optimum moisture contents for different environments are shown in the chart in Fig 1.9 and this can be supplemented by the following recommended *maximum* moisture contents for building and constructional woodwork.

External

Doors and windows	12 to 18
Curtain walling, panel walling, weatherboarding, wall sheathing, shingles, roof sheathing	17 to 20

Internal flooring

Intermittent heating	12 to 15
Continuous heating	9 to 11
Underfloor heating	6 to 10

Wall and ceiling linings

Intermittent heating	12 to 15
Continuous heating	10 to 12

Doors

Intermittent heating	12 to 15
Continuous heating	10 to 12

Joinery

Intermittent heating	12 to 14
Continuous heating	10 to 12

RELATIVE HUMIDITY AND ESTIMATED MOISTURE CONTENT OF TIMBER WHEN MEASURED BY A HUMIDITY METER

EMC for wood at low and high temperatures

RH%	EMC% at 40 to 60 deg F	EMC% at 65 to 80 deg F
76	15.2	14.9 – 14.6
70	13.4	13.0 – 12.8
66	12.6	12.0
60	11.3	11.0 – 10.7
56	10.5	10.1
50	9.4	9.2 – 9.0
46	8.8	8.6 – 8.3
40	7.8	7.6 – 7.4
36	7.3	7.1 – 6.9
30	6.3	6.0

Recommended RH is one of 50% averaged over several weeks.

Testing for moisture content: oven-drying method

1 Select a board or plank (or several) which is considered to be a representative sample.

2 Because the ends of the board may be drier than other parts in its length, cut away the first 230mm (9in) to 305mm (12in) of the board and then cut the sample for testing which need only be 10mm (3/8in) to 12mm (1/2in) in length in the direction of the grain. If of greater length than 12mm (1/2in) the wood will merely take longer to dry.

3 Scrape away all loose sawdust and whiskers of wood and then weigh the sample, preferably on a chemical balance using metric weights which give more sensitive and accurate results. This weight is known as the Wet Weight or Initial Weight.

4 Then place the sample in a well-ventilated drying oven of which there are several kinds, including electric and water-jacketed types, and subject it to a constant temperature of 100 deg C (212 deg F). The aim is to drive all the moisture from the wood by heating it without reducing the weight of the wood itself; that is, without driving off gases or burning the wood.

The above test for moisture content can be carried out with fair accuracy using an ordinary domestic electric or gas cooking oven set to a temperature not exceeding 100deg C (212 deg F), and kitchen scales. The sample of wood needs to be much larger – say 0.22kg (1/2lb) – in weight and, because of the increased size, it will take longer to dry completely, possibly many hours.

5 After a period of time, take the sample from the oven and allow it to cool for a few minutes in a dessicator where it will be unable to absorb atmospheric moisture. Then quickly weigh it again, note the weight, and replace it in the drying oven for a further period of time. Repeat this procedure several times if necessary. When two or more consecutive and identical weight readings are obtained it may be assumed that all the moisture has been driven out of the wood. This last reading is known as the Dry Weight or Final Weight.

To calculate the percentage of the dry weight, multiply the weight of moisture lost by 100, and divide the result by the dry weight.

Timber Measurement, Dimensions, and Terms

Timber measurement

The trade sizes of hardwoods, softwoods, and boards are shown in the chart in Fig 1.10: the tinted area in the softwood section shows the sizes available.

Nominal and finished sizes

It is important to understand the difference between the two, as it can radically affect the price when you buy timber. Nominal sizes are those to which the timber is cut at the sawmill, while finished (or machined) sizes are those which result after the timber has been re-sawn and planed. Thus a piece which measures, say 305mm (12in) wide by 25mm (1in) thick in the nominal sizes, will be reduced to about 300mm (11 13/16in) by 22mm (7/8in bare) as finished sizes, but will still be referred to as 305mm by 25mm nominal (12in by 1in). Length does not enter into the matter.

It follows, then, that if you present a cutting list to a timber supplier which calls for 25mm (1in) finished thickness, he will have to prepare it from 29mm or 32mm (1 1/8in or 1 1/4in) stuff, which will mean wasted timber for which you will have to pay. Bear this particularly in mind when buying softwoods which have been planed all round (PAR), as, for instance, a strip that is nominally 50mm by 25mm (2in by 1in) will be only about 45mm by 20mm (1 3/4in by 3/4in).

Softwoods

These are measured by the 'metre-run', that is, at the price charged for a length of one metre; the price varies according to the sizes of the cross-section. Thus, the metre-run price of a piece which is 50mm by 25mm nominal (2in by 1in) will be about half the price of a piece 100mm by 50mm nominal (4in by 2in).

Hardwoods

These are measured according to the cubic content and, in metric terms, this means measuring the piece and expressing all its dimensions in centimetres; when the dimensions (length, width, and thickness) are multiplied by each other the result is the cubic

Hardwood

Length from 1.8m rising by 100mm increments
Width from 150mm rising by 10mm or 25mm increments
Thicknesses: 19mm
25mm
32mm
38mm
50mm
63mm
75mm
100mm
125mm
thereafter by 25mm increments

Softwood

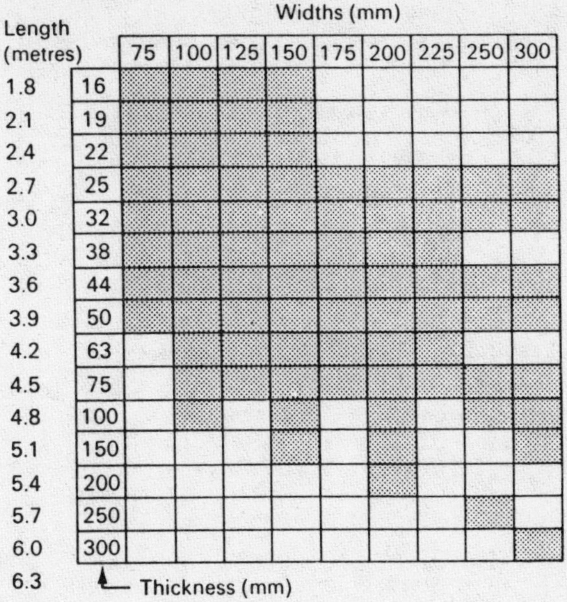

Length (metres): 1.8, 2.1, 2.4, 2.7, 3.0, 3.3, 3.6, 3.9, 4.2, 4.5, 4.8, 5.1, 5.4, 5.7, 6.0, 6.3

Thickness (mm) \ Widths (mm)	75	100	125	150	175	200	225	250	300
16	■	■	■	■					
19	■	■	■	■					
22	■	■	■	■					
25	■	■	■	■	■	■	■	■	■
32	■	■	■	■	■	■	■	■	■
38	■	■	■	■	■	■	■		
44	■	■	■	■	■	■	■	■	■
50	■	■	■	■	■	■	■	■	■
63		■	■	■	■	■	■		
75		■	■	■	■	■	■	■	■
100		■		■		■		■	■
150				■		■			■
200						■			
250								■	
300									■

Boards

Face sizes (mm)	Thickness (mm)
915	3.2
1220	5.0
1525	6.5
1830	8.0
2135	9.5
2440	12.5
2745	16.0
3050	19.0
3660	22.0
	25.5
	32.0
	35.0
	38.0
	41.0
	44.5
	47.5

Fig 1.10

content in 'centisteres'. However, as a centimetre is comparatively small (less than half an inch), the figures tend to become astronomical, and the decimetre (10cm) is sometimes used instead. The following may be of help:

10 centisteres equal 1 decistere, which equals 3.5317 cubic feet; and
10 decisteres equal 1 stere which equals 35.3170 cubic feet

However, many hardwood timber suppliers still use the imperial measurements of inches, feet, and cubic feet. The vital point to remember when calculating cubic content is that all the dimensions must be expressed in the same units; thus, they should all be either metric or in inches or in feet.

As an example, consider a plank 12 feet long by 12 inches wide by 1 inch thick. The first step is to convert the 12 feet into inches by multiplying by 12 which gives 144 inches; the calculation is then (144 × 12 × 1) divided by 1728 (the number of cubic inches in a cubic foot). The answer is obviously 1 cubic foot.

Things can become complicated when the dimensions are, as in real life, difficult to convert into inches. As an example, consider a plank 10ft 7in long by 13½in wide by 1¾in thick. It is possible to calculate the cubic content by using the method given above but it would be quite laborious. In the trade, both time and trouble are saved by using sets of tables contained in a small book called the 'Hoppus Measure'. Anyone likely to become involved in measuring timber is advised to buy one.

Metric equivalents

Here are some tables that may help you

Fractions of an inch to millimetres

in	mm	in	mm	in	mm	in	mm
1/64	0.397	17/64	6.747	33/64	13.097	49/64	19.447
1/32	0.794	9/32	7.144	17/32	13.494	25/32	19.844
3/64	1.191	19/64	7.541	35/64	13.891	51/64	20.241
1/16	1.588	5/16	7.938	9/16	14.288	13/16	20.638

(Continued on p. 8)

5/64	1.984	21/64	8.334	37/64	14.684	53/64	21.034
3/32	2.381	11/32	8.731	19/32	15.081	27/32	21.431
7/64	2.778	23/64	9.128	39/64	15.478	55/64	21.828
1/8	3.175	3/8	9.525	5/8	15.875	7/8	22.225
9/64	3.572	25/64	9.922	41/64	16.272	57/64	22.622
5/32	3.969	13/32	10.319	21/32	16.669	29/32	23.019
11/64	4.366	27/64	10.716	43/64	17.066	59/64	23.416
3/16	4.763	7/16	11.113	11/16	17.463	15/16	23.813
13/64	5.159	29/64	11.509	45/64	17.859	61/64	24.209
7/32	5.556	15/32	11.906	23/32	18.256	31/32	24.606
15/64	5.953	31/64	12.303	47/64	18.653	63/64	25.003
1/4	6.350	1/2	12.700	3/4	19.050	1	25.400

Square inches and square feet to square metres

in 2	m 2	in 2	m 2	ft 2	m 2	ft 2	m 2	ft 2	m 2
5	0.0032	100	0.0645	1	0.0929	11	1.0219	21	1.9510
10	0.0064	110	0.0710	2	0.1858	12	1.1148	22	2.0439
20	0.0129	120	0.0774	3	0.2787	13	1.2077	23	2.1368
30	0.0193	130	0.0839	4	0.3716	14	1.3006	24	2.2297
40	0.0258	140	0.0903	5	0.4645	15	1.3936	25	2.3226
50	0.0322	144	0.0929	6	0.5574	16	1.4865	26	2.4155
60	0.0387	150	0.0968	7	0.6503	17	1.5794	27	2.5084
70	0.0451	160	0.1032	8	0.7432	18	1.6723	28	2.6013
80	0.0516	170	0.1097	9	0.8361	19	1.7652	29	2.6942
90	0.0580	180	0.1161	10	0.9290	20	1.8581	30	2.7871

Cubic feet to cubic metres

ft 3	m 3	ft 3	m 3	ft 3	m 3	ft 3	m 3	ft 3	m 3
1	0.028	11	0.311	21	0.595	31	0.878	41	1.161
2	0.057	12	0.340	22	0.623	32	0.906	42	1.190
3	0.085	13	0.368	23	0.651	33	0.934	43	1.217
4	0.113	14	0.396	24	0.680	34	0.963	44	1.246
5	0.142	15	0.425	25	0.708	35	0.991	45	1.274
6	0.170	16	0.453	26	0.736	36	1.019	46	1.302
7	0.198	17	0.481	27	0.764	37	1.047	47	1.330
8	0.226	18	0.510	28	0.792	38	1.076	48	1.359
9	0.255	19	0.538	29	0.821	39	1.104	35.315 ft 3	
10	0.283	20	0.566	30	0.849	40	1.132	= 1 m 3	

Decimals of an inch to millimetres

in	mm	in	mm	in	mm
0.001	0.025	0.01	0.254	0.1	2.54
0.002	0.051	0.02	0.508	0.2	5.08
0.003	0.076	0.03	0.762	0.3	7.62
0.004	0.102	0.04	1.016	0.4	10.16
0.005	0.127	0.05	1.270	0.5	12.70
0.006	0.152	0.06	1.524	0.6	15.24
0.007	0.178	0.07	1.778	0.7	17.78
0.008	0.203	0.08	2.032	0.8	20.32
0.009	0.229	0.09	2.286	0.9	22.86

Terms used to describe dimensioned timber
Once a log has been converted (that is, sawn) the following terms are used to describe the sawn pieces, depending on size:

Baulk: log squared up ready for further conversion. Minimum sizes 115mm square (4½in square), but usually much larger

Half-timber: a baulk cut in half along its centre. Minimum sizes 115mm × 58mm (4½in × 2¼in)

Flitch (softwood): Minimum sizes 305mm × 102mm (12 × 4in)
Board (hardwood): Any widths up to 32mm (1¼in) thick

Flitch (hardwood): Minimum sizes 204mm × 102mm (8in × 4in)

Plank: 280mm (11in) or more wide by 51mm to 150mm (2in × 6in) thick

Deal (softwood): 230mm to 280mm (9in to 11in) wide by 50mm to 102mm (2in to 4in) thick

Strip: Under 102mm × 50mm (4in to 2in)

Batten (softwood): 127mm to 203mm (5in to 8in) wide by 50mm to 102mm (2in to 4in). The term is applied loosely these days to what are, strictly speaking, tiling or slating battens: up to 90mm (3½in) wide by 12mm to 32mm (½in to 1¼in). Common sizes are 38mm or 50mm (½in or 2in) by 19mm (¾in)

Square: piece of square section with sides from 50mm to 150mm (2in to 6in)

Scantling: from 50mm to 115mm (2in to 4½in) wide by 50mm to 102mm (2in to 4in)

Slab: random pieces sawn from the outside of the log to square it up. They are convex on one side and flat on the other, and the bark is often left on. Regarded as waste but useful for covering stacked timber.
Planks and boards are sold either 'square-edged' (S/E) when the edges have been sawn at right angles to the face, or 'waney-edged' (W/E) when the natural edge of the tree is left on one or both edges.

Timber Grades

Apart from log-sawn material, that is, timber which has waney edges or one square edge, timber is graded according to the visual quality of one face.

FAS (first and seconds) refers to boards with one face free from all 'defect'. The reverse face may contain certain minor defects specified by the grading rules of the exporting country.

No 1 C&S (No 1 common and selects) This is the next grade down, and again one face is clean enough, its precise condition varying with the shipper and the species: there may be one or two relatively small departures from FAS standards, such as a higher proportion of sapwood and slight but sound discolouration. More blemishes are permitted on the reverse. These grades originated in America, but are now used by many other countries such as Japan and the African nations.

'Merchantable' ('select merchantable' and 'standard and better'). These are other lower grades; the last, however, refers more often than not to south-east Asian woods of fairly plain appearance, while the first two are not encountered very often.

Home-grown hardwoods Usually graded as first-quality (or prime) and second-quality, with merchantable perhaps being available as well.

Any given parcel of timber is a mixture of boards from many trees – and not necessarily all from their boles: some will come from limbs and branches. The overriding point, however, is this: although higher grades are assessed fresh from the saw to give the maximum freedom from 'defects' and the minimum variation in grain and texture, beauty is still in the eye of the beholder. Plenty of interesting material can be selected from even the lowest grades.

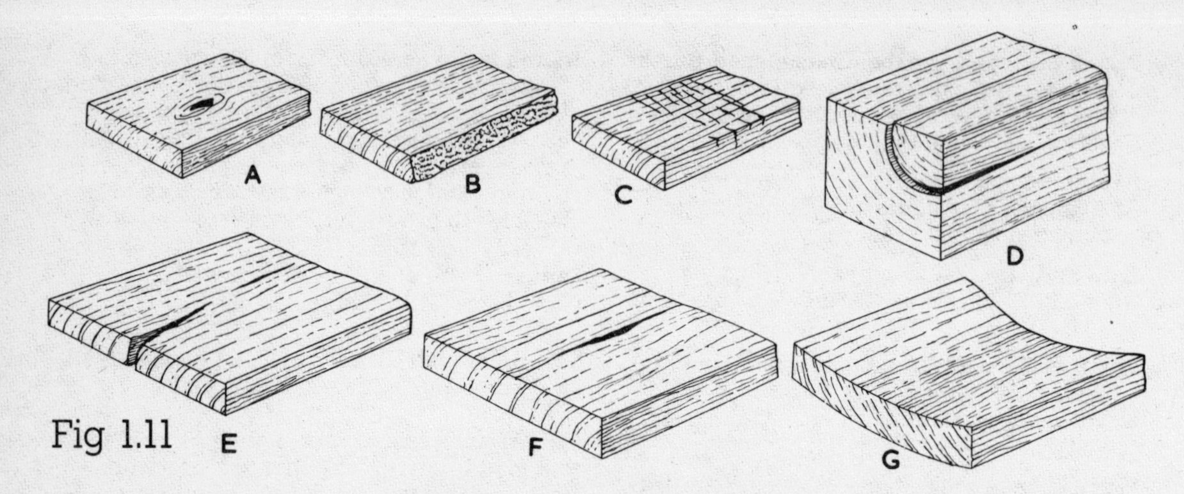

Fig 1.11

Defects in Timber

Knots (A) Avoid timber containing knots (Fig 1.11). Cut out dead knots which have a black ring around them. (B) shows a waney edge which is sometimes left on hardwoods. It consists of bark and sapwood, both of which must be removed. (C) illustrates felling or compression shakes and the parts containing them will have to be cut out. (D) is a 'cup' shake caused by the heartwood drying out more quickly than the rest, and it should be discarded. (E) must also be cut away as it is an 'end' shake although sometimes you can saw lengthwise to eliminate it. (F) is a shake which can either extend part-way through the board or penetrate it completely. In both cases the affected area must be cut away. (G) shows a warped board. If the warping is crosswise as shown, the board will have to be cut into narrow strips lengthwise; if the warping is lengthwise, however, the board can be sawn into short lengths across it.

Heart and Heart-wood Any reference to avoidance of 'heart', not 'heartwood', really means awareness of 'pith'. On the end grain of a complete section of round wood there is a tiny pith which is actually the compressed original sapling around which all subsequent growth is formed. Due to the various conditions during the growth of a tree, such as attempted resistance to gales and storms, site conditions, etc, a tree develops within itself certain stresses. In some cases, because of the type of growth conditions the pith on the end of a felled log may be offset, which is an indicator of extreme stress.

In the conversion of logs into timber, and here we are talking generally of the main stem or trunk, it is often the practice to make the first cut through the pith, that is, a 'breaking cut' in order to relieve much of the growth stress; this is why splitting logs down their length into half-rounds is recommended. When softwoods like pine and spruce, which are relatively small trees, are converted, the breaking cut is often not made, with the result that some planks contain the pith. Some writers on the subject of selection may well advise rejection of these pieces because, in each of them, there is a relatively small volume of wood in which the stresses are closely confined.

In the case of thickish timber, this can result in ultimate splitting; and in the case of thin boards it leads to a tendency for the wood to cup. Hence the loose phraseology at times of 'heartwood up' or 'down' as the case may be, but the reference is to the pith, since all the wood surrounding the pith is heartwood.

Since the original sapling had growing tips to make height in the case of the main stem and to spread into the crown, even small diameter branches and 'lops and tops' will have a pith. Generally speaking, because of the small volume of wood involved, growth stresses in these pieces will be very slight so all that is needed is careful drying to reduce the tendency of the wood to split.

The Strength of Timber

Strength is a rather vague term when applied to any material and especially so when it relates to wood. It may mean impact strength, that is, resistance to shock loading; tensile strength, which is resistance to fracture by pulling; or any one of many other methods of measuring strength. With timber, one of the most important properties is its resistance to bending. In applications as far removed as shelving and floor joists, it is essential to know how much bending will occur when weights or loads are placed on the timber before an acceptable structure can be designed.

The bending strength of timber varies greatly from species to species. As a rough guide, a broad division can be made as shown in the table. Knowing the actual bending strength of a material, and given its dimensions and the load it has to carry, the deflection can be calculated. This calculation is relatively simple and will be used to illustrate one design later.

Formula for shelves

Shelf thickness = (the shelf length multiplied by W) divided by 100. The factor W is 2.0 for mahogany and most hardwoods; 3.0 for red deal and most softwoods; and 4.4 for chipboard ('high density' chipboard can have values of W as low as 2.7).

It will be apparent that timbers with a high bending strength will support a greater load than those with a low bending strength.

Looked at another way red deal, for example, will need to be heavier in section for a given load than mahogany to give the same resistance to bending. In building construction, heavy sections can be used since they are usually hidden from view. In furniture making, however, where design must incorporate some aesthetic appeal, the overall shape will often dictate the dimensions of the timber so that a limited range of timbers will be available for selection.

In order to illustrate this with a common example consider the design of a bookcase. The shelf length is one metre and the width 200mm. The human eye is very sensitive to out-of-square and out-of-flat discrepancies so that bending in excess of 1mm at the centre of the shelf will be noticeable. Take a book load of 15kg (33lb) as an example. Using the simple formula it will be seen that the thickness of, say, mahogany required for the shelves is about 20mm. This is quite in keeping with the overall appearance. If red deal were to be used, the thickness would need to be nearly 30mm. Using proprietary brands of veneered chipboard 18mm thick, the deflection would be over 2mm – not acceptable. Should it be necessary to use red deal or chipboard, the shelf length would need to be reduced in order to lessen the deflection. To avoid the necessity for calculation, graphs can be drawn to obtain the shelf thickness for any practical shelf length.

Table of bending strengths for timber:

Group 1	**Group 2**	**Group 3**
Strength 700 & below	*Strength 1,200*	*Strength 2,000*
Veneered chipboard	Red deal	Mahogany
Plasterboard	Cedar	Beech
	Elm	Ash
		Teak

Timber Specifications

The following list shows readily available timbers. All are hardwoods except when marked (SW), which denotes a softwood.

Column A shows the average densities in kilogrammes per cubic metre which are classified as follows: very light less than 320; light 320 to 465; medium heavy 465 to 630; heavy 630 to 800; very heavy 800 to 1040; extremely heavy over 1040. The densities quoted are for timber with a moisture content of 12%, which is acceptable for general woodwork.

Column B gives details of colours, and the following abbreviations are used: BP = brownish pink; DB = dark brown; DR =

dark red; LB = light brown; LR = light red; MB = medium brown; PB = purple brown; RB = reddish brown; WH = whitish; YB = yellowish brown; YW = yellowish white; V* = variegated colours which are described in the 'Remarks' column. Bear in mind that most timbers darken in colour after prolonged exposure to light.

Column C shows the liability of the timber to shrink, swell, twist, or otherwise move consequent upon any marked departure from the normal 12% MC. B = bad stability; M = medium stability; G = good stability. Botanical names have been omitted except where required to distinguish one timber from a related species.

Timber	*A*	*B*	*C*	*Remarks*
Abura	560	LB	G	Sometimes shows pink tinge. Sharp tools needed as it has a fibrous surface. Stains and polishes well.
Afara (or Limba)	545	YW	G	Tends to split when screwed or nailed. Irregular grain: used in plywoods.
Afrormosia (or Kokrodua)	690	LB	G	Colour darkens on exposure. Iron or steel will stain it when damp. Sometimes has dark streaks.
Afzelia (or Doussie)	820	RB	G	Interlocked grain makes working difficult. Irritant dust. Stains and polishes well. Sapwood is yellow.
Agba	515	LB	G	Straight grain, even texture. Works well but can be gummy.
Apitong (*see* Keruing)				
Ash, European	690	WH	M	Long-grained and tough; good working qualities; reasonably good to stain and polish. One of the best timbers for bending.
Beech, European	720	YW	B	Easy to work as the grain is even and the texture fine. Only used in small dimensions as it is unstable in wide pieces. Also used in plywood. Steamed beech is pinkish colour.
Birch, European and American	655	WH	B	Straight and even grain; works easily. Takes stain readily and is often stained to match other woods.
Cedar, English (SW) *(Cedrus spp)*	560	LB	M	Softish wood easily worked, and polishes well. Usually in veneer form.
Cedar, American (SW) *(Cedrela spp)*	480	RB	G	Works easily but tends to split: it is also brittle and lacks strength. Stains and polishes well.
Cedar, African Pencil *(Juniperus procera)*	545	LR	G	Strong timber which works and carves beautifully. Stains and polishes well.
Cedar, Western Red (SW) *(Thuja plicata)*	370	V*	G	Colour varies from light pink to chocolate brown. Soft, with even, close, straight grain. Very stable, can be used near central heating. It contains a natural preservative oil and can be used out-of-doors without further treatment when it weathers to a silvery grey colour.
Cherry, European and Japanese *(Prunus avium)*	610	RB	M	Fine grain; works reasonably well; good for turning. Stains and polishes easily; sapwood sometimes attacked by beetle.
Cherry, American *(Prunus serotina)*				As above but sapwood not attacked by beetle.

Timber	*A*	*B*	*C*	*Remarks*
Danta	735	RB	M	Fine grain and texture but feels slightly greasy. Works, turns, stains, and polishes well.
Douglas Fir (SW)	530	V*	G	Heartwood brownish pink, sapwood yellow. Attractive grain, works easily. Stains and polishes well. Mostly in veneer form.
Doussie (*see* Afzelia)				
Edinam (*see* Gedu Nohor)				
Elm, European *(Ulmus spp)*	625	LB	B	Cross-grained and difficult to work. Requires carefully controlled seasoning. Attractive grain; hard to stain.
Elm, Rock (American) *(Ulmus thomasi)*	700	LB	G	Close-grained, fine texture; works well. Very durable in wet conditions and is used in boat-building.
Gedu Nohor (or Edinam)	545	RB	G	Interlocked grain makes it tricky to work, but stains and polishes well. Ribbon stripe figure when quarter-sawn.
Guarea	575	RB	G	Fine, even texture sometimes with a mottled figure. Easy to work but can be gummy – difficult to polish.
Gurjung (*see* Keruing)				
Hemlock, Western (SW) (or Alaskan Pine)	480	LB	G	Fine uniform texture; stains and polishes well. Good for panelling and interior joinery. Used for plywood.
Idigbo (or Black Afara)	545	YB	G	Coarse texture and irregular grain make it difficult to work, but stains and polishes well. Very strong wood. Stains yellow in contact with water – do not use water-based adhesives.
Imbuya (or Brazilian Walnut)	720	DB	M	Fine texture but variable grain makes it difficult to work, and dust can be an irritant. Stains and polishes well.
Iroko (or Mvuli or African Teak)	640	DB	G	Irregular grain but works reasonably easily; stains and polishes well. Good for interior and exterior work and as a substitute for true teak.
Jarrah	800	DR	M	Very strong timber that has been used for paving blocks. Hard, dense grain but quite easy to work; stains and polishes well.
Jelutong	470	YW	G	Straight-grained but small (latex) pockets can mar the surface, so can only be utilised in short lengths. Tends to be woolly and split; does not stain or polish well. Sometimes holed by (defunct) borer beetles.
Kapur (Borneo Camphorwood)	740	RB	M	Even close grain, works easily. Does not stain or polish well. Smells of camphor. Stains in contact with iron. Borer beetle holes (defunct) sometimes present.
Keruing (or Apitong, Gerjun, or Yang)	720	RB	B	Interlocked and variable grain make it difficult to work and it does not polish well. Gum exudation can cause trouble. Good for structural work.
Laurel, Indian	850	DB	G	Close-grained with firm texture; works and polishes well. Strong and durable and a

Timber	*A*	*B*	*C*	*Remarks*
				good cabinet-making wood. Difficult to obtain except as veneer.
Limba (*see* Afara)				
Lime, European	545	WH	M	Light in weight and not a strong wood. Close and even grain make it easy to work both with and across the grain – ideal for wood-carvers and turners.
Mahogany, African *(Khaya spp)*	700 (average)	RB	G	There are several varieties and all except Lagos and Sapele (qv), are rather coarse-grained with an open texture. Easily worked but sometimes needs the grain filling before polishing. Lagos mahogany is close and even-grained, easy to work and polish; it is quite light in weight (560) and is not a constructional timber.
Mahogany, American *(Swietenia spp)* including Colombian, Costa Rican, Cuban, Guatemalan, Honduras Nicaraguan, Panamanian)	545 (average)	RB	M	There are two principal varieties: Cuban and Honduras. The first is about 640 weight and is hard, close-grained and silky in texture; it works and polishes perfectly and the veneers are superb. Costa Rican and Colombian mahoganies are very similar; all are now extremely scarce either as solid or veneer. The second (Honduras) is 550 weight, not so close-grained or silky but easily worked and polished – it mellows to a warm golden brown shade. Guatemalan, Nicaraguan, and Panamanian mahoganies are similar and are all first-class cabinet-making woods.
Makore (or African Cherry, Cherry Mahogany)	625	V*	G	Interlocked grain with stripy figure; works reasonably well and polishes excellently. Colour varies from light brownish pink to a purple brown shade after exposure to air.
Mansonia	600	V*	M	Fine, close-grained wood, easily worked – the dust can be an irritant. Polishes well. When first cut is a purple colour; after exposure sapwood becomes yellowish brown and heartwood grey brown with darker stripes.
Melawis (*see* Ramin)				
Meranti (or Seraya, or Lauan)	530	V*	G	Two principal kinds – dark reddish brown, or (from Malaya) yellowish white. A strong close-grained wood which works and polishes well. The reddish brown variety resembles mahogany.
Muninga	625	DB	G	Medium texture and fairly close grain. Works and polishes well. The grain is sometimes streaky.
Mvuli (*see* Iroko)				
Niangon (or Nyankom)	625	RB	M	Coarse texture and has tendency to split around fastenings. Gumminess is a problem and makes it difficult to work and polish. Sometimes suffers from brittle-heart.
Oak, American	700	MB	M	A strong timber; grain straight and close. Colour uniform throughout. Works and polishes well.

Timber	*A*	*B*	*C*	*Remarks*
Oak, British	800	MB	M	Very strong and durable. Grain and texture unpredictable and knots are often present. Difficult to work but polishes well.
Oak, Japanese	650	MB	M	Straight-grained and with fine texture, it is easily worked and polished. Good for special finishes such as fuming, antiquing, or liming.
Obeche (or Obechi, Arere, WaWa)	385	YW	G	A soft timber but some spots have a roey grain which makes them tricky to work. Undistinguished plain grain; suitable for light, hidden work such as drawer stuff. Stains easily if the grain is previously filled. Much used in plywood manufacture.
Opepe	740	RB	G	Yellow when first cut. Interlocked grain with a striped figure. Tricky to work but stains and polishes well.
Padauk, African	850	RB	G	Similar to East Indian Padauk (qv) but with a more open grain and paler colour. Works and polishes well.
Padauk, East Indian	735	DR	G	Moderately hard, heavy and durable. It is often difficult to work due to irregular grain. The red colour is often streaked with darker red.
Parana Pine (SW)	545	V*	B	Straight-grained, even-textured and easy to work as it is relatively soft. Generally light brown in colour with reddish streaks; the sapwood is yellowish white. Polishes reasonably well.
Pine, Scots (or Red Baltic) (SW)	510	BP	M	This is one of the most-used softwoods in DIY and building. Works easily: polish, paint, varnish can be applied if knots are treated to stop resin bleeding.
Pine, Pitch (SW)	690	BP	M	Highly resinous wood which should be painted or varnished but not polished. Easy to work but becomes brittle in dry conditions – best stored in damp situation. Ideal for boat-building.
Pine, Yellow (SW)	385	YW	G	Even grain and firm texture make it easy to work; ideal for interior joinery which is to be painted or varnished. Sapwood is whitish, heartwood creamy yellow.
Plane, London *(Platanus acerifolia)*	625	RB	M	Rarely obtainable except as veneer – known as 'lacewood' when quarter-cut. The wood is called 'sycamore' in Scotland.
Podo (SW)	515	Y	M	Straight-grained and even texture; easy to work. Colour is uniform throughout but it does not respond well to staining or polishing. A good timber for bending.
Ramin (or Melawis)	660	Y	B	Medium to coarse texture and straight-grained. Easy to work both with and across the grain; stains and polishes readily and can be matched to be almost indistinguishable from light oak. Colour is uniform throughout; splinters can cause painful irritation.

Timber	*A*	*B*	*C*	*Remarks*
Rosewood, Brazilian and East Indian *(Dalbergia spp)*	890	V*	G	Brownish purple with darker streaks. Dense and heavy wood with alternating grain which makes it difficult to work. Liable to develop minute cracks in the grain even when polished. Both varieties have same characteristics. Mainly available as veneers.
Sapele (same species as Gedu Nohor and Utile qqv)	625	RB	M	Hard and close-grained, with a roey striped figure. Works reasonably easily; polishes well. Veneer widely used on interior doors.
Seraya (*see* Meranti)				
Sycamore *(Acer pseudo-platanus)*	610	WH	M	Close-grained, silky texture, works easily. Stains and polishes well (harewood is sycamore stained grey with copperas). Normally undistinguished figure but when quarter-sawn has a slight mottled ripple.
Teak	640	LB	G	Coarse and open-grained; is greasy and joints should be de-greased before gluing. Rather difficult to work. Polishes well. Uniform colour except for thin black streaks which sometimes appear. Very durable in exterior and adverse conditions.
Utile	660	RB	M	Close and even texture with interlocked grain which is difficult to work but polishes well. Sapwood is light brown; heartwood reddish brown. Liable to have (defunct) beetle holes.
Walnut, African *(Lovoa klaineana)*	545	YB	G	Has similar colour and black streaks to European Walnut (qv). Works and polishes easily.
Walnut, American Black *(Juglans nigra)*	600	PB	G	Straight grain and even texture make it easy to work and polish – a first-class cabinet-making wood.
Walnut, European *(Juglans regia)*	700	DB	G	Strong and tough timber which can be worked both with and across the grain. Takes a superb polish. Figure often includes thin black streaks – veneers can exhibit magnificent figure when in curl or burr form.
Yang (*see* Keruing)				
Yew	770	V*	G	Strong and elastic timber with a lustrous grain which is reasonably easy to work. The overall colour is a pale red, but has patches which can darken to a plum colour. Tends to be scarce. Polishes well.

Wood Pests

Dry Rot *(Merulius lacrymans)* This requires more or less constant conditions of humidity (not saturation), and timber with a moisture content of slightly more than 20% is ideal for its growth, provided there is also a lack of ventilation. The first indication is a scorched appearance on the surface of the wood on which fungal growths *(mycelium)* develop; they look like fluffy white cotton wool, and may grow a felted pearly-grey skin. The surface becomes cracked into cuboidal shapes which finally disintegrate into a crumbly dust. Usually the rot starts on softwood and then migrates to hardwood.

There is also a characteristic musty, mushroomy smell.

The migratory factor makes this type of rot pernicious as it can spread even through brickwork. As the nutriment in the wood is used up, dark brown or blackish water-tubes *(rhizomorphs)* appear and are capable of passing through cracks in brickwork or behind plaster to carry water to a new colony. The effect is further compounded by the formation of fruiting bodies called *sporophores,* which can be anything from a few centimetres to a metre or so in diameter. When ripe, a *sporophore* will liberate spores in fantastic numbers; the spores are so minute that they can be carried by the slightest breeze and will eventually settle as a brown snuff-like dust; provided the surface is hospitable the spores will, of course, grow.

Dry rot can devastate a building and it is advisable to seek professional help at the first suspicion of an attack. Some immediate precautions which can be taken include: removal and burning of affected wood up to 460mm (18in) away from the last signs of attack; any *sporophores* should be sprayed with a strong fungicide and any brown stains should also be wiped over with a cloth moistened with it. Brick and plasterwork which has been affected, and the immediate area around it, should be sprayed with the fungicide or burned off with a blow-lamp (but beware of the fire hazard if working in confined situations such as an attic). And, of course, the primary cause of the dampness must be traced and eliminated.

Wet Rot or **Cellar Fungus** *(Coniophora cerebella)* This is found on wood in the open air as well as in enclosed areas, but it needs far wetter conditions than those for dry rot and the wood needs to be saturated. It attacks both hard and soft woods.

Unlike dry rot, it does not form *mycelium* although it may grow a thin yellowish-brown skin and dark brown strands. Affected wood cracks into cuboidal pieces, generally along the grain, and will eventually disintegrate into crumbs. This type of rot, however, is not as pernicious as dry rot, as it does not spread, but it can affect the interior of a board while leaving the outer surface looking superficially sound.

Affected wood should be cut out and replaced by sound wood which has been treated with an insecticide. Provided the source of dampness is found and removed, the problem should be solved.

Furniture Beetle or **Woodworm** *(Anobium punctatum)* The first evidence of this pest is the appearance of flight-holes about 1mm in diameter and, if the surface is flat, a light coating of 'frass' (the wood dust expelled by the beetles).

The beetle itself is very small, about 3 to 4mm (1/8in to 3/16in) long, reddish-brown and plump, and able to fly. Its life cycle begins with the male and female beetles mating at any time from late May to early August. The female then lays her eggs in any convenient crack or crevice such as a slightly-opened joint, a split, or even an old flight hole. An egg hatches into a small white grub which burrows through the wood for a year (sometimes two years) before turning into a chrysalis just beneath the surface of the wood. After a few weeks, it turns into a fully-fledged beetle that bites a flight-hole in the wood surface and emerges to re-start the whole cycle.

From the above it is clear that, once the flight holes appear, the damage is done. Consequently, an annual spraying with a proprietary insecticide is a good practice as it not only renders the wood surface repellent to the female beetles, but will also kill any eggs laid on the surface. A special injector is needed to force the insecticide down into the holes to kill any more beetles which may be lurking there. Incidentally, woodworm rarely attacks timber of the true mahogany species.

Powder Post Beetle *(Lyctidae)* These infest unseasoned or recently dried hardwoods, and ash, elm, oak, sweet chestnut, and some imported hardwoods are the most likely to be attacked. One of the deciding factors is that the pores of the timber should be large enough to admit the ovipositor of the female when she is laying eggs. Another factor is that the grubs which hatch from the eggs feed on the starch in the timber and, therefore, they choose only the sapwood – if the wood has been cut for some time the starch will have leached out and the grubs will die of starvation.

The beetles vary in colour from reddish-brown to black, are somewhat flat and elongated and about 5mm (3/16in) long, and can fly. They are active from April until late summer, and the life-cycle from egg to mature beetle takes one year.

Treatment consists of spraying or brushing

on a proprietary insecticide and is most effective in spring or summer. If found among sapwood in the workshop, any other sapwood should be burned. It is also worth spraying any timber in outdoor stacks.

Pin-hole Borer *(Ambrosia)* These normally attack freshly-felled logs in tropical and sub-tropical regions. Any bore holes seen on seasoned timber in this country are an indication of now-defunct infestation and there is no danger of recurrence.

House Longhorn Beetle *(Hylotrupes bajulus)* Normally attacks seasoned softwoods and can therefore do severe damage to structural timbers.

The beetle is quite large, 10mm to 20mm ($\frac{3}{8}$in to $\frac{3}{4}$in) in length and usually brown in colour, although some males are black. Like the furniture beetle, the beetle lays her eggs in splits or crevices and after two to three weeks they hatch out into larvae and begin to bore into the wood. A mature larva is about 25mm to 30mm (1in to $1\frac{3}{16}$in) long, fleshy white in colour, and with deep grooves dividing it into segments. It remains in the wood for a period of three to ten years or even longer, doing immense damage, and then emerges through a flight-hole during July, August, or September. The holes are larger than those of furniture beetles, being about 6mm to 10mm ($\frac{1}{4}$in to $\frac{3}{8}$in) in diameter.

Sometimes there is frass near the scene of infestation, and as the beetle is larger than the furniture beetle the frass is larger, too, and consists of wood crumbs, dust, and pellets of excrement. It is also possible to detect their presence by the appearance of corrugated swellings on the wood surface which are caused by their burrowing. The pest needs professional treatment and in some areas it should be notified to the Pest Control department of the local authority.

Death Watch Beetle *(Xestobium rufovillosum)* This beetle only attacks timber which has already started to decay and hardwoods are the usual targets, although softwoods are not immune.

The beetle is about 6mm to 10mm ($\frac{1}{4}$in to $\frac{3}{8}$in) long, dark brown in colour with patches of short yellow hairs which give it a variegated appearance. They are seldom seen to fly. The eggs are white and lemon-shaped, and about 3mm ($\frac{3}{32}$in) long; they are laid in small clusters of three of four. After two to three weeks they hatch out and crawl over the timber until they find an old exit hole or a suitable crevice which will enable them to bore into the timber. The larvae are about 1mm to 8mm ($\frac{5}{16}$in) long and are covered with yellow hairs.

Their life-cycle is much the same as that of the furniture beetle; they do, however, emerge earlier in the year in April, May, and June, and their exit holes are larger, being about 3mm ($\frac{1}{8}$in) diameter.

Although professional advice should be sought, it is possible to take steps to limit the problem. These include: removal of frass and other debris before using an insecticide; two brush-or-spray applications of insecticide during April and June; annual repeat applications for at least four years; annual inspection of the site for up to ten years; and the spraying of insecticide on any replacement timbers.

CHAPTER TWO

Man-made boards: specifications and uses

MAN-MADE boards are a comparatively recent introduction and have become so widely used over the last ten to fifteen years as to be indispensable and they have revolutionised modern woodworking and design. Large DIY supermarkets normally carry a restricted range of these boards and you may well have to visit specialist woodworking centres to find the more unusual kinds.

Fig 2.1

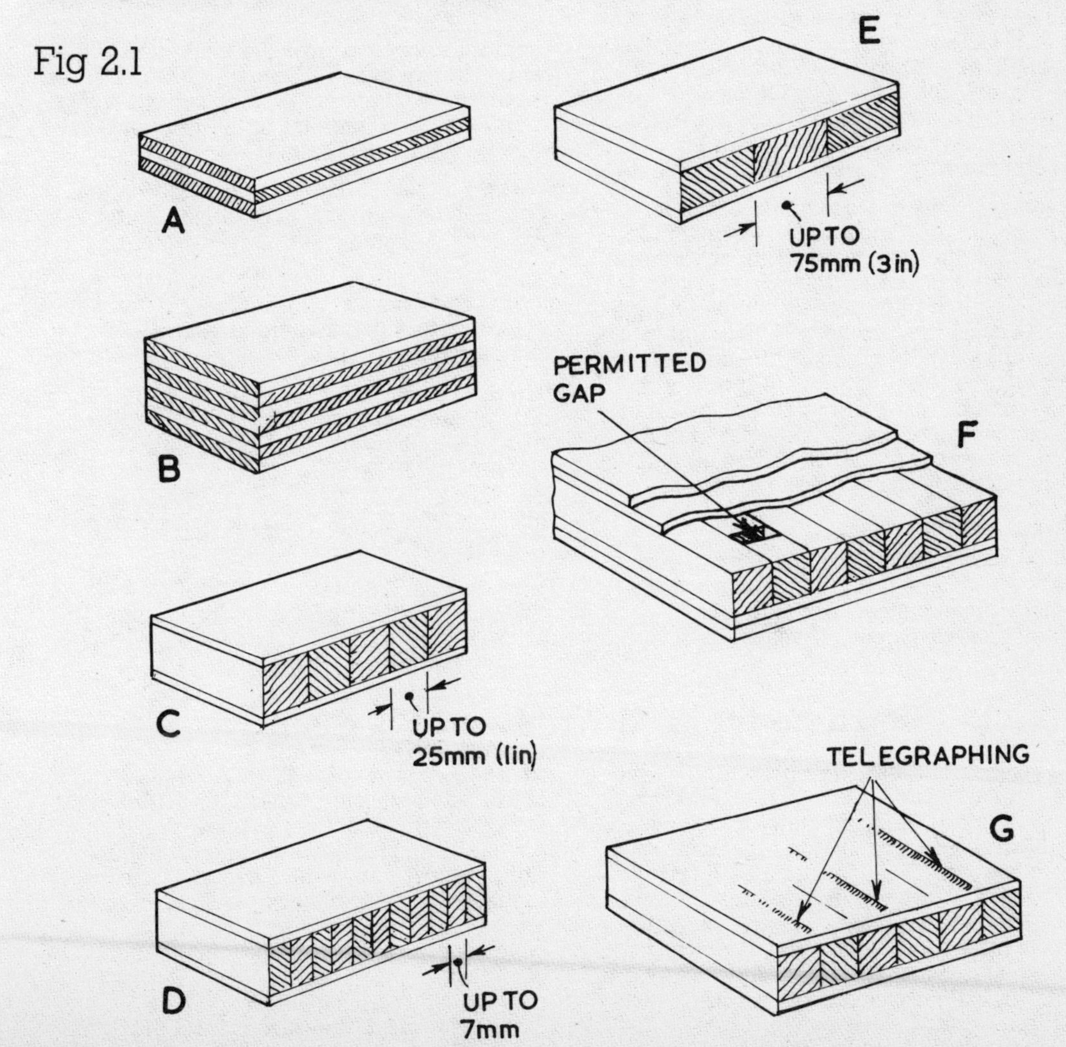

Blockboards and Laminboards

Blockboards and laminboards consist of a core of rectangular strips of wood which are aligned edge to edge and then sandwiched between outer plies. In Fig 2.1, (A) shows three ply; (B) multi-ply; (C) blockboard; (D) laminboard; (E) battenboard; (F) the permissible gap between core strips in blockboard; and (G) how 'telegraphing' affects the outer veneers of blockboard.

Blockboard The core strips can be from 8mm ($^5/_{16}$in) up to 25mm (1in) wide and they may be assembled with or without adhesive. When there is one outer veneer on each side, the board is called a 'three-ply'; other boards can have two outer veneers each side and are then called 'five-ply'. As a general rule if the length of the board exceeds the width then it should be a five-ply. The core strips always run the length of the board, and there may be small gaps up to 3mm ($^1/_8$in) wide between the strips. This is not detrimental.

Laminboard This is a heavier and more expensive type of blockboard in which the core is built up from wood strips or veneers glued face to face and from 1.5mm-7mm wide ($^1/_{16}$in-$^5/_{16}$in). It is particularly suitable for high-class work as the fault of 'telegraphing' which can happen with blockboard does not occur. Telegraphing is when the core strips of the blockboard impart a ripple to the appearance of the outer veneers and this effect, Fig 2.1G unfortunately, often does not show up until the board has been given a high finish.

Gradings

All of these boards are for interior use only unless there is a specific statement to the contrary. In manufacture end-butt joints between core strips are permissible providing they are staggered. Glue bonding is the same as for plywood. Apart from bonding the boards are specified in grades by the quality of the face veneers as follows:–

Grade S Specially selected veneer as specified.

Grade 1 Smooth-cut veneer with any edge joints close and matched for colour. Jointed pieces not less than 254mm (10in) wide. Free from knots, glue stains, and other defects. Slight local discoloration and closed splits allowed.

Grade 2 Veneers not necessarily matched for colour, nor of equal width. Small glue stains and other discoloration permitted. Can have clean inserts.

In three-layer boards the thickness of the veneers is between 2.5mm and 3.6mm. When there are two veneers at each side (5-layer) the combined thickness of the two veneers is between 3mm and 5mm.

Facing veneers Woods used include agba, beech, birch, gaboon, gedu nohor, limba, African mahogany, obeche, poplar, and seraya.

Core strips Woods used include fir, gaboon, obeche, pine, poplar, spruce, and Western red cedar.

Principal sizes 5100mm × 1830mm (16ft 9in × 6ft); 4575mm × 1525mm (15ft × 5ft); 4495mm × 1525mm (14ft 9in × 5ft); 3660mm × 1830mm (12ft × 6ft); 3660mm × 1525mm (12ft × 5ft); 3480mm × 1830mm (11ft 5in × 6ft); 3050mm × 1525mm (10ft × 5ft); 2440mm × 1525mm (8ft × 5ft); 2440mm × 1220mm (8ft × 4ft).

Thicknesses 13mm ($^1/_2$in); 16mm ($^5/_8$in); 18mm ($^{11}/_{16}$in); 19mm ($^3/_4$in); 22mm ($^7/_8$in); 25mm (1in); 38mm (1$^1/_2$in); 48mm (1$^7/_8$in).

Particle (chip) Boards and Flaxboards

The definition of a particle board is one which is made from wood chips alone, or wood chips plus other ligno-cellulosic material such as bagasse board (which is made up from the residue of sugar cane), or flax board (which is made from flax shives, the residues from processing the flax plant). In each case, the particles are bonded with a synthetic resin adhesive and/or other binder. The boards are for interior use only unless otherwise specified.

Extruded chipboard Shown in Fig 2.2A. Made by forcing the mixture through a die with the result that the particles align themselves in a perpendicular formation at right angles to the board surface. This formation is inherently weak and the boards are not recommended for any kind of structural work but only for infilling and cladding.

Platen-pressed chipboard Shown in Fig 2.2B

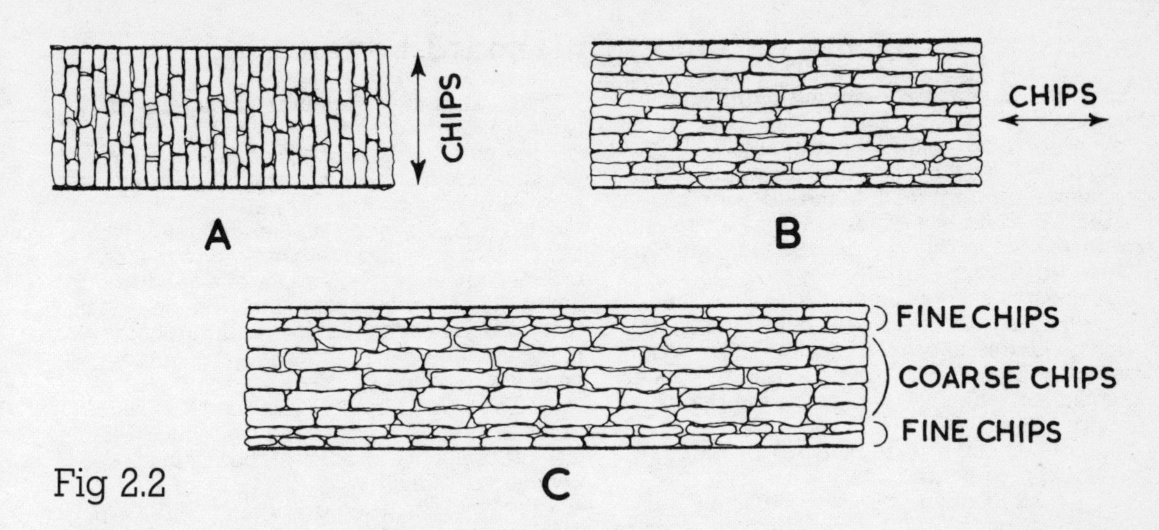

Fig 2.2

and made by pressing the chip-plus-adhesive mixture between platens (rollers) so that it emerges pressed to the required thickness. This is the material commonly known as 'chipboard' and is the type widely used in woodwork. Chipboards are graded according to their density into high, medium, and low densities as follows:

High density A minimum of 800.9kg per cubic metre (50lb per cubic foot).

Medium density A minimum of 400.5kg per cubic metre (25lb per cubic foot).

Low density Less than 400.5kg per cubic metre (25lb per cubic foot). However, the general trade custom is to classify boards from the lightest usage upwards, thus: extruded grade (400 density); furniture grade (500 density); furniture/building grade (600 density); building grade or flooring grade (680 density); and heavy-duty building grade (700 and 720 densities).

Graded-particle board This is shown in Fig 2.2C and is a multi-layer (usually three layers) particle board in which at least two or more layers of particles differ in size.

Some boards contain additives which confer a special quality. For instance, small quantities of paraffin wax can be introduced during manufacture to give moisture resistance, while the addition of borax helps fire resistance. Some boards are rot-resistant because of insecticides or fungicides incorporated during manufacture.

Surface finishes Boards can be obtained in a variety of surface finishes. On some, sawdust is sprinkled on the surface in the final stages of manufacture to give a smooth, fine finish while others purposely have large particles embedded near the surface to impart a mottled appearance. Wood veneers are often used as a facing material and in this case the reverse side of the board should also be veneered to prevent 'bowing'. This veneer is called a 'balancer' and compensates for any pulling force exerted by the surface veneer.

Plastic laminates are also employed as a facing material, and details are given later.

Particle board principal sizes: 1220mm × 2440mm (4ft × 8ft – this is the most commonly sold size); 1220mm × 2745mm (4ft × 9ft); 1220mm × 3050mm (4ft × 10ft); 1220mm × 3660mm (4ft × 12ft); 1220mm × 4880mm (4ft ×16ft); 1220mm × 5185mm (4ft × 17ft); 1525mm × 2440mm (5ft × 8ft); 1525mm × 4880mm (5ft × 16ft); 1525mm × 5185mm (5ft × 17ft); 1725mm × 2745mm (5ft 8in × 9ft); 1830mm × 2440mm (6ft × 8ft); 1830mm × 3660mm (6ft × 12ft); 2440mm × 3660mm (8ft × 12ft).

Thickness 9mm (3/8in); 12mm (1/2in); 15mm (5/8in); 18mm (3/4in); 22mm (7/8in); and 25mm (1in). Only the 15mm and 18mm are readily available through DIY and similar stores.

Flaxboard Similar to a medium density chipboard, although it is lighter in weight. It has a large-scale factory use as a core for veneered stock; it is normally sold commercially and not to non-trade buyers, so no further details are given.

Notes on Using Chipboard Panels

Edge treatments for veneered chipboard panels (Fig 2.3)
(a) shows how a chipboard panel is first edged with a solid wood lipping which has the veneer laid over it flush to the edge of the panel. As there is a danger that the edge of the veneer may lift or 'pick' up, it is lightly bevelled off with a sander.
(b) again, a solid wood lipping is used but this time the edge of the veneer butts against it. It is a good idea to bevel the edge of the veneer very slightly so that if the bead and the panel should move against each other, the gap will not be noticeable.
(c) here, a veneer strip is glued on with the grain running horizontally.
(d) uses a tongued lipping – the small gap left at the bottom of the groove makes a space for the adhesive which would otherwise be squeezed out.
(e) is a neat way of 'lining up' a chipboard panel – that is, giving it a thicker appearance as is sometimes desirable for worktops etc.
(f) shows the use of an 'iron-on' self-adhesive strip. These are ironed on with a domestic electric iron in accordance with the manufacturers' instructions.
(g) a proprietary metal trim which is screwed on; the plastic insert is pressed in and hides the screw heads.

VENEER EDGE BEVELLED

a

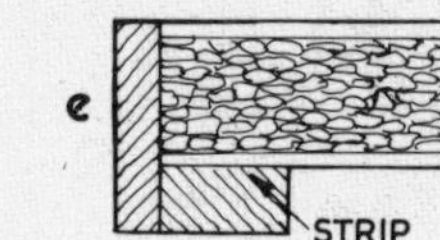

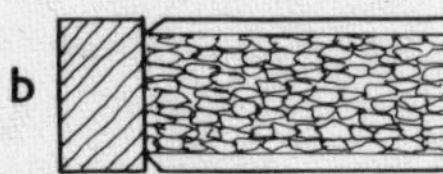

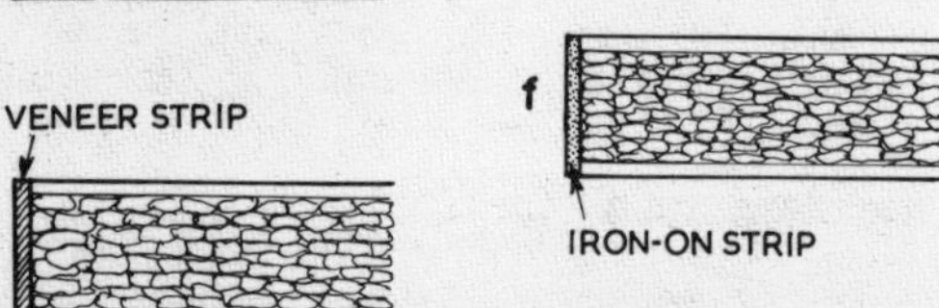

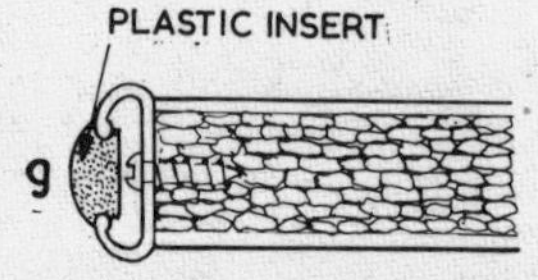

Fig 2.3

Edge treatment for laminate-faced boards (Fig 2.4)
(a) the panel is faced on both sides with a plastic laminate, the edges being bevelled off at an angle of about 30 degrees.
(b) the panel is faced on the underside with a plastic laminate and the panel edge is then grooved to accept the tongue of a solid wood lipping. Another laminate is laid on the upper face to cover both the panel and part of the moulding, and once more the edge of the laminate is bevelled off.
(c) a solid wood lipping is pinned and glued to the edge of the panel; the overhang of the lipping protects the edge of the laminate and gives a neat finish.
(d) the edge is masked with a self-adhesive 'iron-on' tape.
(e), (f), and (g) are all proprietary trims.

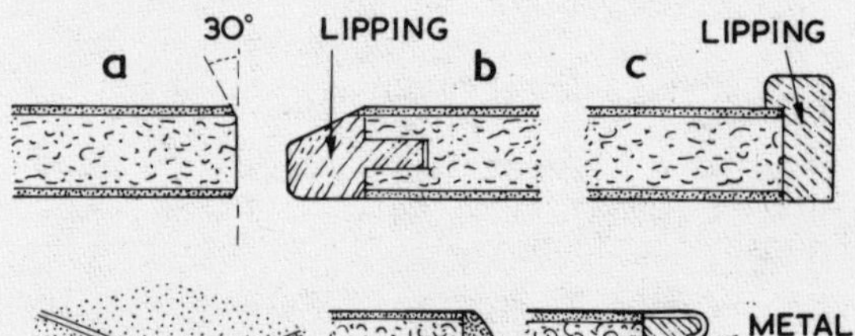

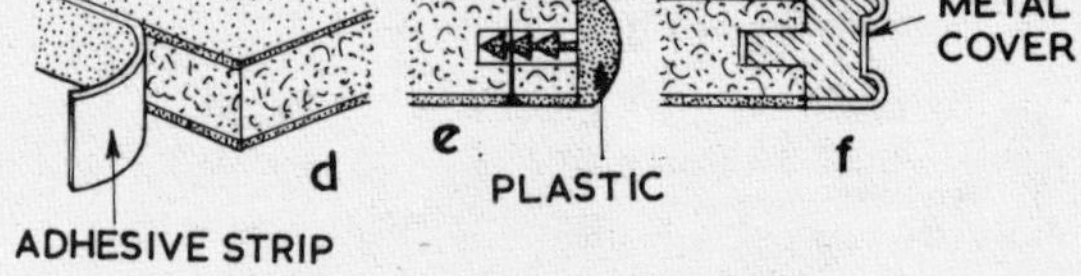

PLASTIC

g

METAL COVER

Fig 2.4

Joints for chipboard panels (Fig 2.5)
(a), (b), and (c) all rely on adhesive only for the strength of the joint; they should only be used where the panels will not be subjected to stress. They can all be made considerably stronger if dowels can be incorporated in the joint.
(d) a butted corner joint with reinforcing glue blocks stuck into the angle.
(e) and (f) both have hardwood tongues glued into grooves. The grain of the tongue runs lengthwise in both cases. Note the small space at the bottom of each groove to allow space for the adhesive.

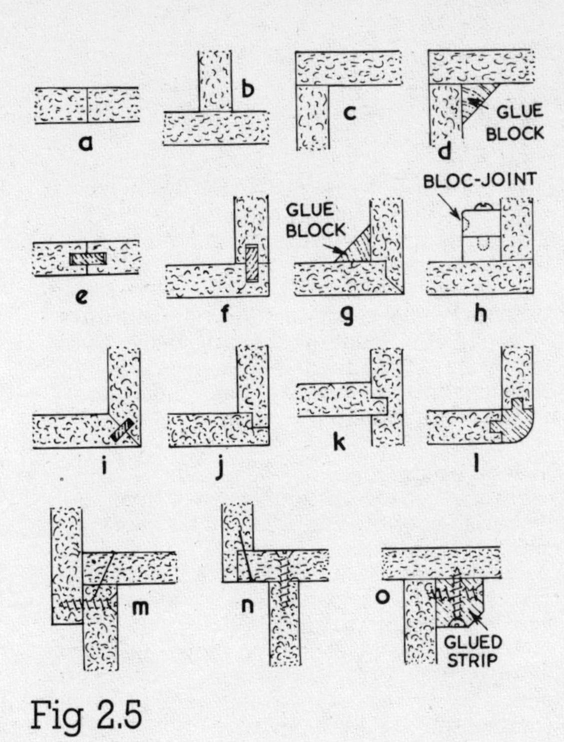

Fig 2.5

(g) is a mitred and rebated joint that calls for accurate machining: the glue block acts as a reinforcement.
(h) is a simple butted joint which is reinforced with a proprietary *Bloc-joint*. If a PVA adhesive which has an adequately long setting time is used, the parts can be glued as well, and a very strong joint will be achieved.
(i) is a tongued mitre joint. The grain of the tongue should run lengthwise, and the grooves should be set back as far as possible from the outside corner, otherwise the joint could split.
(j) and (k) are both rebated joints which are glued and could also be pinned. The fact that the parts are rebated into each other gives extra strength because there is a 'locking' effect, and also there is a large area to be glued.
(l) is a corner joint which requires quite complicated machining, but is both strong and neat.
(m) and (n) are two joints which could be used for attaching a plinth to the bottom of a carcase; the adhesive, plus the pins and screws, should give a very strong fixing.
(o) is the 'workshop' equivalent of the proprietary *Bloc-joint* in (h).

All of these joints can be made successfully using a 'biscuit jointer'.

Plywoods

Plywood boards are composed of veneers or plies bonded together and pressed under heat to form sheets.

It is important to note the method by which a sheet of plywood has been dried and glued. The 'dry cementing' process and the 'semi-dry' process are employed for boards which are not of high quality. They are more likely to warp and twist and also to contain tiny surface splits called 'checks' which may render the boards unsuitable for painting, varnishing, polishing, or veneering.

The component veneers are laid at right angles to each other to distribute their longitudinal strength in both directions and to give rigidity and stability. As the grain of the face veneers on the opposite sides of the sheet must run in the same direction to balance out the opposing strains of the individual veneers, it follows that any board must always have an odd number of plies (eg 3, 5, 7, 9 and so on) and never an even number.

Bonding: plywoods classed as Interior Grade
This grade is used for most furniture and may be bonded from any one of the following three adhesives:

Animal glues Made with glues manufactured from hide or offal. These give a good bond under dry conditions but are very susceptible to moisture and to moulds and fungi. However, they are quite suitable for normal domestic environments.

Blood albumen glues These give a moderately strong bond, but in damp conditions can be liable to breakdown through fungal or mould attacks.

Casein glues These consist of a mixture of milk curds, hydrated lime, and other chemicals and the resulting bond is a good strong one. They must not be exposed to prolonged conditions of damp, otherwise fungal or mould attack will destroy them.

Bonding INT The adhesive used must make strong and durable bonds under dry conditions, although they will tolerate a limited amount of moisture. In addition, they need not be resistant to micro-organisms such as fungi.

Bonding MR Includes adhesives which may last for a few years in full exposure to the weather. They will also withstand cold water (eg damp) for a long period and are highly resistant to micro-organisms.

Bonding BR Has good resistance to weather but will eventually fail under full exposure. Highly resistant to micro-organisms and to cold water conditions.

Although these gradings specify the exact qualities of the adhesives, it cannot be guaranteed that the wood itself will measure up to the same standards.

Bonding: plywoods classed as Exterior Grade

Plywoods bonded with synthetic resin adhesives These include urea-formaldehyde (UF), urea-melamine-formaldehyde (UMF), phenol-formaldehyde (PF), and resorcinol-formaldehyde (RF).

Moisture-resistant plywoods Classed as MR, and using a UF adhesive which imparts a high bonded strength. The bond will withstand prolonged soaking in water at normal temperature and will survive out-of-doors in moderate conditions, but will break down under continuous exposure to extreme weather conditions. Immune from attack by micro-organisms such as fungi.

Boil-resistant plywoods Classed as BR, and so-called because of their resistance to immersion in boiling water, which is one of the standard tests. In dry conditions the bond-strength is the same as MR, but it will survive more severe conditions out-of-doors. As with MR, it is immune from attack by micro-organisms. The adhesive used is UMF.

Weather and boil-proof plywoods Classed as WBP, these are bonded with PF, and are particularly suitable for exposed and adverse weather conditions, surviving long periods without breakdown. They are also immune from micro-organism attack.

RF adhesives Too expensive to be used widely in plywood manufacture, except for special purposes. They are, however, used as fortifiers in conjunction with other adhesives, as their resistance to severe exposure is second-to-none.

Extenders

These are mixed with the expensive synthetic resin adhesives to make them easier to manipulate and go further, bearing in mind that the general method of spreading the adhesive is by rollers.

Some typical extenders are rye flour, soya flour, and other vegetable flours, while resins and/or blood albumen are also used. Obtain data from manufacturers of the adhesive before mixing in any extender.

Surface treatments

There are several different ways of treating the surfaces of plywood. One of the most common is to veneer the face side with a decorative veneer, in which case the reverse face should be veneered with a 'balancer' – usually a cheaper, plainer veneer.

Another finish needing no further treatment is created by applying polyester lacquer in the factory by means of a 'curtain-coater', and this is called 'pre-finished' plywood. It is available either as a plain finish, or with light V-grooves cut in the surface to give the impression of planking.

'Printed plywood' is a fairly recent development and involves spraying a coat of basic colour on to the surface. After drying, the board is passed through several printing rollers to produce the desired pattern and colours. As the surface is a dull finish, it only needs an occasional rub over with wax polish.

There are also plywoods for special purposes, such as formwork for concrete shuttering, ships' bulkheads, or with flame-retardant properties, but these are outside our scope.

Classification of plywoods

There seem to be no internationally accepted standards and what are first-class boards in one country are graded differently from the same class in another. However, the following arbitrary standards may be used for guidance:

Grading of face and back veneers

This refers to the quality of the veneers of the face and back, not the core. It does not take bonding into account. In British-made ply the front and back veneers are assessed separately in numbers 1 to 4. Thus a ply may be marked 1/2, this having a face veneer of grade 1, and back veneer of grade 2.

Grade 1 veneer Firm smooth veneer, free from knots, splits, beetle holes, glue stains, etc. There should be no end joints and any edge joints should be reasonably matched for grain and colour. The jointed pieces should not be less than 254mm (10in) wide, and should all be approximately the same width.

Grade 2 veneer Should have a solid surface without open defects. A few sound knots are permitted; also minor glue stains and local discoloration. Neat repairs of wood inserts are allowed, and edge joints need not be matched for colour and grain. No end joints permitted.

Grade 3 veneer May have knot holes up to 19mm (3/4in) diameter; stains, tight knots, worm holes, and open joints up to 5mm (3/16in), and small areas of rough grain. Decayed wood not allowed.

Grade 4 veneer Knot holes up to 51mm (2in) diameter permitted, also splits up to 25mm (1in) wide, and grain at joints need not match in either colour or grain. Discoloration and stains allowed if they are not caused by rot, and so do not seriously impair the strength of the plywood.

Foreign grading
Many foreign countries use similar terms in grading, but the standards may vary. In Europe the lettering system is widely used, and the following can be regarded as a rough guide though there may be variations. Similar classification is used in some African countries.

A First quality with no blemishes though edge joints may be allowed. Sometimes small knots are permitted. Compares roughly to British grade 1.

B Small pin knots and discoloration permitted. Also edge joints in most cases, and slight roughness.

BB Small knots, inserts, and some discoloration permitted. Sometimes unsanded. Larger knots may be allowed on the back.

C, WG, BBB, or X All defects permitted but well glued.

Canadian Douglas fir May be classified as G2S (good 2 sides); C/S (good one side, solid reverse); G1S (good one side); Solid 2S (solid 2 sides). Solid 1S (solid one side).

Gaboon May be Premier grade with occasional small knots and properly matched if jointed, or Standard grade with small knots, and occasional open splits well filled.

Japanese ply In three grades: AA, first quality; AB second quality; BB, third quality.

Nigerian plywood In three grades in the following order of quality; gold, silver, and blue.

US ply In grades A, B, C, D, in that order of quality.

Defects
Some of these may be permissible in accordance with the particular grade of ply, as follows:

Gap Opening between two core veneers. Not permissible in quality plywood as local shrinkage is inevitable.

Overlap May occur between two core veneers in low grade plywood, resulting in a local ridge at the surface.

Pleat Similar to overlap, but caused by core veneers becoming folded.

Delamination Separation of face veneer from core, usually caused by veneers being glue-starved.

Insert Piece of sound veneer let in to cut out a knot or similar defect. Also known as inlay, patch, or plug.

Edge joint Joint between veneers across the grain. Not allowed except in low-grade plywood.

The term 'veneered ply' refers to plywood which has a decorative veneer laid on one or both sides. Any such decorative veneer should be laid with its grain at right angles to that of the outer layer of the plywood, otherwise hair cracks are liable to develop. This also applies to laminboards and blockboards.

Sizes of plywood boards The first dimension quoted is always the way the grain runs; thus a board measuring 2440mm × 1220mm (8ft × 4ft) will have the grain of the exterior surfaces running parallel to the 2440mm (8ft) dimension, and is called a 'long grain' board. Its converse, a board measuring 1220mm × 2440mm (4ft × 8ft) would have the grain running parallel to its shorter dimension and would be called a 'cross-grain' board.

Boards are normally in any combination of the following sizes: 915mm (3ft); 1220mm (4ft); 1525mm (5ft); 1830mm (6ft); 2135mm (7ft); 2440mm (8ft); 2745mm (9ft); 3050mm (10ft); 3660mm (12ft) by 915mm (3ft); 1220mm (4ft); 1270mm (4ft 2in); 1525mm (5ft); 1830mm (6ft).

Thicknesses Range from 3mm (1/8in) to 25mm (1in) in one millimetre increments. 3mm (1/8in) ply is sometimes called 'aircraft ply' in Britain owing to its wartime use for that industry. Plywood which has over five veneers is usually referred to as 'multi-ply'.

Plastic Laminates

Properties are as follows:

Resistance to dry heat Normally, laminates can withstand surface temperatures up to 180C (356F) for short periods although there may be a slight dulling of the glossy surface. However, temperatures up to 120C (248F) can be borne for several hours. If using plastic laminates in a fire surround, remember that not only will the laminate grow hot, but so will the core to which it is bonded. This can lead to cracking and splitting and the maximum permissible temperature in these conditions is 60C (140F).

Although normal laminates have good resistance to cigarette burns, if any particular area is continually subjected to this treatment (as on the counter-top of a cocktail bar) it would be worth investing in a 'cigarette-proof' laminate which has a metal foil layer incorporated to take care of this problem.

Plastic laminates have good resistance to boiling water. Test samples are required to be immersed in boiling, distilled water for two hours without showing any deterioration.

Resistance to abrasive wear Plastic laminates can stand up to normal wear and tear for many years although the cutting action of knives or similar edge tools can score them. As a general practice, do not clean them too often with scouring powders, leaving it until absolutely necessary. In most cases stains can be wiped off with a damp cloth.

Stain resistance: Acetone, household ammonia, amyl acetate (as used in nail-polish remover) carbon-tetrachloride (dry-cleaning fluid), detergents, mustard, petrol, shoe polishes of all kinds, urine, and wax crayon can all be wiped off. Alcohol (and methylated spirits), citric acid (in orange, lemon and lime juice), coffee, fountain-pen inks (washable), malt vinegar, milk, and tea may cause a temporary stain which can be removed by rubbing lightly with a fine scouring powder. Ballpoint-pen ink, berry juices, caustic alkalis (as used for cleaning toilets), household bleaches, hydrochloric and other acids can leave a permanent stain and should be wiped off immediately.

Sizes
762mm × 1525mm (2ft 6in × 5ft); 762mm × 1830mm (2ft 6 in × 6ft); 762mm × 2135mm (2ft 6in × 7ft); 762mm × 2440mm (2ft 6in × 8ft); 762mm × 2745mm (2ft 6in × 9ft); 762mm × 3050mm (2ft 6in × 10ft) – these are all known as 'door sizes'. 915mm × 1525mm (3ft × 5ft); 915mm × 1830mm (3ft × 6ft); 915mm × 2135mm (3ft × 7ft); 915mm × 2440mm (3ft × 8ft); 1220mm × 1830mm (4ft × 6ft); 1220mm × 2440mm (4ft × 8ft); 1220mm × 2745mm (4ft × 9ft); 1220mm × 3050mm (4ft × 10ft); 1525mm × 3660mm (5ft × 12ft).

The most widely-used thickness is 1.2mm (3/64in).

Hardboards

Technically, these boards are composed of ligno-cellulosic fibres (softwood pulp) compressed to give uniform strength in all directions, and additives are introduced during manufacture to provide boards with special qualities. One side has a smooth surface while the reverse has a woven mesh pattern; double-sided smooth faced boards are available.

Basically, there are three types of board – Standard, Medium, and Tempered – which are each re-graded and distinguished by coloured stripes on the edges of the boards.

Standard board This has one blue stripe and the code letter S.

Medium boards These are sub-divided into four classes, HME, HMN, LME and LMN. The letters HM indicate that the board is high density, and LM denotes low density. The suffix E means that the quality is the highest manufactured, but N indicates that the board, while perfectly suitable for normal usage, does not meet the more stringent tests associated with grade E. The colour codings are: HME, 2 black stripes; HMN, 1 black stripe; LME, 2 white stripes; LMN, 1 white stripe.

Tempered boards (also called 'oil-tempered' or 'super') These include additives which make them weather- and water-resistant.

Gradings TE and TN; as with medium boards the suffix E denotes that the board satisfies the most stringent requirements.

Colour codings TE, 2 red stripes; TN, 1 red stripe.

Other hardboards with special finishes or facings are widely available and include plastic-faced boards, metal-faced hardboards, enamelled hardboards, wood-veneered hardboards, embossed hardboards and perforated hardboards.

Sizes in common use 762mm × 1981mm (2ft 6in × 6ft 6in); 915mm × 2135mm (3ft × 7ft); 915mm × 2440mm (3ft × 8ft); 1220mm × 1220mm (4ft × 4ft); 1220mm × 1830mm (4ft × 6ft); 1220mm × 2440mm (4ft × 8ft); 1220mm × 2745mm (4ft × 9ft); 1600mm × 2440mm (5ft 3in × 8ft); 1700mm × 2440mm (5ft 7in × 8ft).

Thicknesses in common use 3.2mm (⅛in); 4.8mm (3/16in); 6.4mm (¼in); 9.5mm (⅜in); 12.7mm (½in).

Notes on using Hardboards

Hardboard is liable to buckle after fixing if its moisture content is not in equilibrium with the surrounding atmosphere, and to prevent this it should always be 'conditioned' before use, as follows:

1. Lightly scrub the 'wrong' (ie the mesh) side with clean, cold water. The correct amount of water to use is 1 litre (approx. 2 pints) per 2440 × 1220mm (8 × 4ft) sheet, although this need only be used as guide.
2. Stack the boards back-to-back for 48 hours to dry out.
3. When dealing with a single board, cover the wetted side with a cloth to prevent it drying out too soon.

Fixing hardboard It is best to use the special

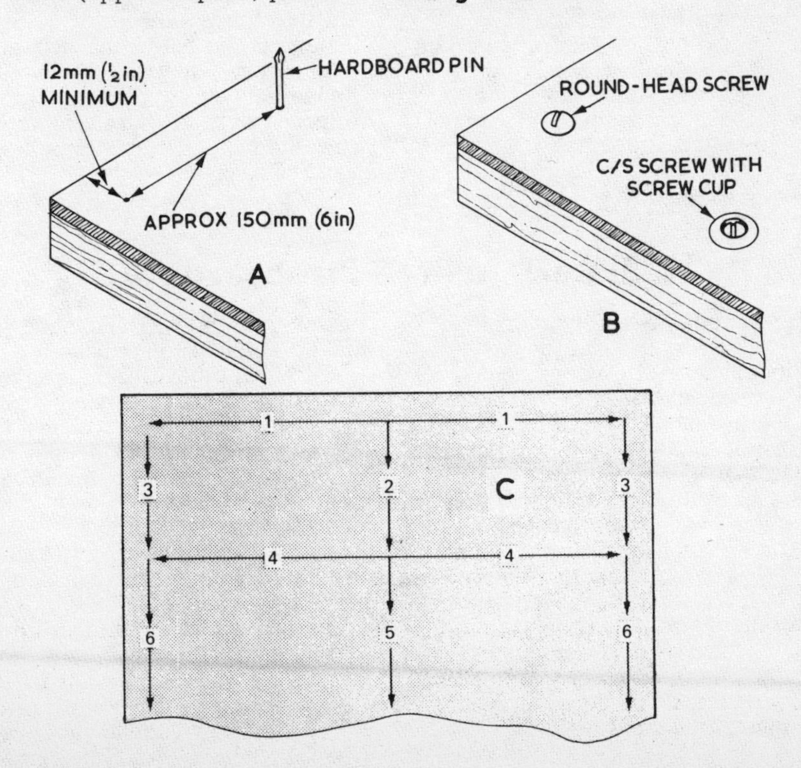

Fig 2.6

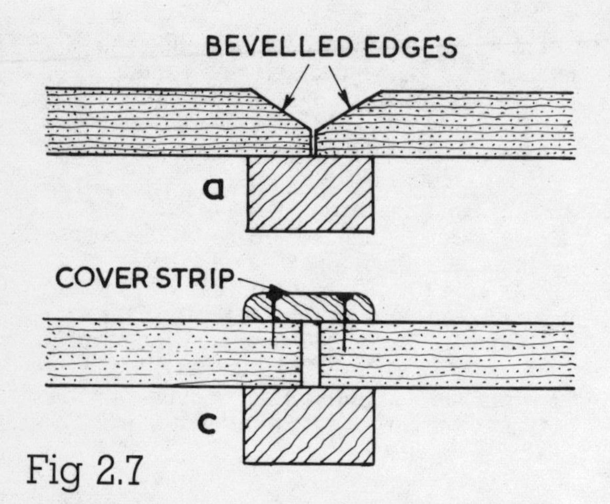

Fig 2.7

hardboard pins which have diamond-shaped heads for this (Fig 2.6A); the heads are punched home and need no filling because of their shape, but other pins will need the heads punching down and filling. If screws are used (Fig 2.6B), they should be either round-heads, or countersunk-heads used with screw cups – countersunk heads used on their own can eventually pull through the board.

When pinning a hardboard panel to a frame, position the outside pins at least 12mm (½in) away from the edge, and space the pins at about 150mm (6in) centres (Fig 2.6A). The sequence of inserting the pins into a hardboard panel on a frame is shown in Fig 2.6C.

Joints between hardboard panels (Fig 2.7) In (a) the meeting edges are bevelled so that any movement of the boards against each other is less apparent. In (b) a length of moulding is interposed between the boards, its face being flush with them. In (c) a cover strip is pinned and glued to the meeting edges. In (d), the edges are chamfered to form a scarf joint, and then glued, with pins driven through into a backing strip.

Cutting hardboard
When sawing hardboard with either hand or circular saws always keep the face side upwards to avoid splintering at the edges. The opposite applies when using a jig or sabre saw; the face side should be kept downwards as such saws cut on the upward stroke.

Medium-Density Fibreboard (MDF)

The basic raw material is timber which has been reduced to a fibrous state (as in hardboard manufacture) by a combination of steam and mechanical grinding. The fibres are then dried to a low moisture content, impregnated with synthetic-resin binders, and transported pneumatically to forming heads. Here they are directed on to a moving belt to form a mat which can be as much as 250mm (9⅞in) thick for a finished board of 12mm (½in) thickness. The fibre mat passes between polished steel belts to reduce its thickness and expel air before being crosscut with a transverse travelling saw and transported into a heated press. The press compresses the mat so that the fibres knit tightly together whilst the heat treatment cures the resin binder. After pressing there is a cooling stage, followed by cutting to usable sheet sizes.

The final product is a large board, usually pale straw in colour, smooth on both sides and ranging in thickness from 6mm (¼in) up to 45mm (1¾in) or more (though 12-22mm (½in-⅞in) is the most common range). In density, MDF is usually about 750kg/m^3 (47lb/cu ft) or more, which puts it in the same class as moderately dense hardwoods. It can be cut, machined, profiled and finished in much the same way as natural timber but is without knots, shakes, splits or other irregularities.

MDF's greatest asset, however, is its homogeneity. Because of its fibrous nature, its consistency is the same throughout its thickness and with minimal variation in density. As a result of this regularity and absence of core voids, edge machining of quite complex profiles is a simple matter. Unlike most other wood-based panel products, MDF usually does away with the need for lipping or edge-banding.

Similarly, because there is little difference between edge, core and face characteristics, incised machining of the face of the board produces excellent results. It is possible, for instance, to machine a single piece of MDF in such a way that it appears like fielded panelling. The smooth, consistent surface of MDF further makes it an ideal substrate for veneering, laminating, or finishing with stains and lacquers.

MDF is often compared with wood chipboards because of its similar range of thicknesses and sheet sizes, and sometimes with hardwoods because of the uses to which MDF is put. Both comparisons can be misleading. MDF needs to be evaluated on the basis of its own individual combination of properties.

This combination has led to its growing use in the furniture and allied industries. A great many manufacturers – and that includes one- and two-man businesses as well as the 'heavy end' – are using MDF for tabletops, unit tops, doors and carcases because of its stability as a core for veneers, its edge-machining qualities and the incised or carved effects which can be achieved. Where veneers are used on the face, profiled edges and incised areas can be stained and lacquered to give a reasonable match for the colour of the face veneer provided total authenticity is not required.

Cutting it into strips – whether for joinery mouldings, like the stiles and rails in flush-door manufacture, or for the production of (say) chair arms – is facilitated largely by the low waste involved. A large sheet of a completely consistent product can be cut to small dimensions without any need for selection of suitable pieces.

Densified Laminated Wood

In its most basic form, densified laminated wood is manufactured from individual veneers of timber which are interleaved with synthetic resin film glues of the phenol formaldehyde type and cured by elevated temperature and pressure. An important factor of its utilisation is the necessity that it should be manufactured to meet, if required, a critical technical specification. This means for example that the arrangement of the constituent laminates – and therefore the predominating grain direction – can be varied to suit the requirements of the completed component.

Compressed wood Is a tough, rigid, electrically-insulating and non-magnetic product with high mechanical strength. It is manufactured from untreated wood veneers which are bonded under a pressure of between 300/400 psi at 300/350F. Compressed wood can be used in situations demanding a reasonable degree of dimensional stability but where resistance to compression and the path of electrical current is of the utmost importance. Because of these properties, compressed wood is very popular with both the textile and electrical industries.

Compreg This is a verbal contraction of 'compressed and impregnated'. Before pressing, each wood veneer is saturated with aqueous resin forming solution (which acts as a plasticiser during pressing) until a quantity equivalent to between 30% or 35% of the dry weight of the wood is absorbed. The veneers are then left for up to two days to allow the solvent (water) to dry out and for the resin to become uniformly distributed throughout the veneer but most important, for the resin to diffuse into the cell wall network. Later moderate heating gels the resin and ensures that all solvent has been eradicated. The individual veneers are then laid up and pressed in a similar manner to that described for compressed wood. The product thus formed exhibits the following advantages over untreated wood: a 65/75% reduction of movement due to ingress/loss of moisture; 10 to 20 times harder; greatly resistant to abrasion; highly lustrous appearance; cut surfaces can be re-sanded and buffed; resistant to decay and insect attack; due to the obvious increased impermeability, more resistant to degrade by acids and alkalis. If required, it may be moulded during the initial stages of manufacture.

Impreg As with Compreg, the veneers are saturated with high penetrating phenol-formaldehyde resin but cured by normal plywood manufacturing pressures. The resultant board possesses shrinkage and swelling properties comparable with Compreg but is inferior with respect to compressive and tensile stresses.

Staypak In contrast to the compressed woods, Compreg and Impreg, the USA production Staypak is similar in most respects to the German-made Lignostone and Lignofol and can be made from either solid wood or veneers. It is wood compressed in its natural state, that is without resin treatment but under very much elevated temperatures and greatly increased pressures, in the region of ¾ to 2 tons per sq in. The manufacture of Staypak involves modifying the heat and increasing the compression conditions sufficiently to allow the lignin to flow.

As lignin is an abundant constituent of wood substance acting as a cementing compound, any internal stresses that would normally be set up as the wood is compressed are dissipated as the lignin commences to flow. The consequent springback (from compression) sometimes found with ordinary compressed wood is eliminated. Although its resistance to swelling is less favourable than Compreg it has almost twice the tensile strength and strength under impact loading.

CHAPTER THREE

Machine tooling specifications, accessories and formulae

TO GET the best out of your machines, whether they are stationary or portable, it is essential to know the correct running and feed speeds, and to choose the accessories that will be most useful.

Machine Saws

Types of machine saws (Fig 3.1)
(a) is a 'plate' saw; that is, one where the thickness is the same throughout. Used for ordinary cross-cutting or rip-sawing.
(b) is a 'hollow-ground' saw, which means that the full thickness is restricted to the rim where the teeth are situated and to the area around the central hole where it is needed for strength. Such saws are used for dimension sawing and leave a planed surface – hence it is sometimes called a 'planer' saw.
(c) is a 'ground-off' saw; its use is limited to cutting very thin strips or boards. With (d) and (e) it completes the group known as 'thin rim saws', which are specifically designed to economise on timber.
(d) is a 'swage' saw and is limited to cutting strips with a maximum thickness of 18mm ($^{11}/_{16}$in).
(e) is a 'taper' saw. It can only cut thin boards down the centre with each cut piece restricted to a maximum thickness of 18mm ($^{11}/_{16}$in).

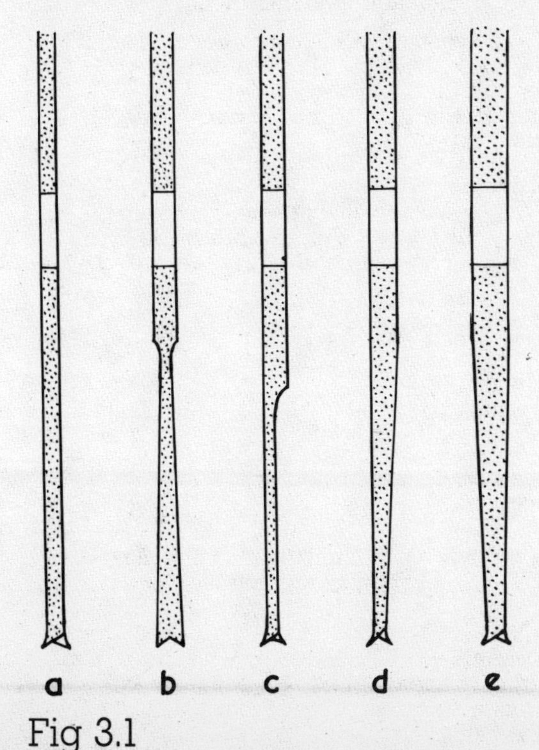

Fig 3.1

Formulae relating to circular saws
The optimum speed of rotation (R) in revolutions per minute (rpm) for a given diameter circular saw can be found from the formula:
R = (1000 × the speed in metres/minute) divided by (pi × saw diameter in mm). The factor of 1000 is included to convert mm into metres; and the value of pi in this and all other examples is 3.14.

Example
A saw of 250mm (10in) dia is required to run at a rim (peripheral) speed of approx 3000 m/min. What is the correct rpm to give this speed?

Answer
R = (1000 × 3000) divided by (3.14 × 250) = 3821rpm, ~ or 63.7rps (revolutions per second), which is obtained by dividing by 60.

The same formula, with the terms transposed, can be used to find the rim (peripheral) speed, thus:

Rim speed = (pi × saw dia × rpm) divided by 1000

3821

Example
Using the same values as in the above formula, the calculation becomes:

Rim speed = (3.14 × 250 × 3821) divided by 1000 = 2999.49 metres per minute or 49.9 metres per second – both these answers are, for all working purposes, 3000 and 50 respectively.

Note: the theoretically optimum rim (peripheral) speed is recommended as approximately 2900 metres (or approx 9500ft) per minute. Obviously, calculations often involve 'rounding-off' some figures, and there is no point in producing answers which are correct to three decimal places if they cannot be applied in workshop conditions.

Theoretical optimum rpm for circular saws

175mm (7in) diameter	5000rpm
205mm (8in) diameter	4500rpm
254mm (10in) diameter	3600rpm
305mm (12in) diameter	3000rpm
355mm (14in) diameter	2500rpm
405mm (16in) diameter	2300rpm

Horsepower required for different sizes of circular saws
(Note: one horsepower = 746 watts)

Saw diameter 175mm (7in)	$\frac{1}{3}$ to $\frac{1}{2}$hp
Saw diameter 205mm (8in)	$\frac{1}{2}$ to $\frac{3}{4}$hp
Saw diameter 254mm (10in)	$\frac{1}{2}$ to 1hp
Saw diameter 305mm (12in)	$1\frac{1}{2}$ to 2hp
Saw diameter 355mm (14in)	2 to 3hp
Saw diameter 405mm (16in)	3 to $4\frac{1}{2}$hp

Pulley sizes
If both the motor and the saw need fitting with pulleys, a ratio must be found for the pulleys; to do this the motor rpm has to be taken into consideration and is usually marked on the motor casing.

Example
A 1500rpm motor is to be coupled to a saw and the required rpm for the saw is 3000. Then the calculation is:
Motor rpm divided by saw rpm, or 1500 divided by 3000 = $\frac{1}{2}$.

Therefore the motor requires a pulley of twice the diameter of the one on the saw.

There are two variations of these calculations, the first one being where the saw pulley already exists, and both the saw rpm and the motor rpm are known – what size of pulley is required on the motor?

Answer
Multiply the saw rpm by the saw pulley diameter and divide the product by the motor rpm. Using the values in the example above and assuming the saw pulley is 50mm (2in) diameter, we have

(3000 × 50) divided by 1500
= 100mm (4in)
for the diameter of the motor pulley.

The second variation is when you need to calculate the size of the saw pulley, when the formula is:
(motor rpm × motor pulley dia) divided by the saw rpm.

Example
With the same values as the first example, this becomes (1500 × 100) divided by 3000 = 50mm for the diameter of the saw pulley.

Portable Electric Circular Saw

The following are the maximum depths of cut for different saw diameters:

152mm (6in)	48mm ($1\frac{15}{16}$in)
178mm (7in)	60mm ($2\frac{3}{8}$in)
203mm (8in)	67mm ($2\frac{5}{8}$in)
228mm (9in)	80mm ($3\frac{1}{8}$in)

Bandsaws

The optimum speed of a bandsaw is based on the linear speed, which averages 2000 metres (approx 6560ft) per minute but can vary down to about 914 metres (3000ft) per minute on small bandsaws.

Linear speed
The formula to find this is (pi × the diameter of the wheels in mm × motor rpm). Divide by 1000 to convert mm into metres.

Example
Find the linear speed of a bandsaw with 450mm dia wheels, and a motor rpm of 950. The calculation is:

(3.14 × 450 × 950) divided by 1000 = 1343 metres (4404ft) per minute.

Table showing typical linear speeds

Wheel dia	*RPM*	*Linear speed per minute*
305mm (12in)	950	approx 914m (3000ft)
457mm (18in)	950	approx 1372m (4500 ft)
610mm (24in)	800	approx 1524m (5000ft)
762mm (30mm)	750	approx 1798m (5900ft)

Length of saw required
To find this, the normal workshop practice is to raise the top wheel to its highest point and then lower it about 20mm (¾in). A length of string is then run around the wheels and its length is regarded as being satisfactory for the length of blade required.

There is, however, a formula for calculating it, as follows:
Length in metres = (3.14 × wheel dia in mm) divided by 1000; add to this result twice the distance from wheel centre to wheel centre after deducting 20mm (for strain).

Bandsaw power required

For 305mm (12in) dia wheel	⅓hp
For 457mm (18in) dia wheel	½hp
For 610mm (24in) dia wheel	1½hp
For 762mm (30in) dia wheel	3hp
For 915mm (36in) dia wheel	3hp

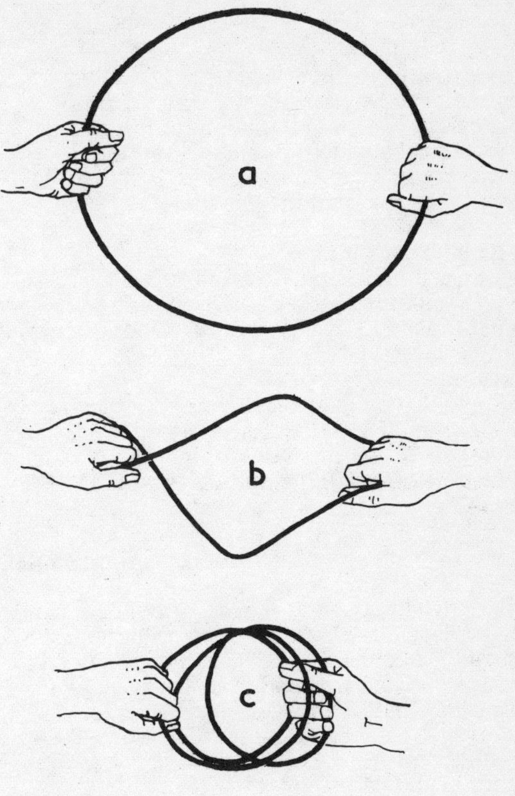

Fig 3.2

Coiling a small bandsaw (Fig 3.2)
This can best be done in three stages:
(a) Grip the bandsaw firmly at opposite sides, with the back of your right hand facing you.
(b) Then twist both hands in opposite directions, one towards and the other away from you, and at the same time allow your hands to come closer together.
(c) The bandsaw should then spring into a triple coil, as shown.

Planers

Cutting speed
This is governed by the rpm of the cutter block, and the diameter made by the cutting edges of the cutters.

In most machines both of these factors are fixed and cannot be altered. The speed can vary between 3000 and 6000rpm and, for machines with a cutter block of 75mm (3in) or less, a speed between 4000 and 6000rpm is suitable.

For industrial machines, the following formulae may be useful:

Peripheral cutting speed
This equals (3.14 × cutter block dia in mm × rpm) divided by 1000.

Correct rpm
This equals (1000 × cutting speed) divided by (3.14 × cutter block dia in mm).

Tracking a cutter block
A 'tracker' is an accessory sometimes fitted to industrial planers. Basically, it is a device which applies an abrasive stone to the cutters while the block is revolving. By so doing it ensures (a) that all the cutters are in fact cutting and (b) that they are all cutting to the same depth.

Although it is not easily apparent to the eye when these conditions are reached, all the cutters will leave a mark on the wood as they rotate – the distance between each cutter

2.22

mark is called a 'pitch'. Under eight cutter marks per 25mm (1in) is considered unacceptable; eight to twelve is satisfactory for exterior woodwork such as garden sheds, fences etc; twelve to eighteen for interior woodwork that is to be painted; and eighteen and over is suitable for surfaces which are to be glasspapered and polished.

Pitch of cutter marks
To calculate this, apply the following formula: Pitch = (1000 × feed speed in metres per minute) divided by (number of cutters × rpm).

Example
Assume that a cutter block with four cutters has an rpm of 4000, and the feed speed is 20 metres (67ft) per minute. We then get: Pitch = (1000 × 20) divided by (4 × 4000) = 1.25mm or 20 cutter marks per 25mm (1in). If the cutter block has only two cutters the pitch will be 2.50mm or 10 cutter marks per 25mm (1in).

Feed speed
The same formula can be transposed to calculate the required feed speed, as follows: Feed speed = (number of cutters × pitch × rpm) divided by 1000 and, if we apply the same values as in the first example, we get Feed speed = (4 × 1.25 × 4000) divided by 1000 = 20 metres (67ft) per minute.

HP for different lengths of cutter blocks

100mm (4in) length	⅓ to ½hp
150mm (6in) length	½ to 1hp
230mm (9in) length	1 to 1½hp
305mm (12in) length	2hp

Lathes

The optimum speed of a lathe depends mainly on the diameter of the wood being turned, although secondary factors such as the nature of the wood and the kind of tool being used also play a part. The following is a rough guide to speeds for different diameters – it must be borne in mind that as a work-piece is being turned its diameter necessarily decreases, thus calling for a different speed.

Lathe speeds

25mm (1in) diameter work-piece	3000rpm
50mm (2in) diameter work-piece	2500rpm
75mm (3in) diameter work-piece	1500rpm
102mm (4in) diameter work-piece	1250rpm
127mm (5in) diameter work-piece	1000rpm
204mm (8in) diameter work-piece	650rpm
305mm (12in) diameter work-piece	570rpm
458mm (18in) diameter work-piece	300rpm
610mm (24in) diameter work-piece	250rpm

A 100mm (4in) lathe requires a motor of ⅓ to ½hp, and a 127mm (5in) a ¾hp motor – the measurements refer to the height of the centres above the bed.

Spindle Moulders

The rpm can vary from 4000 to 10000; generally, the higher the speed the better the finish, especially with difficult grain. Small machines have ⅓ to ½hp motors, but for work using large cutters the horsepower should be ¾ to 1.

Vertical Spindle Moulder (or Shaper)

The principal feature of this machine is the spindle which protrudes vertically through the working table. This can be fitted to carry cutters of various types, such as those shown in Fig 3.3; details are as follows:
(a) is the French head, which has a slot through which a cutter, or a pair of cutters, are introduced and held down by a locking nut and, if required, a packing piece or pieces.
(b) shows slotted collars and two cutters; the lower cutter is dropped over the spindle head first, the cutters follow next, and the top collar is dropped on and held by a set-screw.
(c) is a square block. These vary in size from about 60mm (2⅜in) to 110mm (4⅜in) square and from 51mm (2in) to 120mm (4¾in) long. The bolts which carry the cutters are slid down the grooves in the block and threaded through the slots in the cutters and the securing nuts are tightened.
(d) is a Whitehill cutter block. These are circular and made in two standard diameters,

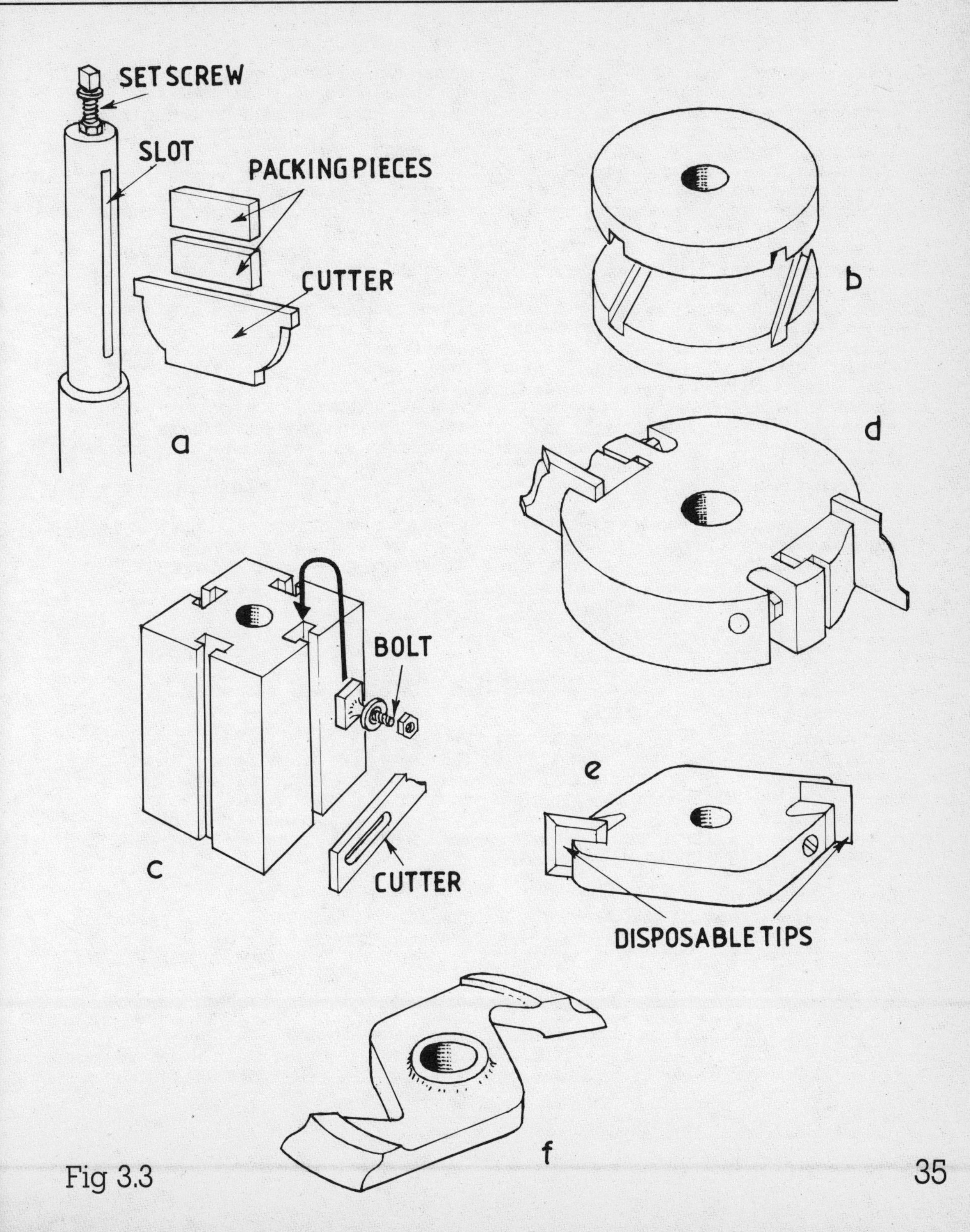
SET SCREW
SLOT
PACKING PIECES
CUTTER
a
b
d
BOLT
CUTTER
c
e
DISPOSABLE TIPS
f

Fig 3.3

125mm (4⅞in) and 137mm (5⅜in) by 23mm (15/16in) thick. Their great advantage is that the cutters can be rotated through 360 degrees so that each edge of the cutter can be used and different profiles can be spindled by simply turning the cutters on their fixing bolts to present the desired shape. All of the above suffer to some extent from balancing problems as the centripetal and centrifugal forces must cancel each other out. If the cutters are out of balance, the machine bearings will be damaged, and in extreme cases a fastening bolt could fracture, allowing a cutter to fly off with disastrous results.

To overcome the difficulty some manufacturers now offer the following patterns: (e) the 'disposable tip' head. The cutters (or tips) are made of tungsten carbide and are therefore particularly suitable for work on particle boards and plywoods. Each cutter has four cutting edges and when these are all blunted, it is thrown away. Cutters should always be put into use or discarded in matching pairs, as using one new one with a partly used one could upset the balance.
(f) the two-wing solid profile cutter. These are expensive and are bought in ready-ground to the required profile by the supplier. Regrinding can be done in the home workshop but is arduous and exacting. The cutters are also supplied with four or six wings.

The following are the rpm of spindles when fitted with various cutting heads: square cutter blocks – 3,000 to 4,000; circular heads such as the Whitehill – 4,500 to 6,000; slotted collars – 6,000 to 7,000; solid profile cutters should be run at the highest speed available.

It is obvious that with cutters and blocks revolving at such high speeds some form of safety guard is essential. One which is often used is a Shaw guard, and this (in its best form) consists of two pressure pads which bear on the work; one pad is arranged vertically and the other horizontally so that the work is fed through a kind of tunnel.

Good though this is, the revolving spindle is left unguarded and loose clothing (for example, a loose tie) could be caught in it. It is therefore best to use the Shaw guard in conjunction with a cage or bonnet which covers the revolving cutters except for a gap through which they project when cutting.

Sanding Machines

Disc sander
The following table gives optimum rpm and horsepower for different sizes of discs:

254mm (10in) dia	600 to 2500rpm	½ to 1hp
405mm (16in) dia	900 to 1000rpm	1hp
610mm (24in) dia	400 to 570rpm	1 to 3hp
760mm (30in) dia	200 to 320rpm	4hp

Single-drum sander
Optimum speed is from 900 to 1500rpm. A 150mm (6in) diameter drum needs a ¾hp motor, and up to 254mm (10in) diameter, 1½hp.

Belt sander
Power required depends on the width of the belt and the kind of work done, but generally a 102mm (4in) wide belt needs a ⅓ to ½hp motor, and a 150mm (6in) wide belt ¾ to 1hp.

Belt speed
This is based on the number of metres per minute, and varies between 305 and 915m/min (344 and 3001 ft/min).

Pulley rpm
This depends on the diameter of the pulleys and the belt speed, and the formula for determining it is as follows:
Pulley rpm = (metres per minute of belt × 1000) divided by (diameter of pulley × 3.14).

Example
Where the belt speed is 610m/min (2001ft/min), and the diameter of the pulley is 127mm (5in), we get
Pulley rpm = (610 × 1000) divided by (127 × 3.14) = approx 1521rpm.

The same formula (with the terms transposed) can be used to find the belt speed, thus
Belt speed = (pulley rpm × pulley dia in mm) divided by 3.14; by using the terms in the example above we get

Example
Belt speed = (1521 × 127) divided by 3.14 = 610m/min (2001ft/min).

Routers

Feed speed
The correct speed (the rate at which the router cutter is passed through the work) comes naturally with practice. Because of the diverse range of materials worked with the router, and the variety of cutters used there can be no clear-cut recommendations – only a common sense approach based on experience.

After some while, the operator will learn to gauge feed speed by the 'free-cutting ability' of the router. If the router is fed too slowly, free cutting is inhibited, and friction and burning are inevitable. Conversely, feeding too fast will prevent the cutter from performing its cutting and clearance operations, the motor will be overloaded, and the groove is likely to be 'feather-edged'.

Strangely, if a blunt cutter is used the symptoms of both too slow and too fast a feed will occur simultaneously.

Cutting speeds
Free-running speeds given in sales literature can be misleading, since it is the spindle speed under load which is significant. A powerful router, say of 1200w rating, may only have an 18000rpm speed rating, but under a light load it will barely drop its revolutions at all. Conversely, a 400w router running free at 25000rpm will drop down to 17000rpm very quickly; it should therefore only be used on really light-duty operations.

It is impossible to give a definite rule about cutting speeds because conditions vary from job to job. For guidance, however, one might say that a 6mm (¼in) diameter cutter requires a free-running speed of between 20000 and 24000rpm for the best results. Conversely, a cutter of 19mm (¾in) diameter performs better at a speed of between 14000 and 20000rpm. An important point to remember is that, if the router is under-powered, the cutting speed under load will be drastically reduced and incorrect. A correct speed and a sharp cutter will ensure a good finish – unless the wood is green or moisture-laden, when feathering is to be expected in any case.

Overloading
Several factors affect the life of a motor. In all cases, early recognition of trouble is of paramount importance, because prompt attention can save an expensive re-wiring job. If the motor runs slowly or intermittently, check for carbon-brush wear or bearing failure, and do not put it to work until this has been done. If a bearing is seizing up, it may still be possible to salvage the motor windings.

In operation, the spindle speed will naturally be reduced under load; but it should not drop much below 70% of the free-running rpm. For an indication of whether the tool is being mishandled, listen to the tone or whine of the motor, which will be noticeably lower under excessive load. Your motto should be 'keep a sharp ear out and maintain the revs'. If the drop in revs seems too great when the machine is being correctly used, some maintenance is required as soon as possible. The cause may be a faulty bearing. Do not continue to use a machine in that condition.

Router Cutters

There is a bewildering array of router cutters for various purposes, and the following notes attempt to classify the various types.

Cutters for moulding edges Profiles include: bevel; bullnose; cavetto; chamfer; classic styles; cove; multi-beaded (for reeded edges); ogees; ovolos and matching scribers for rule joints; rebating; rounded-over: staff bead.

Cutters for trimming edges Include TC (tungsten-carbide) cutters for trimming plastic-faced boards at 45/60/90 degrees; combined rebating and trimming cutters.

Cutters for grooving, slotting and channelling Include HSS (high speed steel) and TC cutters for dovetail-housings – the same cutter will also cut dovetails; drip channel; eccentric chuck and single flute cutter for long runs – can only be used with collets with 10 to 12mm capacities; hinge recessing; radius-ended for cutting grooves with rounded bottoms; recessed rebating with stepped grooves for shelf supports; single flute for fast groove cutting; staggered tooth for fast groove cutting and chip clearance; two flute with bottom cut which allows for plunging when cutting mortises; two flute without bottom cut – cannot be plunged; Vee grooving.

Cutters for shaping the edges of panels and for cleaning out sunk panels The edges can be bevelled, ogee, ovolo, or square.

Special cutters Hinge-sinkers which cut clean holes to house circular hinges (20, 25, 26, 30 and 35mm diameters). Keyhole slot-cutters – suitable for 8 and 10 gauge round-head screws; the cutter is plunged 10mm (3/8in) deep into the wood, moved forward about 12mm (1/2in) and then brought back so that the cutter can be withdrawn. Pierce-and-trim cutters which can be plunged to pierce and then cut out apertures in plastic-faced boards or worktops. Tee-slot cutters which cut a recess in which electric cables can be inserted – a 5 or 6mm (3/16 or 1/4in) sawcut has to be made first for the shank to move along.

Cutter sets These are available for cutting tongued and grooved boards which match exactly but are for 10 or 12mm (3/8in or 1/2in) capacity collets only. There is also a range of profile/scriber sets which produce matched positive and reversed mouldings with bevelled, ogee, or ovolo profiles – they fit routers with 6mm (1/4in) capacity collets and a minimum power of 650 watts.

Bits and Drills

See Fig. 3.4. All bits intended for use with the hand-brace are designed for the relatively slow movement which is necessarily a feature of hand-work. To use some of them at the high speeds associated with power would cause difficulties. On the other hand, the ever-growing use of electric power drills has resulted in the production of special drills which are largely dependent on speed for a clean result.

Centre bit 1 Intended for boring shallow holes or for boring right through thin wood. It is liable to wander if used for a deep hole. An essential feature is that the centre point has the greatest projection so that it forms the pivot on which the bit turns, enabling it to start exactly in the required position. The nicker follows so that it cuts in the periphery of the circle (its edge must slope in the right direction or be rounded so that it cuts, not scratches); and the cutter comes last, lifting the waste which has already been severed by the nicker. To sharpen it, the centre point is filled to a triangular section, and the nicker is sharpened on the inside only. Only the bevel of the cutter is sharpened. Centre bits are made in sizes ranging from 6mm to 58mm (1/4in to 2 1/4in).

Screw-point centre bit 2 Its advantage is that it is not necessary to maintain so heavy a pressure since the screw point draws the bit into the wood. It is unsuitable for boring right through thin wood because the screw point obviously is no advantage, and in any case makes a large hole which makes centreing from the opposite side awkward. Sizes range from 5mm to 58mm (3/16in to 2 1/4in).

Forstner bit 3 This bit is guided by its circular rim rather than the centre point, though its small centre enables it to be started in the required position. Relatively slow cutting, and for fine work only. Cuts a clean hole, almost flat-bottomed: holes can also overlap. Sizes from 10mm to 50mm (3/8in to 2 in).

Shell bit 4 Used almost entirely for screw and similar small holes. Can be repeatedly sharpened until too short for practical use. Has largely been replaced by the faster-cutting drills. Sizes from 3mm to 12mm (1/8in to 1/2in).

Spoon bit 5 Used for purposes similar to those of the shell bit, but can be started more accurately and cuts a cleaner hole. Can only be sharpened a few times as when the spoon end is filed away it becomes a shell bit. Sizes from 3mm to 12mm (1/8in to 1/2in).

Nose bit 6 Similar uses to Nos 4 and 5, but slower-cutting; an advantage is that the waste is extracted as the bit is withdrawn. Sizes 3mm to 16mm (1/8in to 5/8in).

Morse drill bit 7 This is an ordinary morse drill but supplied with a shank to fit a hand-brace. Cannot be started accurately unless the position is popped with a punch or a pilot hole bored. Sizes from 2mm to 19mm (1/16in to 3/4in).

Half-twist bit (also called 'diamond' or 'cobra') 8 Used for screw holes. It is fast-cutting but can split the wood if used too near the edge or the end. Sizes from 2mm to 10mm (1/16in to 3/8in).

Snail-horn countersink 9 Used after a hole

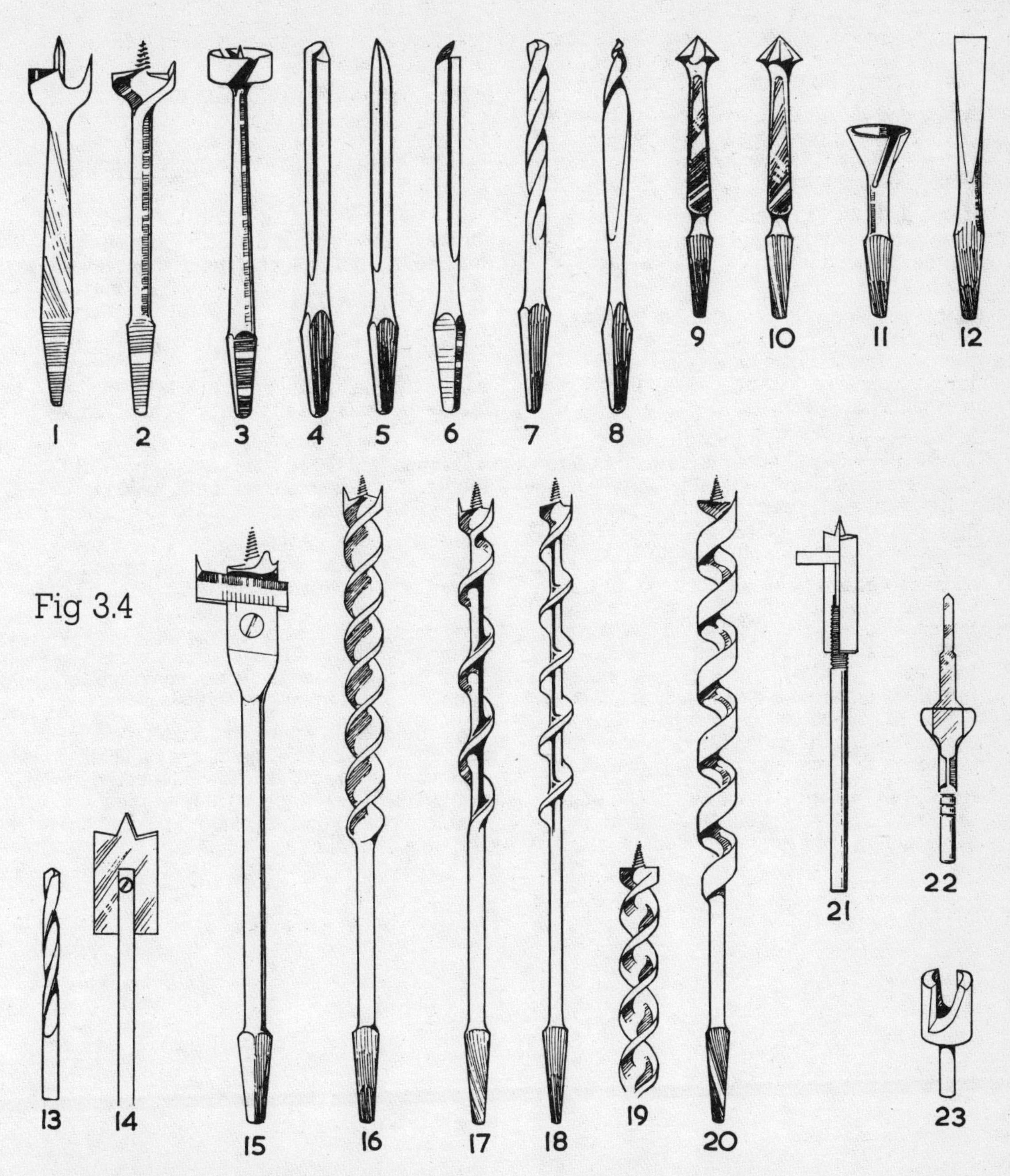

Fig 3.4

has been made to enable a screw head to sink in flush. Gives a smooth finish if kept sharp, with the edge slightly undercut. Sizes from 10mm to 22mm ($^3/_8$in to $^7/_8$in).

Rose-head countersink 10 For countersinking holes in brass and soft metals. Sizes from 6mm to 25mm ($^1/_4$in to 1in).

Dowel sharpener or beveller 11 Takes off the sharp, square edges of a dowel enabling it to start easily in its hole. As the end of the bit is usually about 25mm (1in) across cannot be used when the dowels are closer together than 12mm ($\frac{1}{2}$in) centres.

Turnscrew bit 12 Enables screws to be driven in quickly, and gives great leverage for large screws, although heavy downward pressure is essential. Sizes 6mm to 16mm ($\frac{1}{4}$in to $\frac{5}{8}$in).

Morse drill 13 The familiar drill used with power drills; intended for metal but frequently used for wood. Wide range of sizes.

Flatbit 14 Used with power drills. It bores a clean hole quickly. Not suitable for use with the hand-brace as the slow speed would probably cause tearing out. Sizes from 10mm to 32mm ($\frac{3}{8}$in to $1\frac{1}{4}$in).

Expansive bit 15 For larger holes – it saves keeping a wide range of centre bits. Centre cutter removes waste before the larger outer cutter comes into operation. Made in two sizes for boring 12mm to 38mm ($\frac{1}{2}$in to $1\frac{1}{2}$in) holes, and 22mm to 76mm ($\frac{7}{8}$in to 3in).

Jennings pattern twist bit 16 Used for deep holes as when dowelling. The spiral enables the chips to escape, and at the same time keeps the bit in alignment since the sides bear on the wall of the hole. Nickers cut the periphery ensuring a clean hole, and the cutters remove the waste. Standard lengths are from 202mm (8in) to 254mm (10in) overall; from 5mm to 38mm ($\frac{3}{16}$in to $1\frac{1}{2}$in) diameters.

Irwin or solid-centre twist bit 17 Generally reckoned to be stronger than No 16, and has the advantage of easier chip clearance. Same lengths as No 16; diameters from 3mm to 38mm ($\frac{1}{8}$in to $1\frac{1}{2}$in).

Irwin single-nicker twist bit 18 Similar to No 17, but the single nicker and cutter give better clearance for green wood and other difficult timbers. Sizes from 6mm to 25mm ($\frac{1}{4}$in to 1in).

Scotch twist bit 19 Used for rough work where splintering out does not matter (eg fencing, sheds, etc). Lengths from 202mm to 254mm (8in to 10in); diameters from 3mm to 38mm ($\frac{3}{16}$in to $1\frac{1}{2}$in).

Single auger bit 20 Has a spur on the point to ensure smooth edges. Can be used in the hand-brace, although special bits are made for power drills. Sizes 6mm to 25mm ($\frac{1}{4}$in to 1in).

Superspandrill 21 For use with a power drill; it bores a clean hole from 10mm to 25mm ($\frac{3}{8}$in to 1in) diameters.

Counterbore bit 22 Used entirely for screw-holing with a power drill. The end bores the thread hole in which the screw bites, the next part forms the shank hole, and the shouldered part the countersinking. The spring stop (when fitted) permits of flush countersinking, recessing, or counterboring. In sets of four for various screw-sizes.

Plug cutter 23 To enable plugs to be cut for pelleting, although the plugs are parallel instead of tapered. A shallow hole of the outside diameter of the bit is bored first to enable the latter to be started. The resulting plug is 10mm ($\frac{3}{8}$in) in diameter.

CHAPTER FOUR

KD fittings and general cabinet hardware

TODAY there is a wide range of hinges and fittings of all kinds which can save you valuable time otherwise spent in making complicated joints or special constructions, and most of them are designed for use with man-made boards. The following is a comprehensive summary of those which are readily available.

Angle plate Fig 4.1 A handy mild steel plate for strengthening and squaring up corners of carcases etc. The central hole is for the flush-fitting of lightweight wall cabinets.

Angled shrinkage plate Fig 4.2 For strengthening corners in carcases etc made of natural wood where shrinkage may be a problem – the slots on one of the leaves allow for this. Roundhead screws should be used in these slots and not driven home too tightly.

Flush-fitting flap hinges Fig 4.3 Made in 35mm diameter size only. The hinge is fitted by drilling a 35mm dia hole to a depth of 12mm; the centre of the hole on both base and lid should be 12.5mm from the edge of the board. When the two parts of the hinge are brought together it is possible to make adjustments in three dimensions.

Cam fitting Fig 4.4 The cranked nylon dowel is fitted into a 8mm diameter hole drilled centrally in a panel up to 18mm thick and centred at 9mm from the inside edge on wider panels. The hole should be 25mm deep, and a steel pin is driven into the dowel to lock it in place. A 25mm blind hole is then drilled 12mm deep to take the circular boss of the fitting. When the two pieces of board are brought together, the dowel is accepted into the cam and a half-turn on the slotted head will tighten the joint.

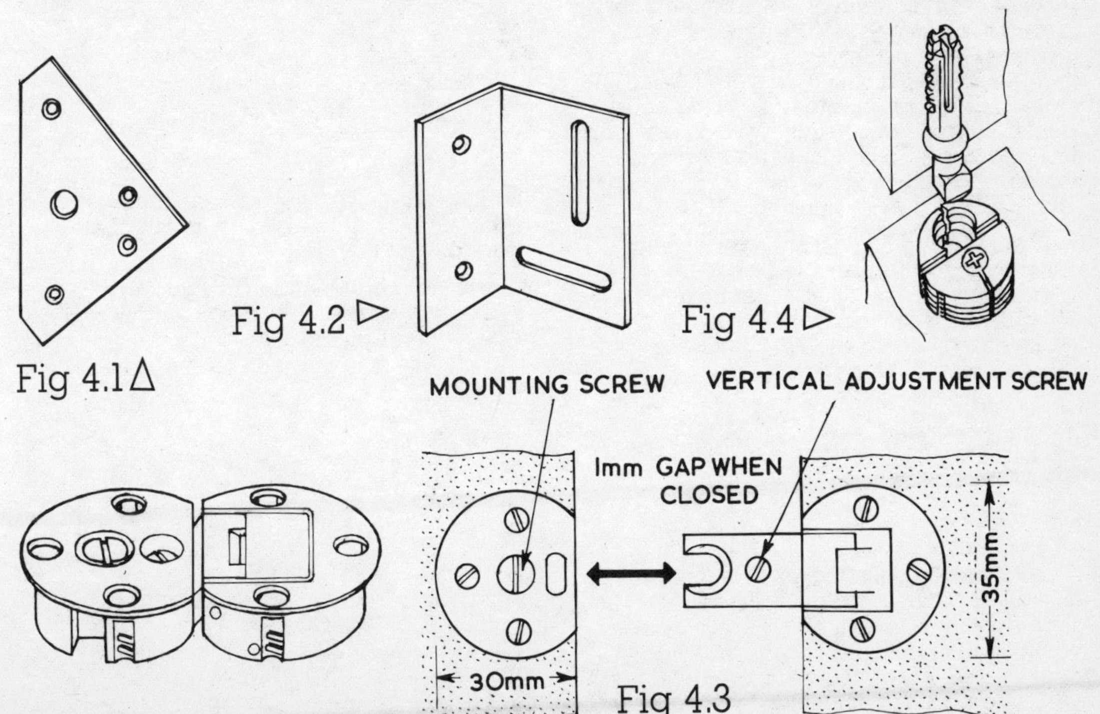

Fig 4.1△

Fig 4.2▷

Fig 4.4▷

Fig 4.3

Cabinet hanger Fig 4.5 This is designed to hang wall cabinets and allows for adjustments in all directions up to 12mm. It also allows the cabinet to be lifted off the wall when decorating etc.

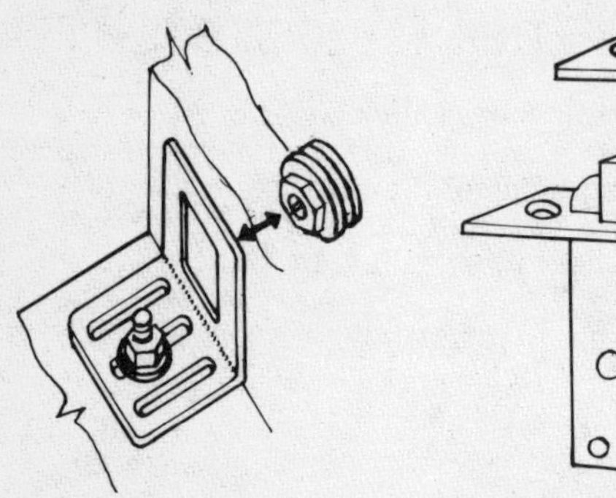

Fig 4.5

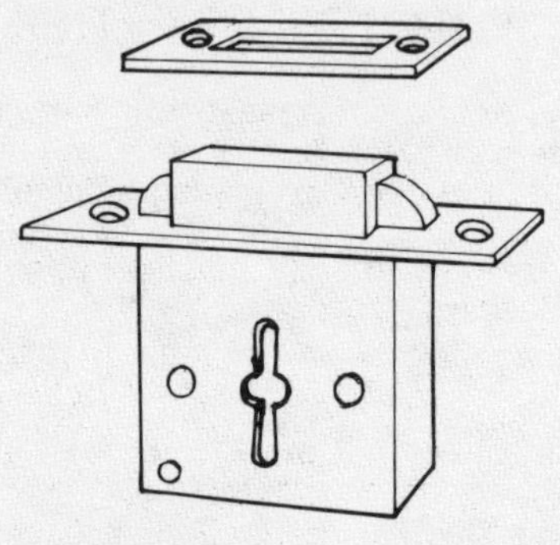

Fig 4.6

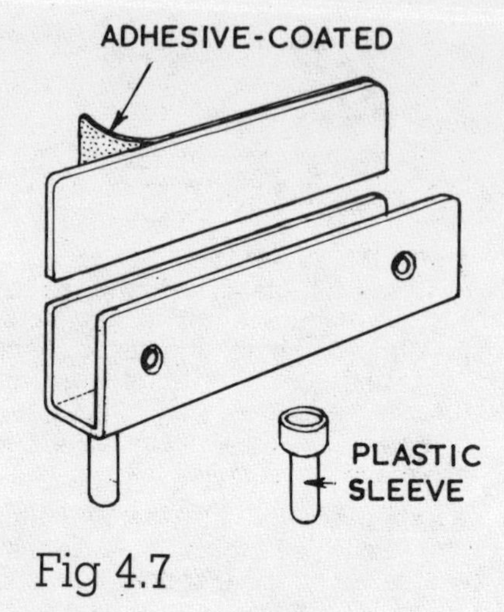

Fig 4.7

Bird's beak lock Fig 4.6 Suitable for locking any vertical door, flap, or front (such as a tambour or roll-top desk) which relies upon gravity to close. The two 'beaks' are sprung and engage into a locking plate.

Glass door pivot hinge Fig 4.7 Suitable for inset frameless glass doors of 4 to 5.5mm thickness such as those on glass-fronted hi-fi record cabinets. It is supplied with fixing screws, load-bearing pressure plate, and plastic pivot sleeves, each of which is simply inserted into a 8.5mm diameter hole drilled in the top and bottom of the cabinet. The hinges are supplied in handed pairs.

Wardrobe fitting Fig 4.8 A powerful cam-action fitting which provides a secure joint where large flat panels meet at a corner. A screwdriver is inserted in the slot and turned which causes a tongue to slot into the receiver plate, 45mm wide.

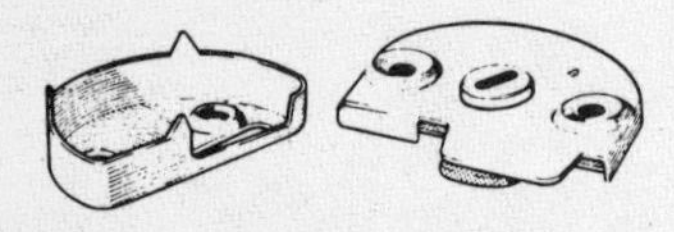

Fig 4.8

Door-lift mechanism Fig 4.9 Designed for use on wall cupboards, the fitting has a dual purpose as it acts as a hinge and stay combined. The door-lift mechanism allows cupboard or locker doors to open upwards, while the spring action holds the door in the open position. The mechanism consists of a right- and a left-hand fitting, both spring-loaded.

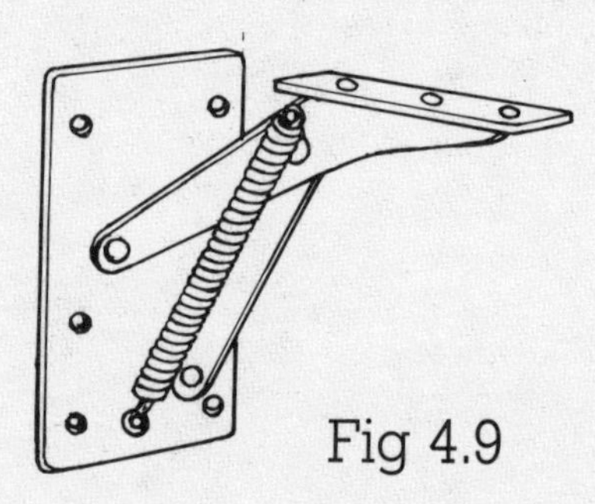

Fig 4.9

Wardrobe hanging-tube fittings Fig 4.10 (a) cup end bracket; (b) end bracket for oval tube; (c) end ring socket.

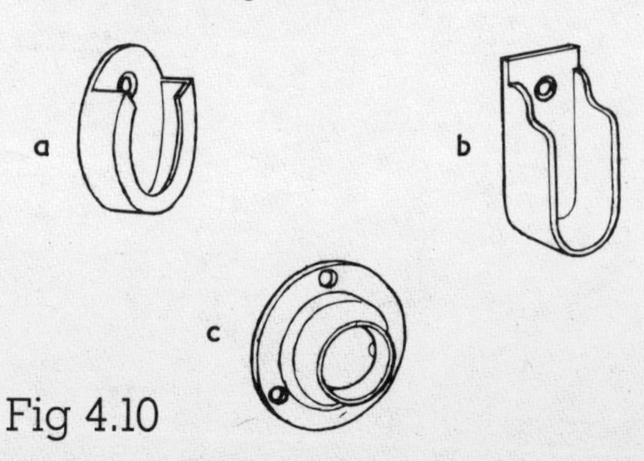

Fig 4.10

Cabinet suspension fitting Fig 4.11 For fitting inside wall cabinets. The fittings are capable of supporting weights up to 120 kilograms (approx 264lb). Vertical and horizontal adjustments of up to 4mm are possible.

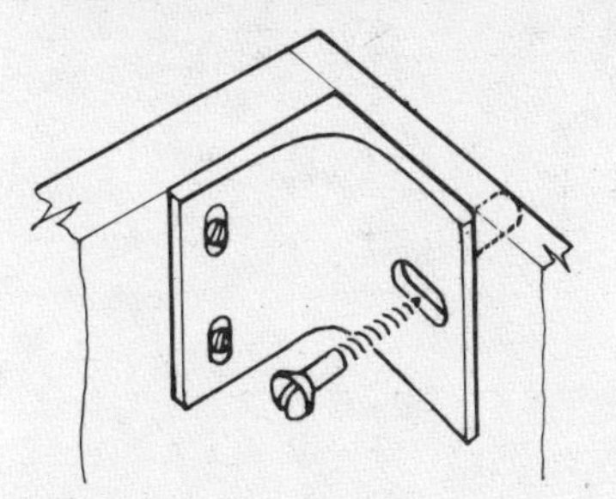

Fig 4.11

Base plate Fig 4.12 and 4.13 All concealed hinges require matching base plates. The hinge itself is attached to the door, the base plate is fitted to the carcase, and the hinged door is connected to the base plate.

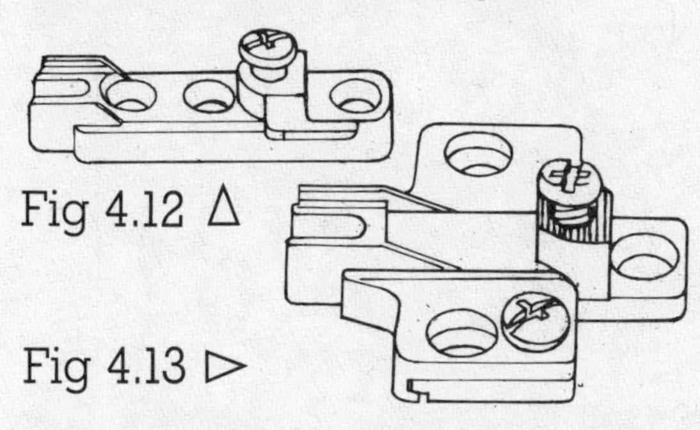

Fig 4.12 △

Fig 4.13 ▷

Concealed Mini cabinet hinge Fig 4.14 This hinge is particularly useful on smaller cabinets and may be suitable when hanging framed doors where the amount of timber is less than with solid doors. Requires a matching base plate which is attached to the carcase; the hinged door is offered up to the base plate and secured by means of a machine screw in the arm.

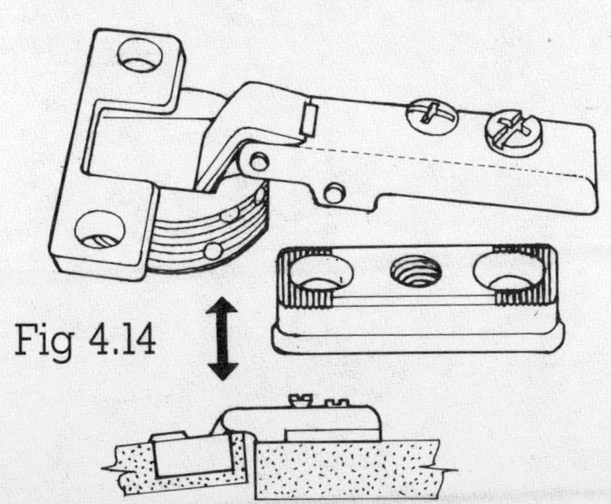

Fig 4.14

Glass door Mini hinge Fig 4.15 With 94 degrees opening angle. This hinge is based on the same design as the Concealed Mini cabinet hinge (qv) and it requires the same base plate. The hinge boss fits into a 26mm diameter hole cut in the glass door (this hole is normally cut for you by the glass supplier). The door is then secured to the hinge boss by a decorative front which is fastened by two small machine screws. The hinge is suitable for hanging glass doors between 4.5 and 7mm thick.

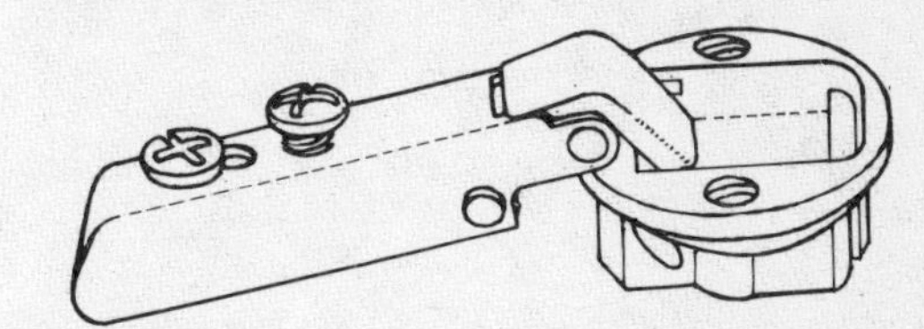

Fig 4.15

'Confirmat' connector Fig 4.16 This is designed with a deep cylindrical buttress thread which bites into the material of chipboard or fibreboards. A 7mm diameter through hole needs to be drilled in one panel and a 5.5mm pocket hole in the other. The panels are then lined up as for a dowelling operation. A cover cap can be fitted to hide the head; if drilling through a melamine-faced board it is advisable to prepare a countersink.

Fig 4.16

Adjustable cabinet support Fig 4.17 The fixing block is attached to the underside of the cabinet so that the end panel is supported. The amount of 'toe-room' or set-back of the plinth will determine the position of the fixing block relative to the front edge of the cabinet. The adjustable leg is a 35mm dia tube with a 77mm dia foot; it is supplied with a pin which marks the standard 150mm height position and the leg can then be adjusted to +19mm or −14mm from this. A screw-on plate (not shown) is fixed to the back of the plinth facing at the required

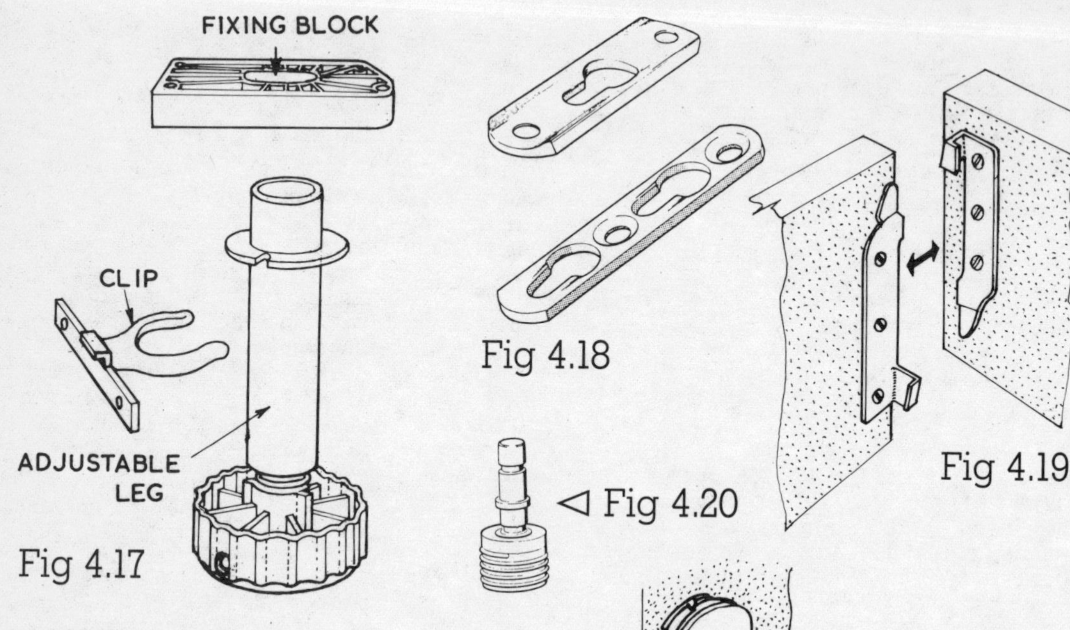

Fig 4.17

Fig 4.18

Fig 4.19

◁ Fig 4.20

height; the clip illustrated slides on to this plate and the whole assembly is clipped to the adjustable leg.

Frame assembly fittings Fig 4.18 Two types of surface-fixing plates which are supplied with special screws for making modern chairs easy to assemble.

Bed fitting Fig 4.19 The fitting is particularly suitable for wooden panel-sided beds or cots. There are two parts which are screwed to the panels to be joined; one part is then slotted over the other.

Tee joint Fig 4.20 A three-part invisible fitting in which identical nylon bushes are glued into each wooden component and connected by a short nylon dowel – the parts come together with a firm press-stud action. The dowel is 22mm long and the bushes 12mm outside diameter.

Assembly fitting Fig 4.21 This has the advantage that it does not require any edge drilling of the boards to be fixed. It is only necessary to drill two 25mm diameter holes in the face of the boards; the two parts of the fitting are then pushed together and the cam screw given a half-turn to tighten the joint.

Hinge sinker Fig 4.22 Made in two sizes – to drill 26 and 35mm diameter holes not exceeding 13mm deep (this depth is sufficient to accommodate the hinge bosses

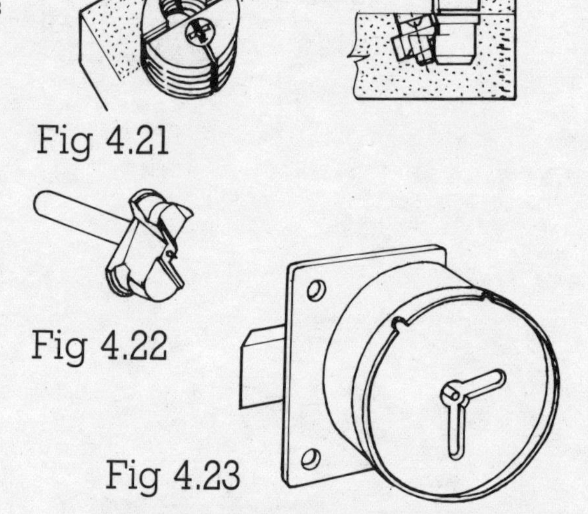
Fig 4.21

Fig 4.22

Fig 4.23

on concealed hinges). Ideally it should be used in a vertical drill stand; it will cut clean, blind holes in chipboard, softwood, or hardwood.

Circular cupboard lock Fig 4.23 Can be used on right-hand doors, or on drawer or lift-up flaps; it is fitted into a 35mm dia hole drilled to a depth of 10mm and secured by two screws. The 35mm dia hole needs to be centred at 20mm from the board edge.

Glass door cylinder lock Fig 4.24 Suitable for glass sliding doors up to 6mm thick without the need for drilling holes in the glass. A ratchet action accommodates door overlaps of 18mm to 83mm.

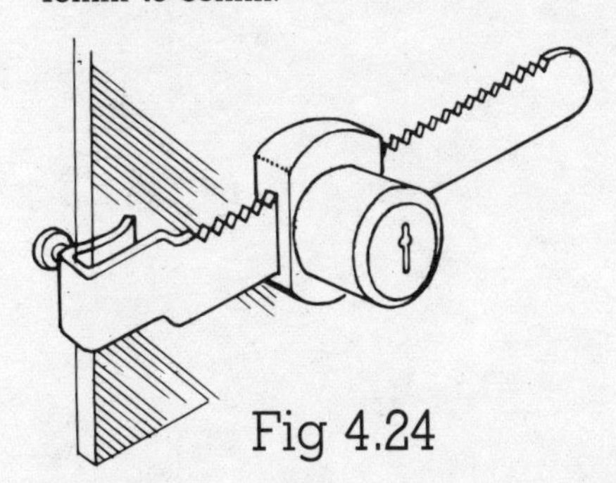

Fig 4.24

Sliding door lock Fig 4.25 A 19mm dia hole is drilled through the outer door and the body of the lock is fitted into it. A socket is fitted into a 8mm dia hole, 11mm deep, which is drilled directly behind the lock cylinder. The locking action includes a push-button mechanism which extends a bolt to locate in the rear door socket to secure both doors.

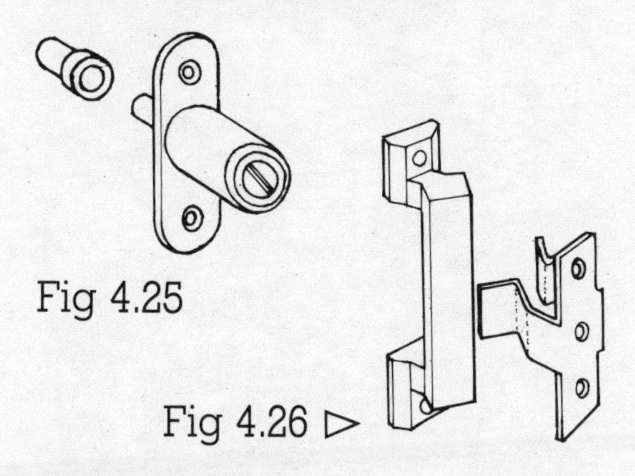

Fig 4.25

Fig 4.26 ▷

Plinth connector Fig 4.26 This consists of a hardened plastic pillar connector which is attached to the carcase, and a strong steel spring clip which is fitted on to the plinth front and engages on to the connector. This enables the plinth front to be removed easily for access to wiring etc.

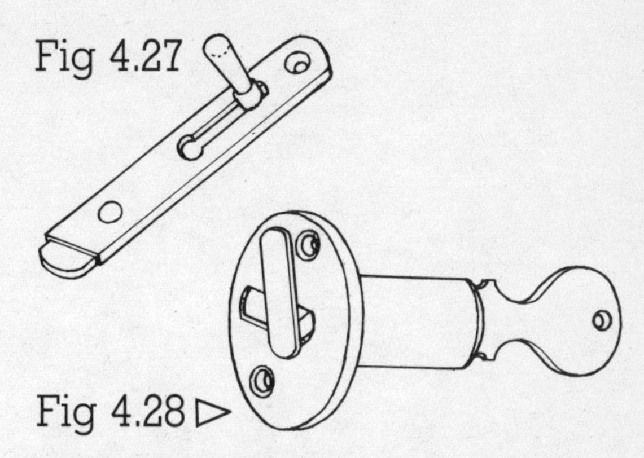

Fig 4.27

Fig 4.28 ▷

Automatic furniture bolt Fig 4.27 This bolt locks in the closed position and the slide button has to be pulled out before it can be slid back, so making it difficult for young children to operate.

Fall-flap lock Fig 4.28 This is primarily for use on pieces such as bureaux and cocktail cabinets where there are fall-flaps, but it could also be adapted for small cabinet doors. The lock and bolt are flush with the surface when the flap is open; the key can only be removed when the flap is locked.

Concealed cabinet hinge with 100 degree opening angle Fig 4.29 Designed for use with lay-on doors, ie where the door covers part or all of the carcase frame. It is so constructed that when the door is fully opened it does not protrude beyond the outside edge of the cabinet. They are made unsprung and sprung – the spring-loaded closing mechanism retains the door firmly shut against the frame of the cabinet and there is no need to use any other kind of door

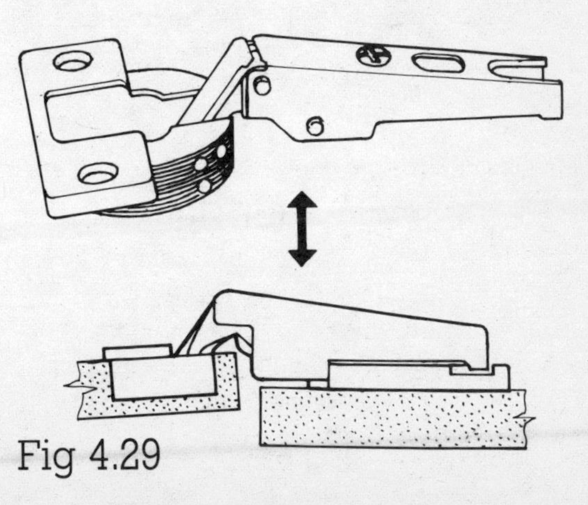

Fig 4.29

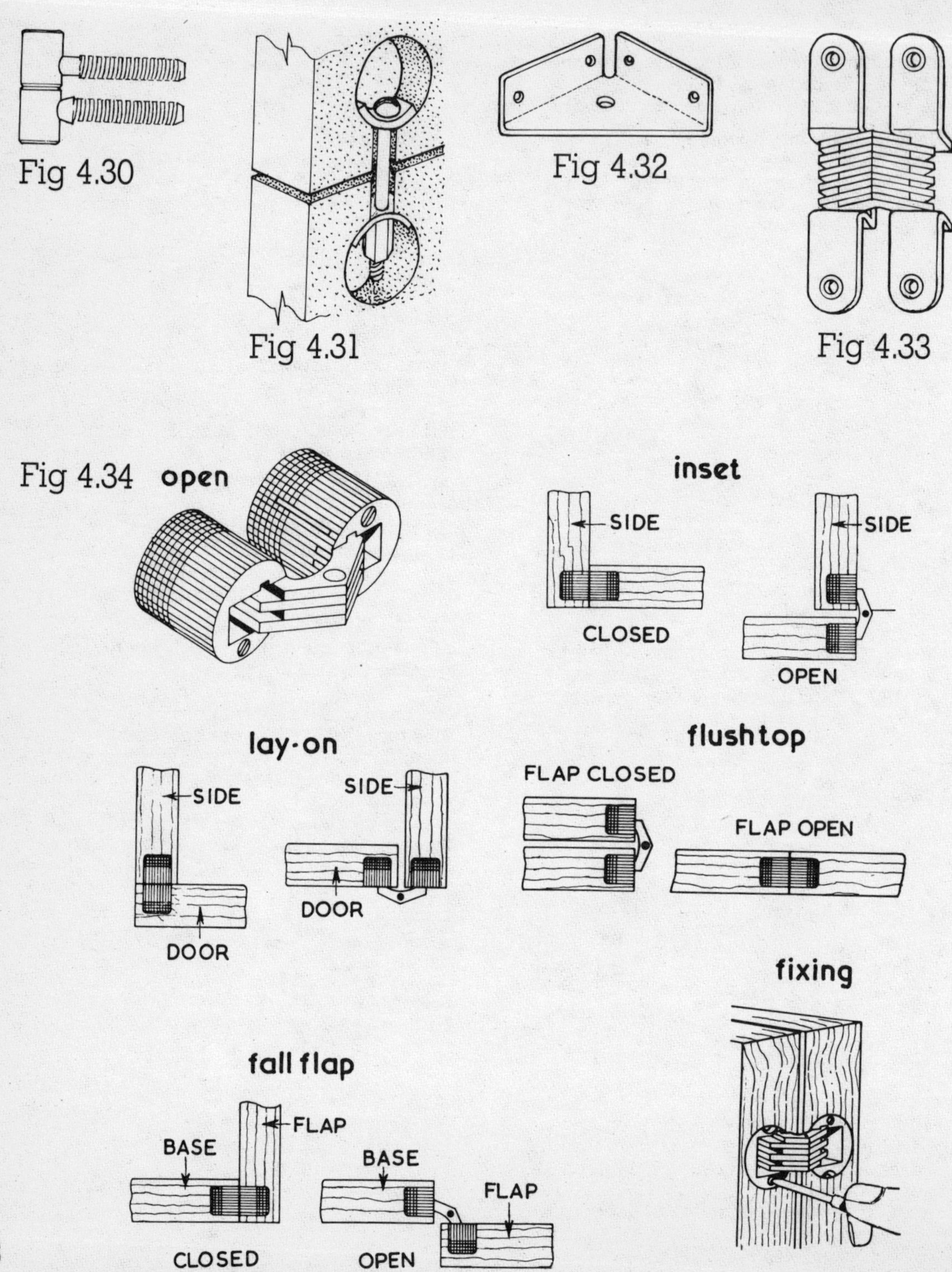

Fig 4.30

Fig 4.31

Fig 4.32

Fig 4.33

Fig 4.34

catch. On large doors two sprung hinges could be used, with an unsprung one at the centre. Other models are made with 110/125 degree, and 170 degree opening angles.

Pivot hinge Fig 4.30 Used either for rebated doors or partial lay-on doors where the larger part of the frame is left visible as a design feature. The arms are screwed into 4.5mm diameter holes drilled in the edge of the door and the frame, leaving the butt of the hinge visible as a design feature. Wall plugs can be inserted into the holes when chipboard is used. An advantage is that they are 'lift-off' hinges which are not handed.

Panel butting connector: Fig 4.31 For connecting two butting panels end-to-end (as in a worktop); a 35mm hole is drilled in each panel centred at 35mm from each panel edge, and a 15mm channel is cut from the edge of each hole to the edge of the panel. The fitting is inserted and the hexagonal nut tightened. Made in two sizes – 78 and 150mm.

Corner bracket Fig 4.32 For strengthening and squaring-up the inside corners of cabinets. Wall cabinets can also be hung from the central hole, and the brackets can be used for fastening either individual worktops or across a series of cupboards. For this, the bracket should be inverted and the worktop secured by screwing through the bracket into the underside of the surface. Made in two sizes – 51 and 65mm.

Invisible hinge Fig 4.33 This has an opening angle of 180 degrees and is fully recessed into both the door and the hanging stile. It operates through a series of connected scissor-type joints which makes for an even load distribution of the weight of the door.

Cylinder hinge Fig 4.34 This has a full 180 degree opening angle and can be used for inset or lay-on doors, fall flaps, flush tops, or cabinet folding doors. It is inserted into pre-drilled holes and an adjusting screw is turned to make a tight fit once the hinge is in position. Made in four sizes centre-to-centre, namely 10, 12, 14, and 16mm.

Sepa hinge Fig 4.35 An invisible hinge that has a 180 degree opening angle. The leaves are laid into round-ended recesses on the door and the frame and are concealed when the door is closed. Suitable for lay-on or inset doors, fall flaps, or 'concertina' folding doors.

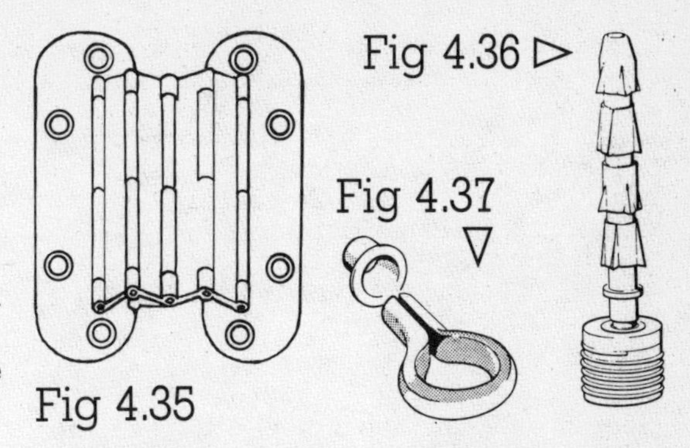

Fig 4.35

Fig 4.36 ▷

Fig 4.37 ▽

Nylon barbed dowel Fig.4.36 Can be used to join invisibly cabinet corners and main partitions by gluing in a bush in the top of the cabinet and attaching it to the dowel which is driven into the end of the cabinet side. The dowels are 50mm long by 6mm diameter, and the bush is 12mm outside diameter.

Shelf support Fig 4.37 Consists of a socket into which a ring-plug is inserted.

Frame connector Fig 4.38 A two-part fastener to join stool or table frames to connecting rails; the fitting is visible but could be used as a design feature. It consists of an aluminium barrel which is tapped to take a steel bolt, which is operated by an Allen key. The hole in the barrel nut is placed off-centre so that the fitting can finish flush with one surface of both 19mm and 22mm rails. The nut is 6mm diameter by 22mm long; the bolt 6mm diameter by 65mm long.

Magnetic catch Fig 4.39 Made in several sizes and shapes but all with the common feature that a steel striking plate is attracted magnetically to a magnet housed in a screw-on case; the latter is capable of being adjusted laterally. The magnetic 'pull' is measured in kilogrammes. As well as their common use for keeping cabinet doors closed, they can be utilised to secure detachable wall panels such as temporary display boards etc.

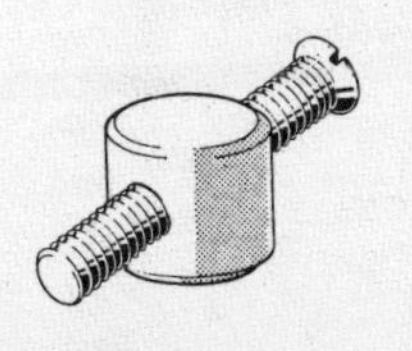

Fig 4.38

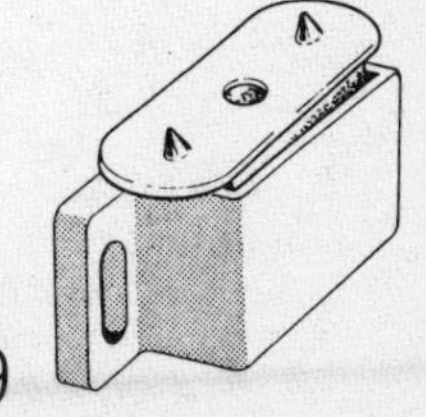

Fig 4.39

Chipboard fastener Fig 4.40 The nylon bush, which is threaded on the outside, is glued tightly into a hole drilled in the board to accept it, and the self-tapping screw is driven in to produce its own screw-thread inside the bush. The glue (such as Cascamite) strengthens the sides of the hole in any relatively weak material. Sizes: 15mm o/dia bush, 38mm long screw; also 12mm o/dia bush, 12mm long screw.

Tee-nuts Fig 4.41 These have a wide application for fastening problems of many kinds; the nuts are hammered in and secured by means of the prongs into softwoods and chipboards, enabling substantial units to be bolted to them.

Table brace fitting Fig 4.42 A three-part fastener which securely anchors table rails and legs together on the inside of the frame; for use on tables which are only dismantled occasionally – such as when moving house. It consists of a metal plate which has its ends slotted into the rails and is also secured with screws; a dowel screw is inserted through a central hole in the plate. One end of the dowel screw is threaded for a wing nut which is tightened against the plate, while the other end is screwed into the wooden leg.

Flushmount fittings Fig 4.43 These are pairs of surface-mounted fittings used for suspending or mounting objects flush, the interlocking tongues ensuring a stable fixing while still allowing the objects to be detached and re-mounted easily. Size: 45mm by 38mm.

Corner fitting Fig 4.44 A cheap and efficient surface-mounted fitting, sold in pairs. Suitable for many purposes, particularly for such pieces as kitchen cabinets where appearance is not important.

Straight leg plate Fig 4.45 Designed to accept screw-in legs of various types; the one illustrated is only one of the many shapes and sizes available.

Taper connector Fig 4.46 Supplied in sets, each consisting of two outer and two inner channels which slide into each other dovetail-fashion. A typical use is fitting the arms to the back of a chair after upholstering.

Chipboard fastener Fig 4.47 A three-part fastener comprising (a) a threaded and tapped nylon bush (not illustrated); (b) a threaded screw with a hole tapped in the head; (c) a cheese-head cover-cap which

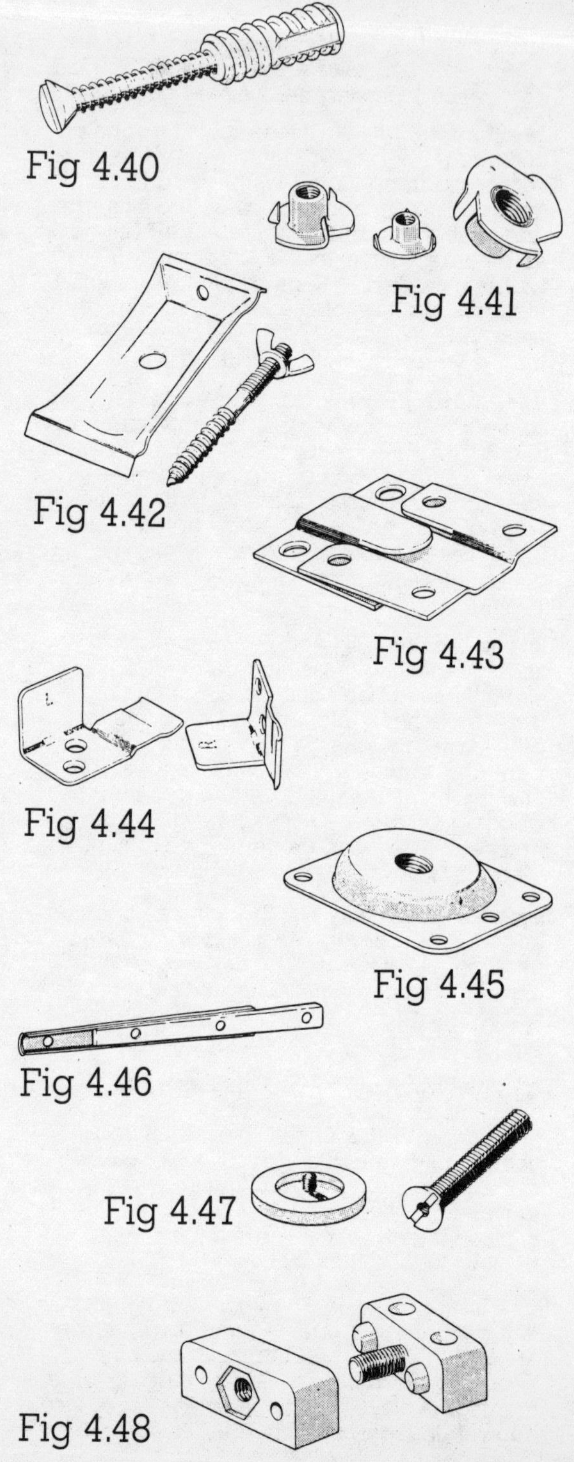
Fig 4.40
Fig 4.41
Fig 4.42
Fig 4.43
Fig 4.44
Fig 4.45
Fig 4.46
Fig 4.47
Fig 4.48

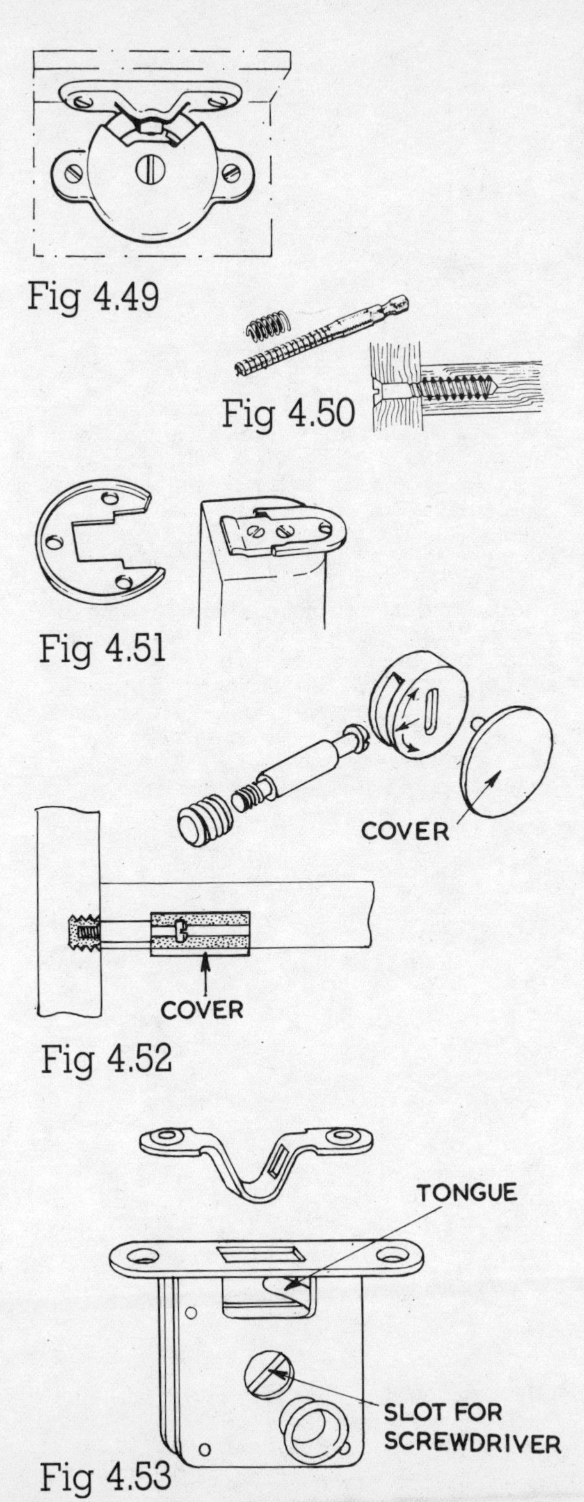

Fig 4.49

Fig 4.50

Fig 4.51

Fig 4.52

Fig 4.53

screws into the hole in the head. Sizes: bush 8mm diameter; screw 6mm dia by 55mm long.

Knock-down block fitting Fig 4.48 Widely used two-part fastener which is surface-mounted and requires no preliminary preparation to the wooden pieces to be joined. The components are first screwed to the surfaces and then secured to each other by means of the bolt which passes through one into a metal bush in the other.

Surface-fixing lock Fig 4.49 A cam-action fitting which is in common use in locations where appearance is not important. A screwdriver is used to turn the tapered tongue through a receiver plate to give a rigid fixing.

'Helicoil' fastener Fig 4.50 A two-part fastener which can be used with all types of manufactured board, being at least twice as effective as conventional wood screws. The coiled insert is fitted on to a special mandrel which is driven into a pre-bored hole, using a joiner's brace. It is then ready to receive the special screw.

The fasteners are normally for trade use as they can only be ordered in minimum quantities of 100. Sizes: inserts 9 to 38mm long; screws 6.5mm diameter by 50mm long. *List of stockists available from Armstrong Patents Ltd, Beverley, Hull, Yorkshire.*

Detachable leg fitting Fig 4.51 For use on light occasional tables; the circular plate is screwed to the underside of the top or frame while the bottom plate is screwed to the top of the leg.

'Fix' cam fitting Fig 4.52 Generally useful for cabinet construction, particularly chipboard. Minimum thickness of parts to be joined is 13mm. The cam can be tightened by turning a screwdriver in the slot when the cam bears on the bolt and takes up any slackness between the parts being joined. A plastic covering cap can be pressed in to conceal the fitting.

Mortise-type KD fitting Fig 4.53 For joining panels end-to-end: the tongue is turned to lock the fitting by turning a screwdriver in the slot.

Pivot hinge for lay-on doors Fig 4.54 Supplied in handed pairs, one being fitted to the top of the door and the other to the bottom. No recessing is needed as they are simply screwed to the surface; the hinge

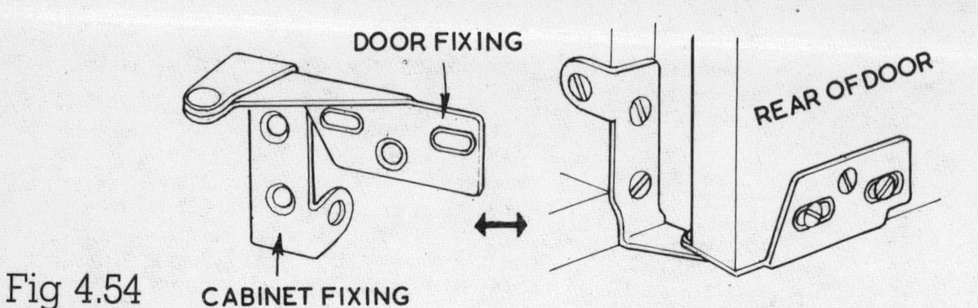

Fig 4.54

allows a 180 degree opening angle. For 15mm thick doors.

Cabinet connecting screw Fig 4.55 Comprises two plastic caps which screw on to a metal studding: after drilling the necessary holes, the caps can be tightened with a screwdriver.

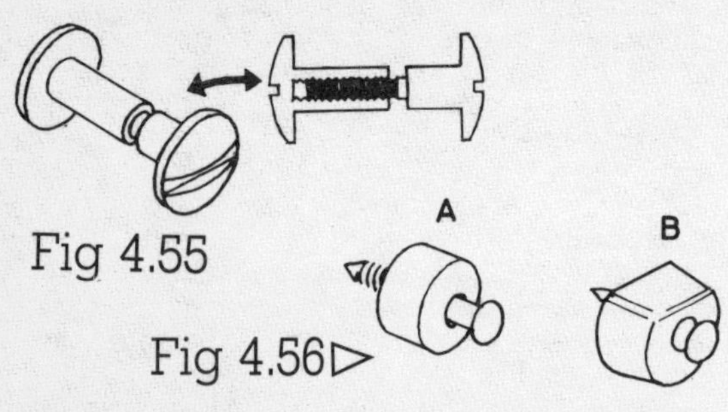

Fig 4.55

Fig 4.56▷

Shelf support studs Fig 4.56 Illustrations are self-explanatory.

Folding-leg fitting Fig 4.57 A strong hinge-type fitting which will accept square legs up to a maximum of 38mm ($1\frac{1}{2}$in). The locking action can be released by finger pressure. No cutting or shaping of the legs is required as they can be simply screwed in place. Supplied in handed pairs.

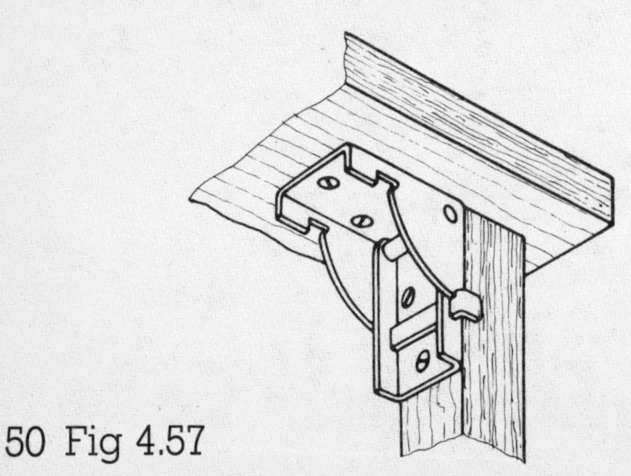
Fig 4.57

'Rollenda' sliding door system Fig 4.58 For heavy doors up to 50kg (112lb). The carriage has nylon rollers and is 55mm long; two are needed for a sliding door, and one for a door which folds. The fixing bracket and support track can be arranged either vertically or horizontally.

Accessories not illustrated are: (a) an end stop; (b) insert guides for single, and double, doors; (c) rubber buffers to stop a door swinging when opened or closed; (d) door pivots which are attached to the carriage and enable doors to fold; (e) a lower guide track which can be sunk into the floor, flanked by a batten along each side, or left as it is.

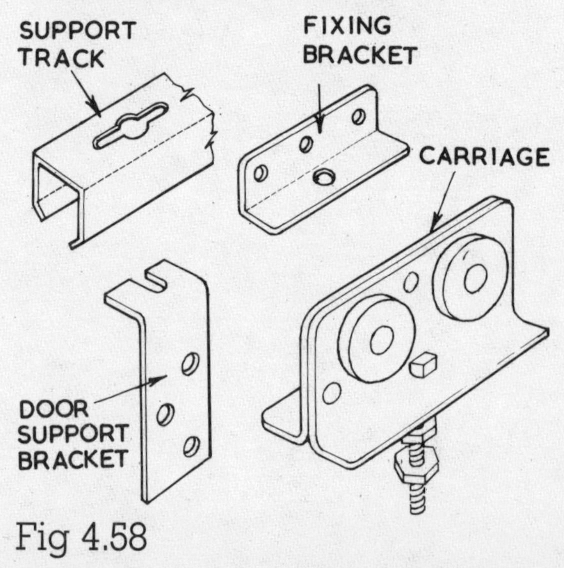

Fig 4.58

Roller-type sliding door system Fig 4.59 For medium weight 12kg (26lb) doors: for example, on a small wardrobe.

Light-weight sliding door system Fig 4.60

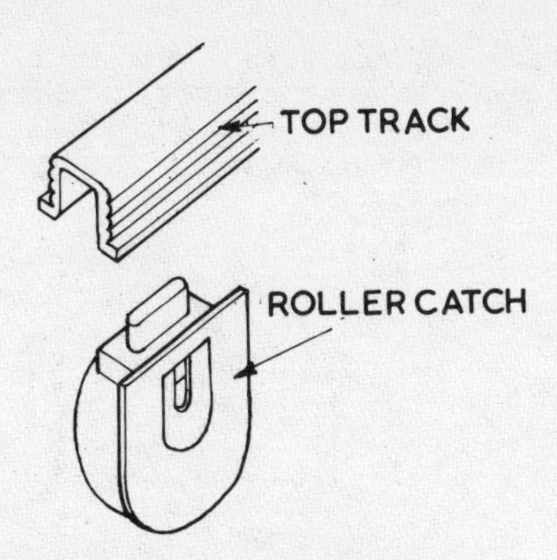

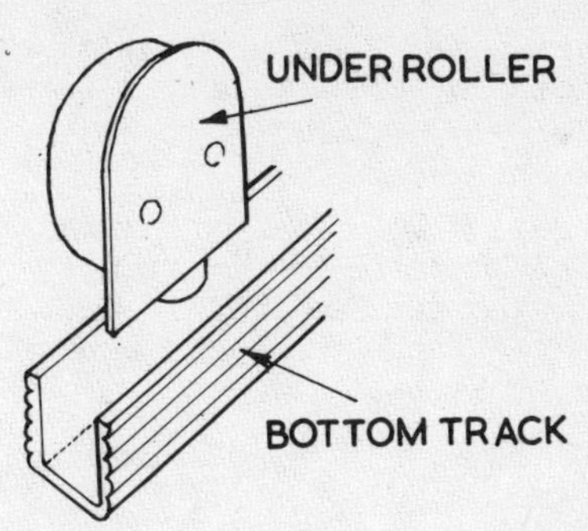

Fig 4.59

Made of graphited nylon for smooth running. The spring pin guide is barbed and fitted into a 9mm dia hole in the top of the door: when the door is to be dismantled it is pushed upwards against the spring in the guide and pulled outwards from the bottom. The lower sliding door guide is also barbed and is fitted into a channel cut in the bottom of the door. There are also upper and lower tracks (not illustrated) which are fitted to the framework.

Single-cranked hinge Fig 4.61 For use on doors with a minimum thickness of 16mm . The hinge can be used either flush or lay-on, and if the cranked portion is fixed to the frame and the flap to the door it can be used on a cupboard mounted over a wardrobe.

Double-cranked hinge Fig 4.62 For use on doors with a minimum thickness of 16mm ($\frac{5}{8}$in). Functions in the same way as the single-cranked hinge in Fig 4.61, but offers greater support on the frame and the door.

Centre hinge Fig 4.63 This is used on doors that cannot be fastened at the butt edge; the hinge flaps are recessed into both the frame and the door. The hinge pivot is fitted with a nylon bearing washer. The hinge is 51mm long × 12mm wide (2in × $\frac{1}{2}$in) when closed.

Card table hinge Fig 4.64 For use on desk flaps and occasional table leaves. 76mm × 12mm (3in × $\frac{1}{2}$in).

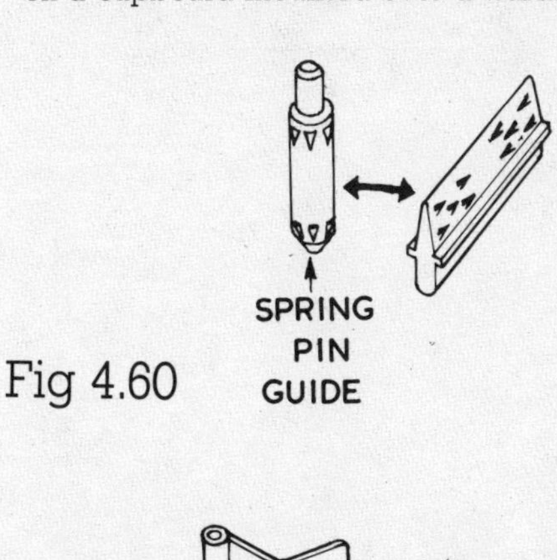

Fig 4.60

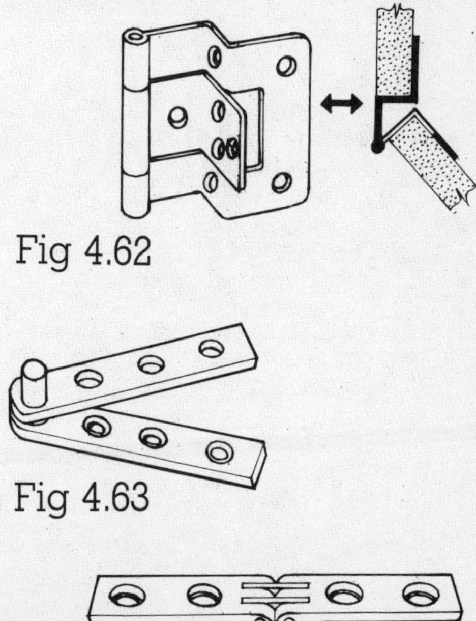

Fig 4.62

Fig 4.63

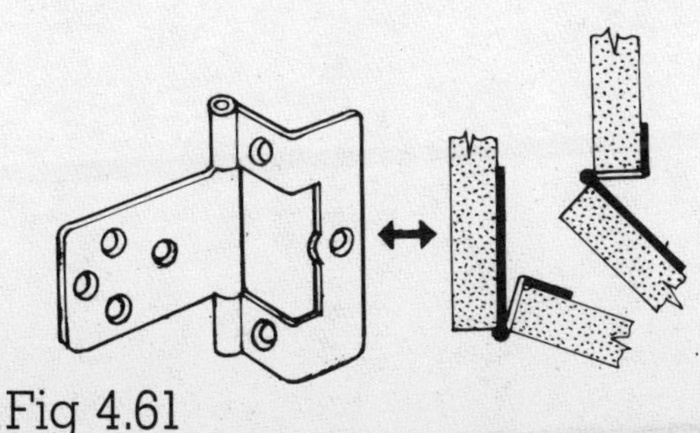

Fig 4.61

Fig 4.64

Radius-end hinge Fig 4.65 Similar in use to the counter hinge (Fig 4.66) but has rounded ends to the flaps. 65mm × 30mm ($2\frac{1}{2}$in × $1\frac{1}{4}$in).

Counter hinge Fig 4.66 Used for counters and lift-up flaps on bar counters. The flaps are linked so that the flap can lie flat on the top when open. 76mm × 25mm (3in × 1in), and 102mm × 32mm (4in × $1\frac{1}{4}$in).

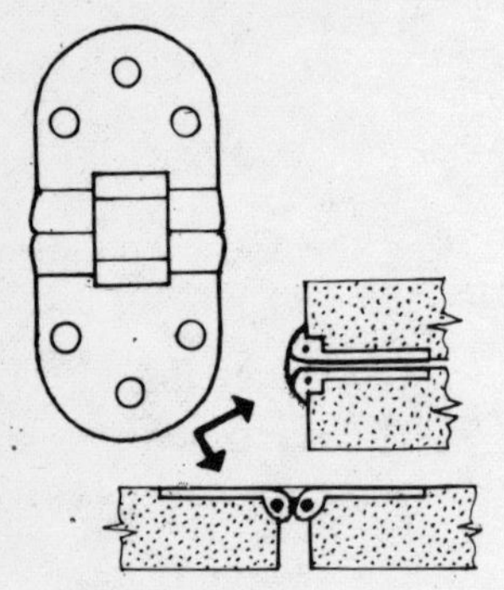

Fig 4.65

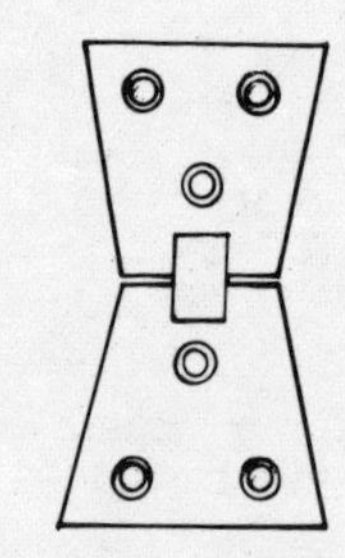

Fig 4.66

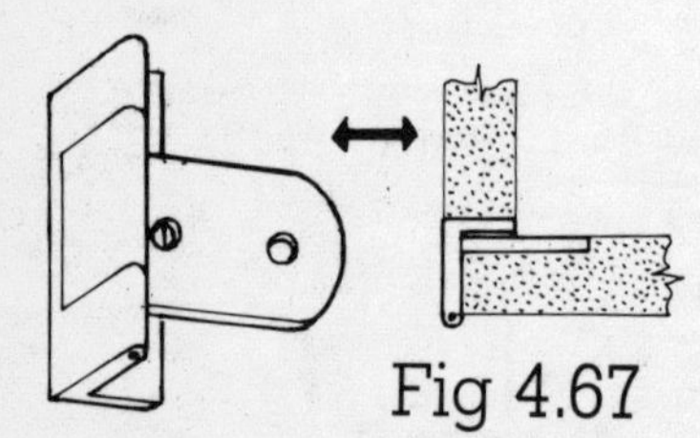

Fig 4.67

'Newform' angle hinge Fig 4.67 Similar in use to the angled cabinet hinge in Fig 4.68, but it is not a 'lift-off' hinge. For 16mm ($\frac{5}{8}$in) thick doors.

Angled cabinet hinge Fig 4.68 When fitted, the blank face of the cranked portion is exposed and as it is polished solid brass, it forms a decorative feature. The hinge is easy to fit as it requires no recessing, and it is a 'lift-off' type, so doors can be dismantled easily.

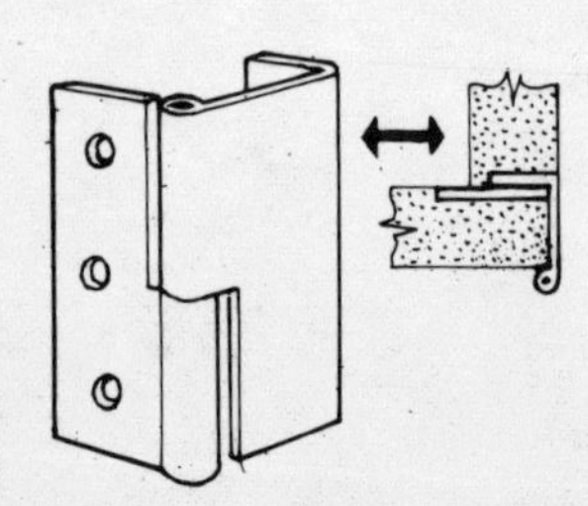

Fig 4.68

Screen hinge Fig 4.69 A three-sectional hinge which is movable in both directions. It accepts 25mm (1in) thick panels and is designed for use with multi-panelled doors or screens.

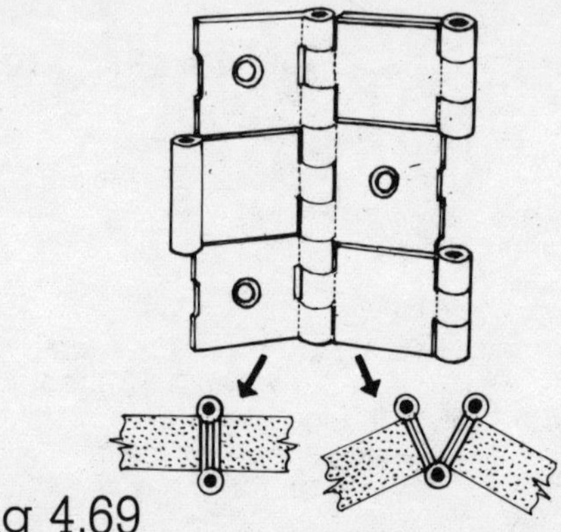

Fig 4.69

H-hinge Fig 4.70 This hinge is useful when door surfaces are not flat along the butting edges (for example, where they are curved vertically) and it prevents the parts fouling each other. Length of hinge varies from 51mm (2in) to 127mm (5in).

Parliament hinge Fig 4.71 For room doors which need to fold back flat to a wall and clear architraves, skirtings, etc. The knuckle protrudes from the door face slightly more than half the greatest projection of the architrave.

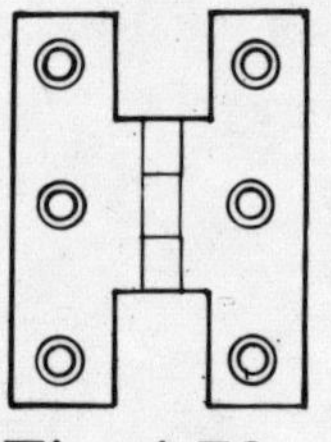

Fig 4.70

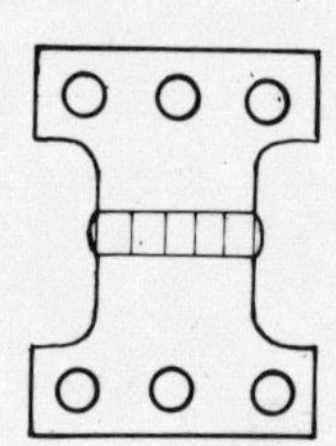

Fig 4.71

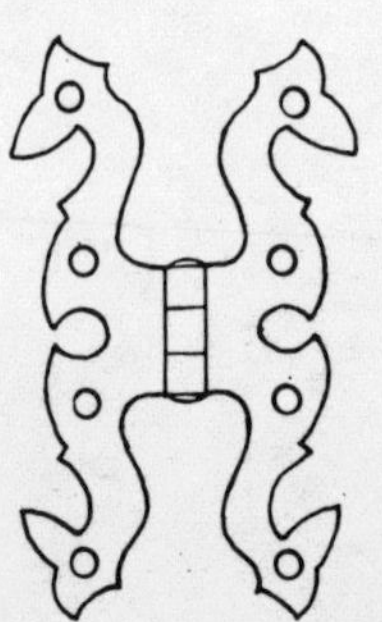

Fig 4.72

Snake hinge Fig 4.72 Also called a cock's head, or serpent, hinge. Lengths 51mm (2in); 64mm (2½in); 76mm (3in); and 102mm (4in).

Cranked clockcase hinge Fig 4.73 For hood or trunk doors.

Longcase clock hood hinge Fig 4.74 For use when the door needs to be thrown outwards as it is opened, so that it may clear obstructions such as pillars or decorations. Can be supplied with or without the pin; the screw holes for fixing to the under-edge of the door need to be drilled by the purchaser to suit the job.

Wardrobe lock Fig 4.75 Made left or right handed; 90mm × 45mm (3½in × 1¾in).

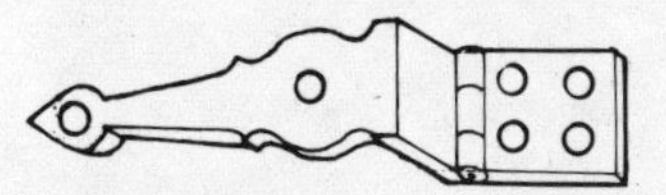

Fig 4.73

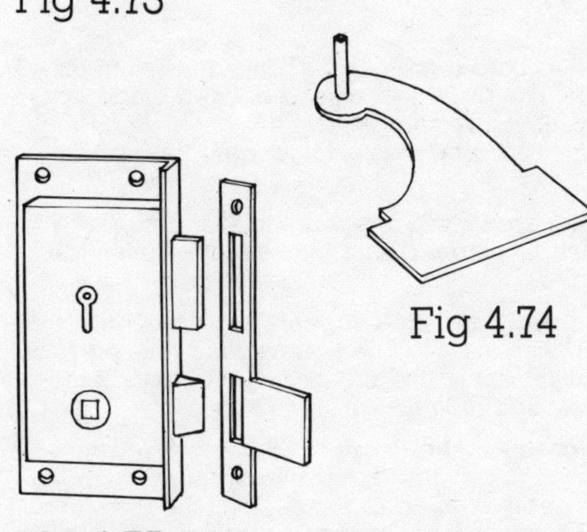

Fig 4.74

Fig 4.75

'Dovil' bracket Fig 4.76 A cantilever type of support bracket. Fixing consists of drilling two holes – one for the pin and one for the screw and wall-plug. The bracket is provided with holes through which to screw into the underside of the shelf. Two sizes: 115mm × 29mm (4½in × ⅛in), and 190mm × 29mm (7½in × ⅛in).

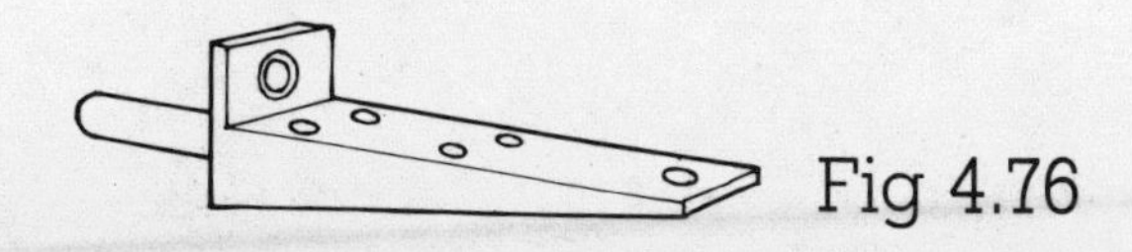

Fig 4.76

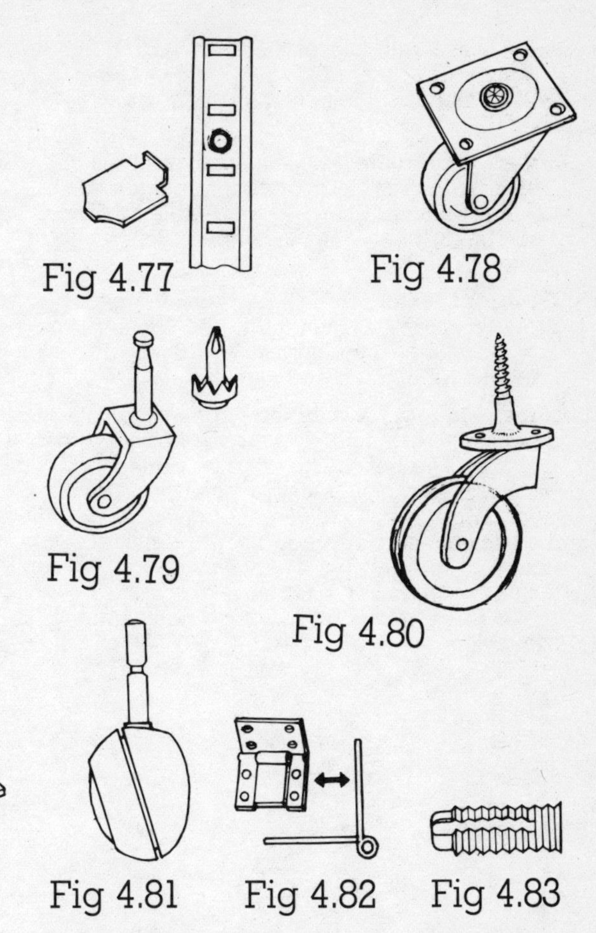

Fig 4.77 Fig 4.78 Fig 4.79 Fig 4.80 Fig 4.81 Fig 4.82 Fig 4.83

Bookcase strip Fig 4.77 Designed for surface fixing; no rebating or recessing needed as the strip is cut to length with a hacksaw and screwed on. The clips locate into the horizontal slots. In 914mm × 4mm (36in × ⅛in full) lengths.

Plate castor Fig 4.78 42mm (1¾in) dia wheel; 51mm (2in) plate; 54mm (2⅛in) overall height.

Peg and socket castor Fig 4.79 Similar to Fig 4.78, but with peg and socket fixing. Peg-hole needs to be 40mm deep × 10mm dia (1½in full × ⅜in).

Dinner wagon castor Fig 4.80 With screw fixing 65mm (2½in) dia wheel: can also be obtained with sprung wheels.

Ball castor Fig 4.81 Designed to be attached to heavy furniture while avoiding damage to carpets and other floor coverings. Supplied in handed sets of four – two right hand, two left hand – and with peg and socket fixing (illustrated) or plate fixing (not illustrated). Ball diameter is 42mm (1¾in) but other sizes available.

Butler's tray hinge Fig 4.82 A hinge fitted with a leaf-spring to retain it in the open 90 degree position. Useful for bed-tables. 64mm × 32mm (2½in × 1¼in) or 64mm × 38mm (2½in × 1½in).

Chipboard fastener Fig 4.83 Typical design; they are made in 12mm (½in) and 25mm (1in) lengths, and of diameters to fit 6, 8, and 10 gauge chipboard screws.

Adjustable foot for cabinet Fig 4.84 Operates on a similar principle to the one shown in Fig 4.16 (qv). The bottom ring can be turned by hand and provision is made for a screwdriver to be inserted into a slot at the top so that adjustments can be made *in situ.* Nominal height 150mm (5⅛in) with allowance for 20mm (¾in) variation; requires a mounting block. Extra fittings for attaching plinths are available.

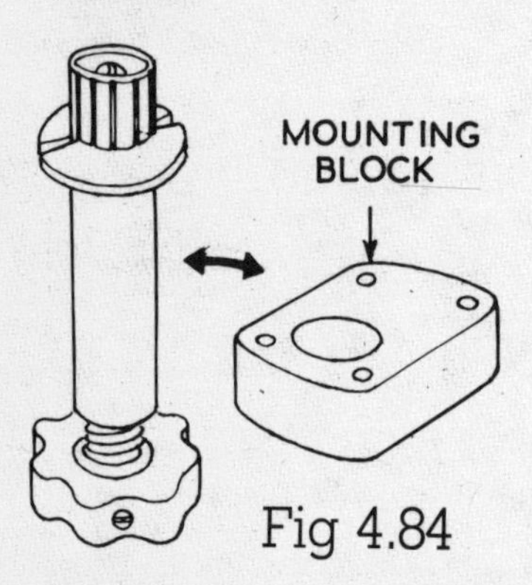

Fig 4.84

Domed-head screw Fig 4.85 A useful screw for fastening mirrors and similar fittings in bathrooms. The screw is inserted and driven in the normal way, and the domed head screws into a specially tapped hole. For 25mm, 32mm, and 38mm (1in, 1¼in, and 1½in) screws. In polished brass, satin brass, polished chrome or satin chrome finishes.

Turntable (or Dumbwaiter fitting) Fig 4.86 Consists of two steel plates with a ball-race mounted between them. Screw holes are provided on both plates. In two sizes of plate – 160mm and 57mm (6¼in and 2¼in) square; 19mm and 11mm (¾in and ⅜in full) overall depth; 50kg (112lb and 56lb) weight capacities.

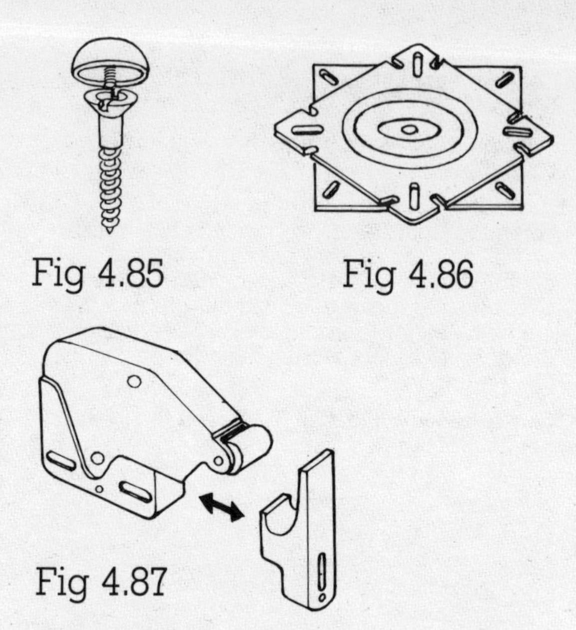

Fig 4.85

Fig 4.86

Fig 4.87

Automatic latch Fig 4.87 Designed to fit on doors so that they can be opened or closed without a handle – push the door closed and the latch operates; another light push and it opens.

Steel stud shelf support Fig 4.88 This stud is simply inserted as a push-fit into a 5mm dia hole.

Flush-fitting shelf support Fig 4.89 The socket is press-fitted into a 7mm dia hole, 10mm deep, and the peg on the bracket is pressed into it.

Two-piece shelf support Fig 4.90 The two pegs are inserted in 5mm dia holes drilled at a distance apart of 15mm PLUS the thickness of the shelf: the wings on the upper peg grip the shelf firmly. Ideal for glass shelves.

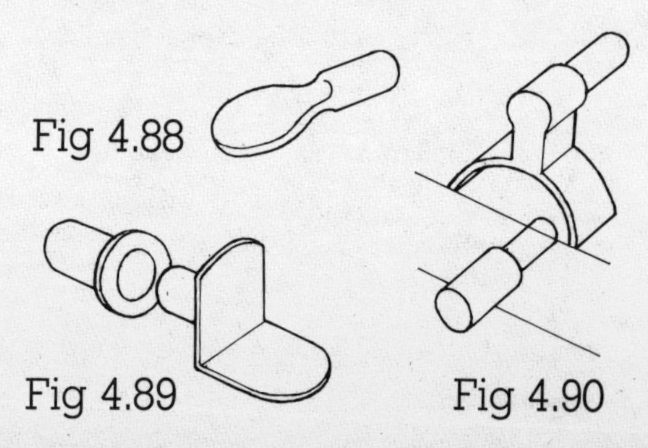

Fig 4.88

Fig 4.89

Fig 4.90

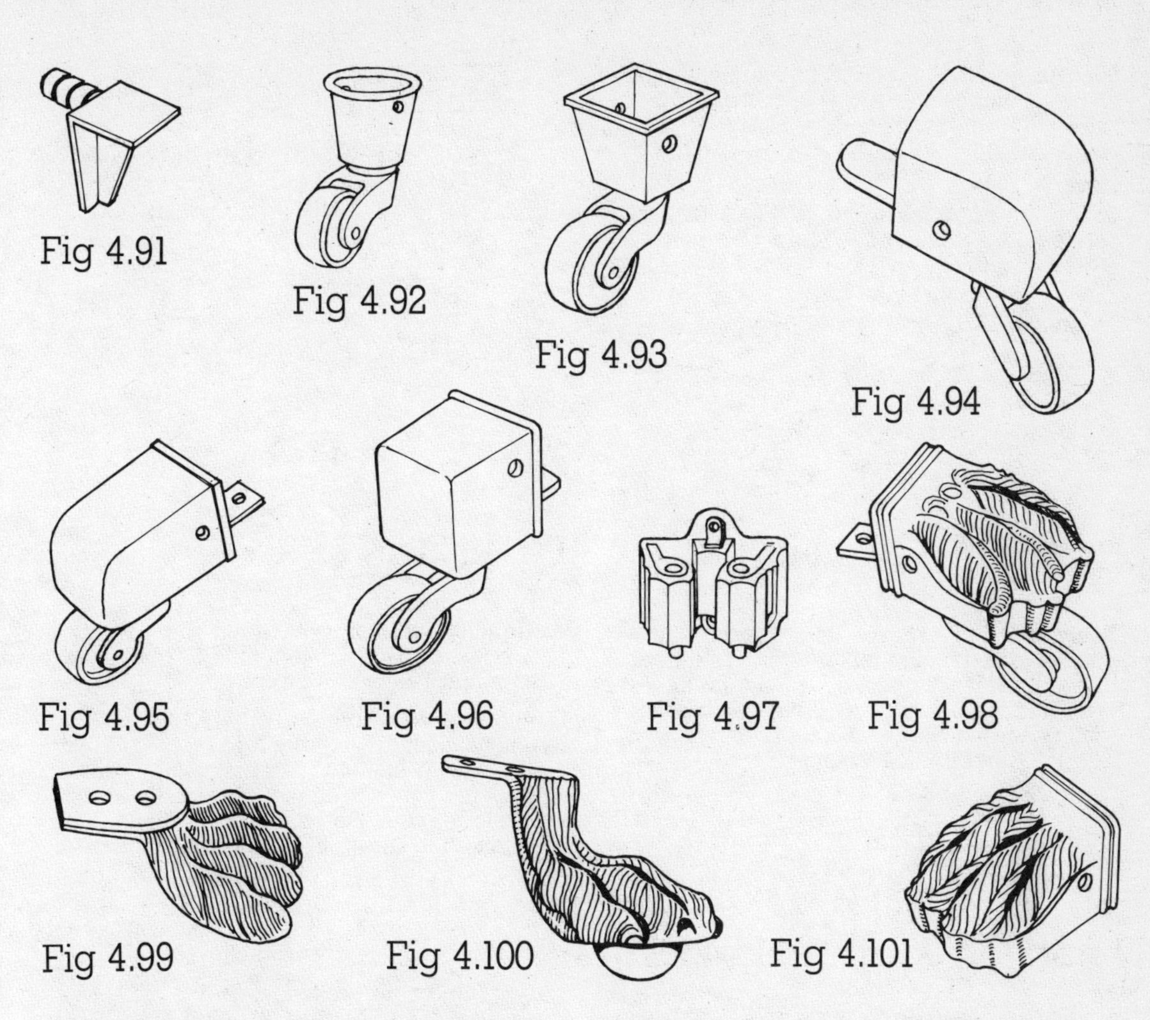

Fig 4.91 Fig 4.92 Fig 4.93 Fig 4.94 Fig 4.95 Fig 4.96 Fig 4.97 Fig 4.98 Fig 4.99 Fig 4.100 Fig 4.101

Shelf support Fig 4.91 Made in plastic, this support incorporates a reinforcing brace which helps to spread the load. It is simply pushed into a 5mm dia hole.

Round socket castor Fig 4.92 Inside diameter of socket varies from 16mm to 38mm ($\frac{5}{8}$in to 1$\frac{1}{2}$in) in 3mm ($\frac{1}{8}$in) increments.

Square socket castor Fig 4.93 Diameter of wheel and plates varies from 19mm to 38mm ($\frac{5}{8}$in to 1$\frac{1}{2}$in) in 3mm ($\frac{1}{8}$in) increments.

Bull-nose box castor Fig 4.94 One size of aperture – 32mm (1$\frac{1}{4}$in).

Round-toe box castor Fig 4.95 One size of aperture – 32mm (1$\frac{1}{4}$in).

Square-toe box castor Fig 4.96 Size of aperture varies from 19mm to 38mm ($\frac{3}{4}$in to 1$\frac{1}{2}$in) in 3mm ($\frac{1}{8}$in) increments.

Broom holder Fig 4.97 Made from galvanised spring steel, the roller-arms on this appliance will grip tool handles of most sizes.

Claw-foot box castor Fig 4.98 Size of aperture varies from 19mm to 38mm ($\frac{3}{4}$in to 1$\frac{1}{2}$in) in 3mm ($\frac{1}{8}$in) increments.

Claw-foot Fig 4.99 Dimension across foot varies from 22mm to 51mm ($\frac{7}{8}$in to 2in).

Claw-foot ball castor Fig 4.100 As claw-foot castor (Fig 4.99) but with ball foot. Dimension across foot varies from 22mm to 38mm ($\frac{7}{8}$in to 1$\frac{1}{2}$in).

Claw-foot box shoe Fig 4.101 Made in two widths, 22mm and 32mm ($\frac{7}{8}$in and 1$\frac{1}{4}$in).

Secretaire catch Fig 4.102 Press-button catch for securing the front of a secretaire. In 3 sizes – 45mm by 25mm (1¾in by 1 in); 50mm by 32mm (2in by 1¼in); 67mm by 35mm (2⅝in by 1⅜in).

Secretaire or 'dolphin' hinge Fig 4.103 For edge-fitting; in 2 sizes – 77mm (3in) and 90mm (3½in).

Fig 4.102

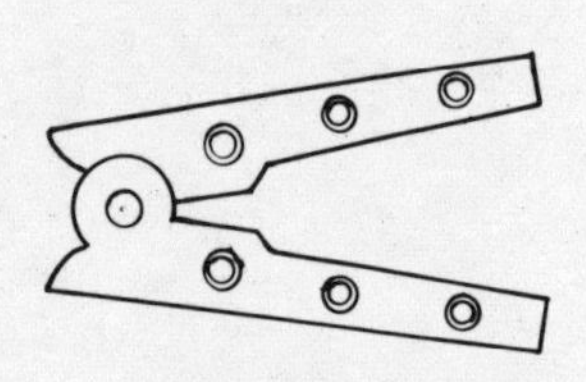

Fig 4.103

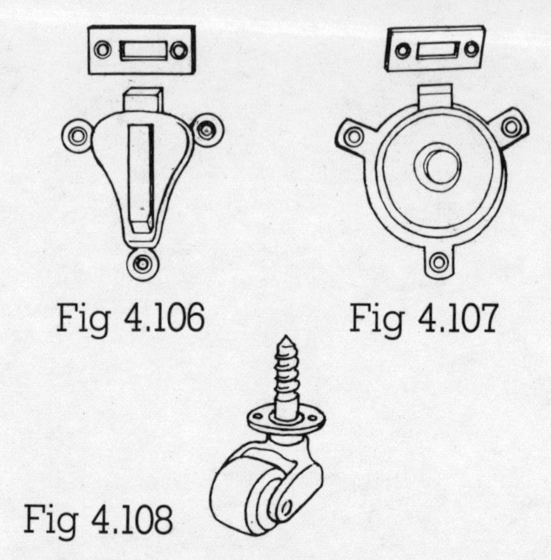

Fig 4.106 Fig 4.107

Fig 4.108

Table fork Fig 4.104 A fitting to secure the leaf of an extending table to the table-bed; one socket is screwed to the underside of the leaf, and the other to the underside of the table-bed. In 4 sizes – 63mm (2½in); 76mm (3in); 90mm (3½in); 102mm (4in).

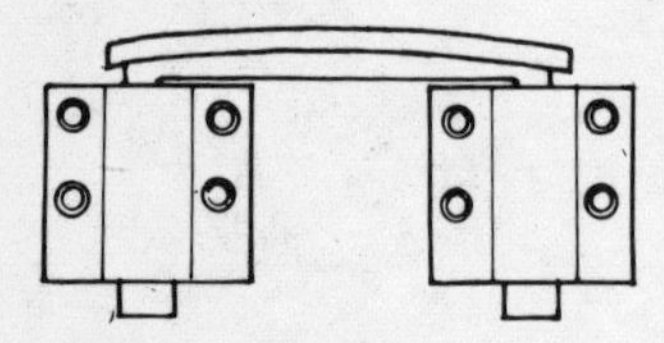

Fig 4.104

Double banjo catch Fig 4.105 For securing the top on a large tilt-top table. One size only 210mm (8¼in).

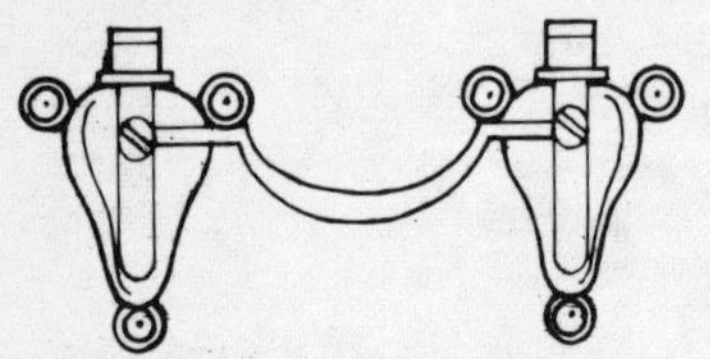

Fig 4.105

Single banjo catch Fig 4.106 For securing the top on a small tilt-top table. Made in 2 sizes – 58mm (2¼in); 76mm (3in).

Round button catch Fig 4.107 A useful press-button catch for many purposes. In 2 sizes – 35mm (1⅜in); 41mm (1⅝in).

Antique squat castor Fig 4.108 Made with 4 dia sizes of plate – 19mm (¾in); 22mm (⅞in); 25mm (1in); 29mm (1⅛in).

Dovetail-slide fitting Fig 4.109 Fulfills a similar function to a table fork (see Fig 4.105); the socket is split into two matching halves, one being screwed to the table-bed and the other to the leaf. One size only – 76mm (3in). The fitting is shown upside-down for clarity.

Fig 4.109

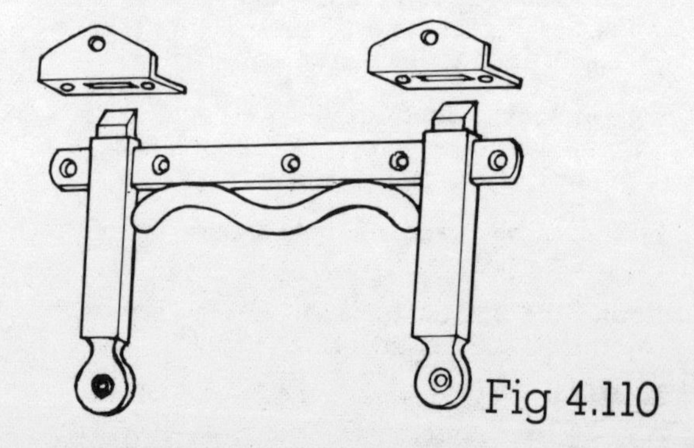

Fig 4.110

Double table catch Fig 4.110 For securing leaves of an extending table to the main table-bed. One size only – 152mm (6in).

Stretcher plate Fig 4.111 'X' denotes dimension quoted as length; 50mm (2in) only. A labour-saving method of fixing stretchers on tables, chairs, and stools.

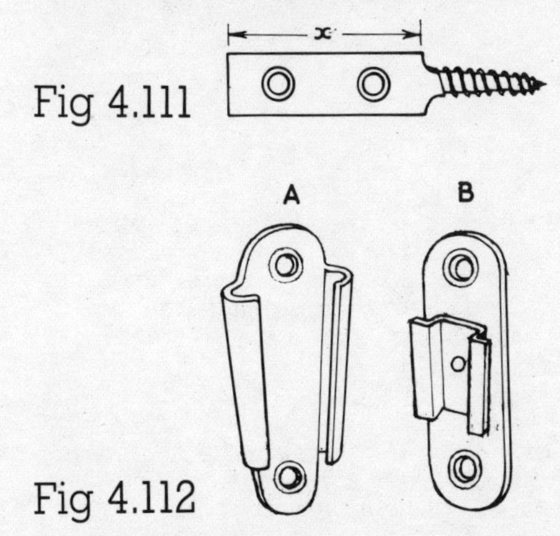

Fig 4.111

Fig 4.112

Mirror pivot Fig 4.112 This fitting enables a mirror to be hung between posts so that it can swing; the piece with the built-in pivoting bracket is fixed to the mirror post and the mating piece is fixed to the edge of the mirror backing. The mirror can be removed without disturbing the brackets. Supplied in pairs, one size only 50mm by 20mm (2in by $\frac{3}{4}$in).

Fitting for revolving chair seat Fig 4.113 Diagram is self-explanatory; supplied in one size only, 230mm (9in).

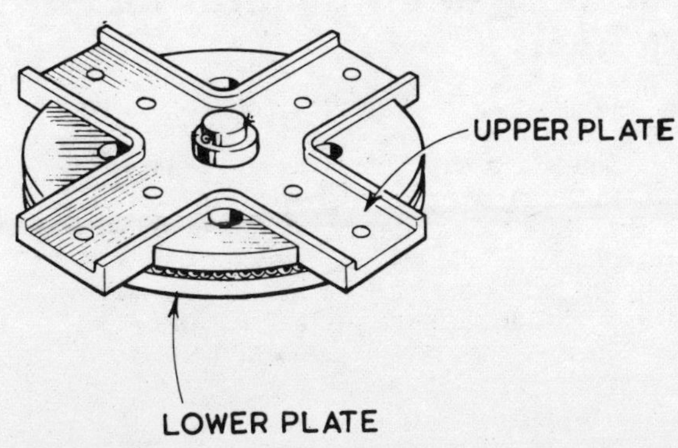

Fig 4.113

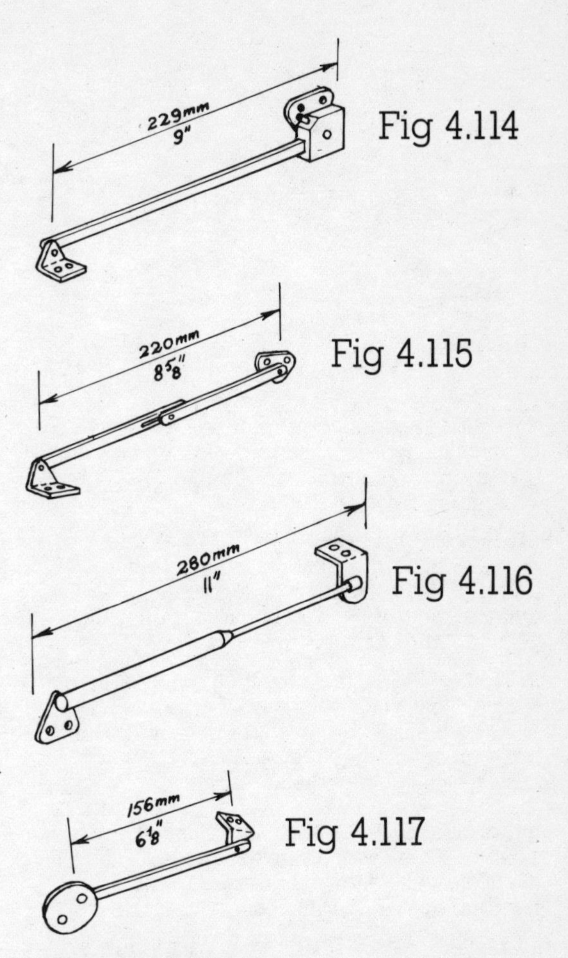

Fig 4.114

Fig 4.115

Fig 4.116

Fig 4.117

Adjustable braking stay Fig 4.114 A friction stay suitable for all fall-flap applications; a screw on the stay-housing can be adjusted to control the speed at which the flap falls. Overall size 250mm ($9\frac{7}{8}$in); supplied in handed pairs.

Joint stay Fig 4.115 This is the basic fall-flap stay which can be used either right- or left-handed. Overall length 220mm ($8\frac{5}{8}$in).

Spring lift-up stay Fig 4.116 The cylinder encloses a spring which holds the flap open; when the flap is closed the spring is tightly compressed and secures it without the need for a separate catch. Can be used right- or left-handed. Overall size 280mm (11in).

'Top Box' stay Fig 4.117 For use on lockers and boxes over wardrobes. When the door or flap is opened to the horizontal position the stay locks and holds it there; by lifting the

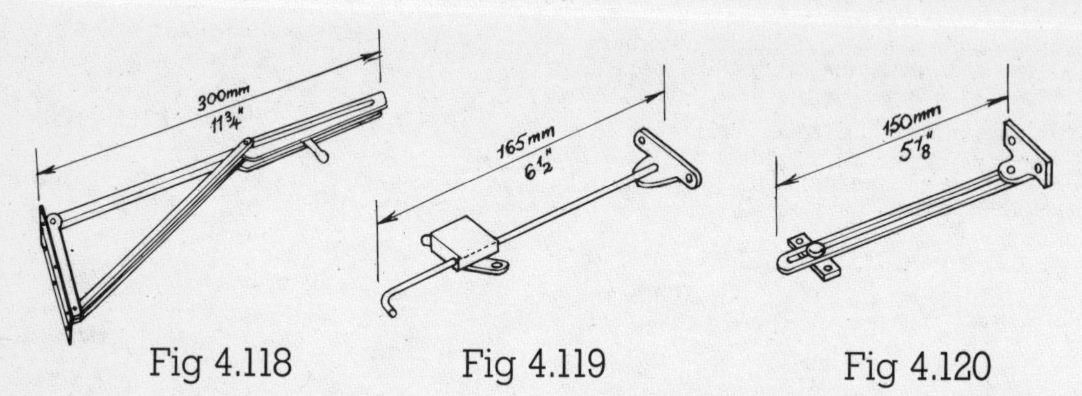

Fig 4.118 Fig 4.119 Fig 4.120

flap slightly the lock is released and can be closed. Supplied right-handed only; only one stay per flap is required. Minimum flap height 290mm (11⅜in).

Self-locking bracket Fig 4.118 Useful for fall-flap tables as the bracket incorporates a quick-release trigger which releases the automatically-locked position. Supplied in pairs; 300mm long (11¾in).

Hi-Fi stay Fig 4.119 As well as its obvious use for Hi-Fi cabinets, this stay can be employed in any situation where a lid needs to be held open as in needlework cabinets, dressing tables etc. The stay has a friction-action which gives exceptionally smooth operation; when closed, the arm projects downwards 172mm (6¾in) which makes it suitable for shallow consoles or cabinets. Supplied handed; overall length 165mm (6½in).

Lid stay Fig 4.120 A traditional design of stay for bureaux etc; there is no braking action but it locks in position when the lid or flap is opened by means of a peg which locates into a notch on the slide arm. To close, the lid or flap is lifted slightly to disengage the peg. Right-hand mounting only; overall length 150mm (5⅞in).

Many of the above fittings can be obtained from your local supplier, but in case of difficulty the following firms can be contacted:
Figs 4.73, 4.74 – Charles Greville & Co Ltd, Willey Mill House, Alton Road, Farnham, Surrey GU10 5EL (0252-715481)
Figs 4.82, 4.92, 4.94, 4.95, 4.96, 4.97, 4.99, 4.100, 4.101, 4.102, 4.103, 4.104, 4.105, 4.106, 4.107, 4.108, 4.109, 4.110, 4.111 – H. E. Savill, 9 St Martin's Place, Scarborough, North Yorkshire, YO11 2QH (0723-373032).

The remainder from – Woodfit Ltd, Kem Mill, Chorley, Lancs PR6 7EA (02572-66421)

Steel Butt Hinges and Back Flap Hinges for general joinery (use Fig 4.121)

Steel butt hinges and backflaps are sized by the length of the flap along their knuckles. The use of varying shapes, relative sizes (that is, the length/width ratio) and weight, and the use of pins of different types, make up the characteristics of the huge range available. Only the more important standard patterns are dealt with but, even so the variety may appear confusing. They are nearly all offered as standard finish in bright steel, but may be available electro-galvanised, sherardised, bronzed (a copper deposit finish), or 'brassed', that is, electro-brass plated. Where it obtains, mention is made under the notes on individual patterns.

There are two distinct types available, cranked or swaged (A), and uncranked (B). The difference is important, because the methods of fixing differ. The cranked type is fitted into a near-parallel rebate, with the knuckle protruding from the face of the work, while the other type is fitted into a taper rebate, and most important of all, is sunk into the work to the centre of its pin.

In practice, it will nearly always be found desirable to increase the depth of rebate away

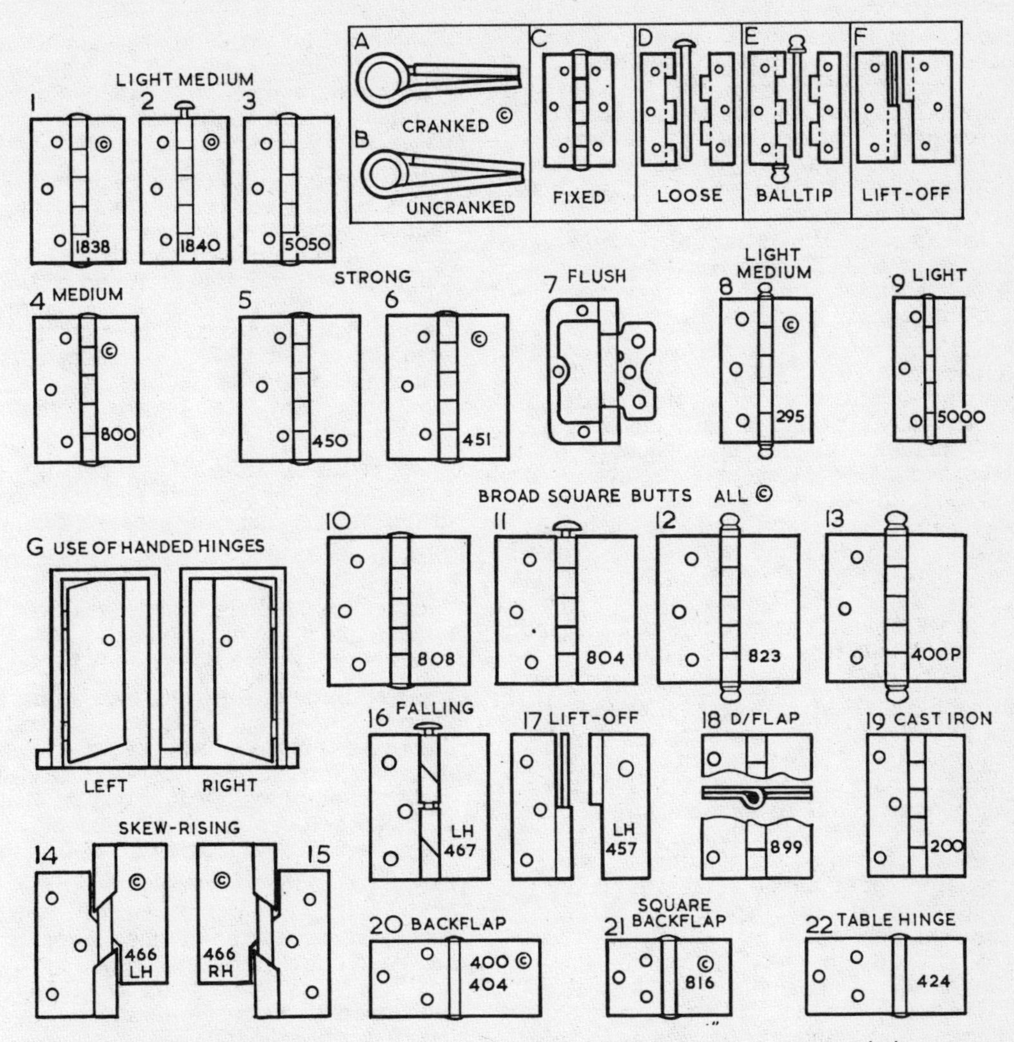

Fig 4.121 Although some hinge leaves are shown blank, the screw holes are nevertheless arranged symmetrically.

from the knuckle, so that the hinge in its closed position will still be slightly open. This will avoid one reason for the hinge binding. Note that nearly all brass butts are uncranked.

The majority of steel hinges have fixed pins (C) made from steel wire which is inserted when the male and female flaps come together during manufacture; it is cut off, and the ends neatly turned over to form the characteristic mushroom head. Brass butts usually have their pins cut off flush, and are held firmly by the tightness of the insertion. It is a criterion of a good hinge that there should be little or no space between the knuckles, and the hinge should be fairly stiff to open when new. Obvious gaps between the knuckle joints can produce something like a 12mm (½in) drop on a 760mm (30in) door.

Loose-pin butts are of two main types – the cuphead (D) which is a fairly loose wire pin with a cup-head, or the ball-tip (E), or the finial head; the latter is a feature of heavier hinges where the stout wire pin carries a decorative ball-shaped end which is used to withdraw the pin. A matching dummy ball is fixed at the bottom of the hinge to balance the effect.

A further variation is the lift-off butt (F), where the pin is fixed in the lower portion; the same method is used in a rising skew butt. Both types are made right and left hand, and the hand is decided by the side which carries the fixed pin (see diagrams 14 and 15). The hand required is determined by viewing the door from the inside, (G). The advantages of loose-pin and lift-off hinges are obvious, and they are easier to fit.

Details of the hinges illustrated follow; the diagrams are of 75mm (3in) butts and 40mm (1½in) backflaps, and the pattern numbers quoted are those most likely to be encountered.

Joiners' butt (No 1) (1838) is a cranked medium-light butt, and most of the doors in this country are hung on its 75mm, 90mm, and 100mm (3in, 3½in, and 4in) versions. Normally supplied in bright steel, it is also available sherardised with steel or brass pins. Exactly the same hinge, but with a loose cuphead pin, is No 2 (1840), and an uncranked version, with a fixed pin, is No 3 (5050). No 4 (800) is a medium cranked butt of heavier weight, but only available in a small range of sizes; and No 5 (450) uncranked and No 6 (451) cranked, are the heaviest designs.

Broad butts (Nos 10, 11, and 12) whose open width is the same as their length, are a good example of the different use of alternative pins. They are all good strong heavy butts, although used infrequently because of their high price. They are probably the best, if only because of their square dimensions, which means a bigger spread of screws, and so helps to prevent grain splitting. A heavy domestic door would be securely hung on three (a pair and a half) of 75mm or 90mm (3in or 3½in) butts of this type, which would be better practice than using only two of 100mm (4in). A still heavier version (No 13), and a non-square lighter one (No 8) are usually 'brassed' or 'bronzed'.

Rising skew butts (Nos 14 and 15) are used when upward clearance is required during opening as when fitted carpets are used, and they also give automatic closing. Generally of bright steel, they are handed, and the most popular size is 75mm (3in) and this is usually adequate, although three (a pair and a half) are recommended for heavier doors. Absolute plumb-line fixing is essential. The top edge of the door must be chamfered away from the hinge face to allow clearance during the initial opening of the door. The bottom of the door must be cut short by 16mm (⅝)in measured from the floor, to allow carpet clearance. The inclined helical surfaces must be kept lightly oiled, and on no account must paint be allowed on these surfaces because it will quickly form an abrasive paste which will cause severe wear.

Falling butts (No 16) are used in exactly opposite circumstances where a door is required to fall open when released from its catch; their design incorporates a loose cuphead pin. Typical uses are on lavatory doors in hospitals and homes for elderly people. Both skew and falling butts are made from other materials – cast iron ones are sometimes available, and brass and bronze, the latter usually being provided with a steel helical bearing surface.

Loose, or lift-off butts (No 17) are also handed, and like loose-pin butts are most useful when a door needs removing quickly.

Flush hinge (No 7) has its flaps designed so they will fold one inside the other, and its thickness is therefore slightly less than half a normal butt; it can thus be fitted flush to both door and frame, and no rebate is needed.

Cast iron butts (No 19) (200) are a relic from the past, but are still used in small numbers. Its devotees make all sorts of rather extravagant claims in its defence; its critics say all its so-called qualities can be matched by butts of steel brass. It is commonly available in 50 and 100mm (2in to 4in) sizes.

Double flap butt (No 18) (899) is a stout steel hinge, and as its name implies, is made from two layers pressed and formed together. It has been largely used to supplant the cast-iron butt, but is not intended as a direct replacement as it is of different outline. No 9 (5000) is a very light cabinet hinge.

Backflaps complete the range; the standard ones (No 20) are made cranked and uncranked, and have equal-sized flaps whose lengths are greater than their nominal sizes. They have many uses, and quite invaluable.

Square backflap (No 21) is used mainly for cabinet-work.

Table hinge (No 22) is also used in cabinet work and is known to cabinet-makers as the Rule Joint hinge; it is a normal backflap with odd-sized flaps, and is countersunk in reverse to suit its use in hingeing the flaps of drop-leaf tables. Provision must be made for the knuckle when fixing as this is sunk into the work, in contrast with normal practice.

Tee, Strap, and Reversible Hinges; also Bands and Hooks Fig 4.122

The range of hinges under this heading includes the bigger and heavier patterns most of which are used outside; the nominal dimension of all of them is the distance between their pins and the extremity of their longer flaps. The drawings are not to exact scale but are in proportion, and some details have been exaggerated to emphasise them. The pattern numbers are makers' numbers in common use, although most of the hinges are more popularly referred to by verbal description.

Steel tee hinges are the modern counterparts of the old hand-made Cross Garnets, or Tee Bands, and are superior to them in all respects. They are made in four different patterns, the sole difference being an increase in the thickness of the steel used, and a corresponding increase in the widths of

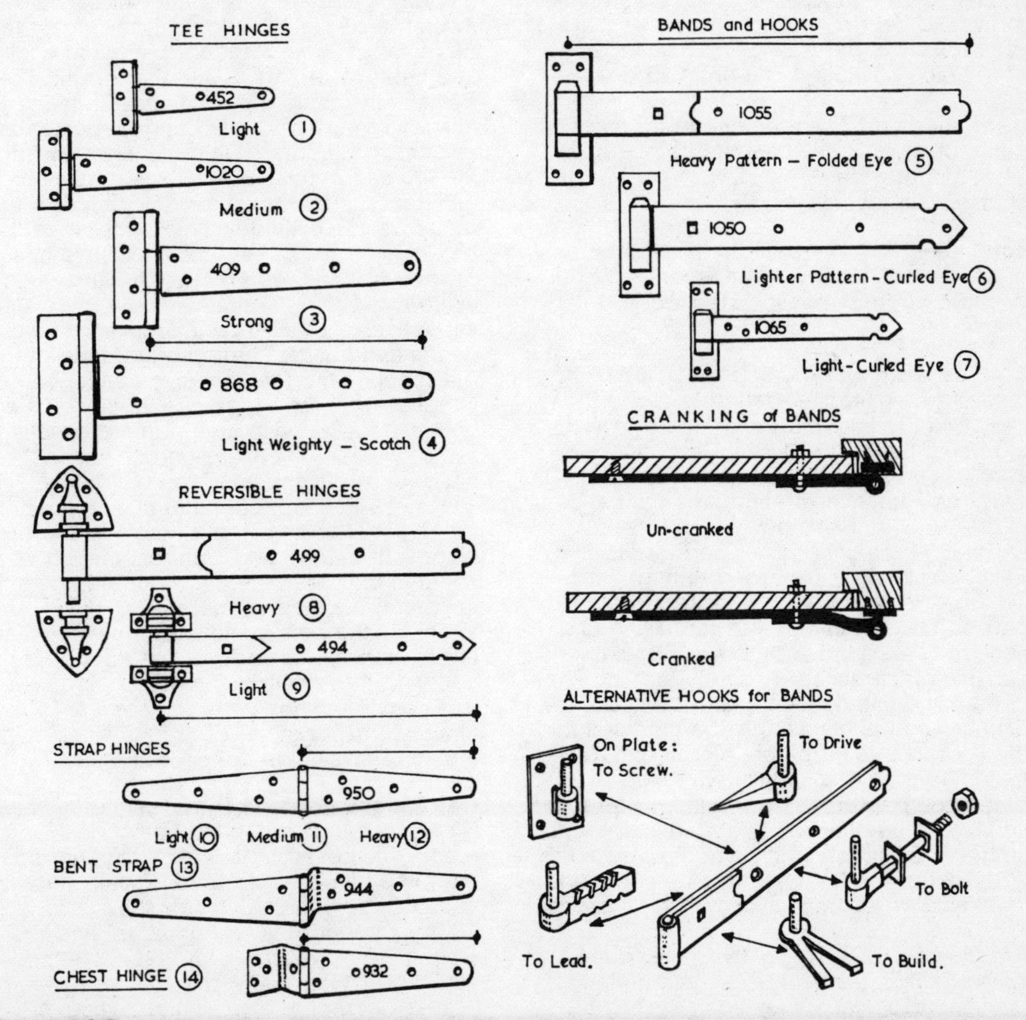

Fig 4.122

their tails and heads. They are produced in an overall range from 75mm (3in) to 610mm (24in), which gives a range of sizes and weights. Those commonly bought over the shop counter are usually black or grey japanned finish; but self-colour steel and galvanised finishes are also available.

Light tees (No 1) are available from 75mm to 305mm (3in to 12in), and are generally used for jobs where no great strength is needed; for example, rabbit hutch and poultry house doors.

Medium tees (No 2) are made in sizes from 255mm to 460mm (10in to 18in) and are used for similar light work where a bigger hinge is required, as in the case of light gates, and light braced, tongued and grooved doors.

Strong tees (No 3) are produced for the whole range of sizes from 75mm to 610mm (3in to 24in) and provide a selection of heavier and stronger hinges.

Scotch tees (No 4) are the heaviest members of the quartet, and are used where strength – because of greater suspended weight – is important.

Standard band and hook (No 5) This is the 'folded eye' pattern so-called because the band is folded around the orifice or eye for the pin of the hook, and then continued for about a quarter of the length of the band. This provides additional strength at a critical part of the band, and also gives a more solid location for the coach bolt used for the first fixing point, which is passed through the square hole provided, and locked from the inside. The design of a standard band and hook involves a minor fault which is happily capable of correction – namely that the back of the band and its hook-plate are in different planes, and the plates must be mortised into the door frames for proper alignment. If the bands have a crank equivalent to the difference between the two planes, the fixing surfaces will be in line, and no cutting-out of timber or brickwork will be necessary. Most types of this kind of band can be supplied cranked; the illustrations show the difference.

Curled eye (No 6) A slightly lighter band and hook in which the hook-eye is a simple circular shape with no extension. They are not normally available cranked.

Curled band hook (No 7) This is a less robust pattern for light work; it is roughly the same weight as a strong tee hinge. Bands are always supplied as standard with hooks on plates, to screw, as shown; all of them can be supplied with hooks suitable to insert into holes cut into brickwork or stone, or to bolt through concrete or wooden posts, or to build into brickwork, or to drive into wooden posts. The last-named is a poor thing, and hooks to bolt through are usually preferable. The illustrations show the various kinds available, and these should be specified when ordering.

Reversible hinges There are two patterns available: heavy (No 8) which is roughly the same weight as a standard band and hook; and light (No 9), about half the weight. Their designs are quite different, insofar as the pin is an integral part of the band and extends on each side into bearing spindles which ride in the top and bottom cups. They are suitable only for face-fixing usually into timber frames. Many people consider them better than bands and hooks – the more positive fixing provided by the top and bottom cups goes some way towards eliminating the play and subsequent 'drop' experienced with ordinary bands and hooks. Their only possible drawback is the fact that they cannot be supplied with the range of alternative fixing hooks, but otherwise they perform exactly the same function. Their design eliminates the need for any cranking of the bands.

Exactly the same general advice is offered for all kinds of bands and hooks as for tee hinges; fit the biggest and best the job would seem to indicate. The aim, with big doors, is to spread the load as much as possible, and to do this the bands should not be less than three quarters the width of the door(s). If in doubt, fit three hinges to each door; this is good advice in any case, for it will help eliminate much of the dropping which is such a feature of this kind of door-hanging.

Strap hinges (Nos 10, 11, 12, 13, and 14) Light No 10; medium No 11; and heavy No 12, are roughly comparable in weight with the first three tee hinges described. Usually supplied in self colour steel, although some sizes of the light pattern may be obtained finished japanned or galvanised. A cranked light version No 13, and the chest hinge No 14, of similar weight are also available; both of these are normally made in self-colour steel.

Abbreviations for Locks and Hardware

B.P.	Brass pin (hinges)
D.A.	Double Action (hinges)
D.H.	Double hand
D.T.	Drilled through (spindles)
D.T. and T.	Drilled through and tapped
E.A.	Easy Action
F.R.	Full rebated
H.B.	Hook bolt
H.R.	Half rebated
I.P.	Iron pin (hinges)
L.H.	Left hand
M.K.	Master key
P.B.P.	Phosphor Bronze pin (hinges)
P.B.W.B.	Phosphor Bronze Washered Butts
R.B.	Reverse bolt or Roller bolt
R.H.	Right hand
S.A.	Single Action or Spring Action
S.B.	Stub bolt
S.C.	Screwed cap
S.R.	Skew rebated
S.W.B.	Steel Washered Butts
W.A.	Weighted Action

CHAPTER FIVE

Timber connectors

THIS chapter deals with methods of joining timber parts together other than by means of joints. Therefore, we give details of nails, screws, nail plates, etc, many of which have been developed over the past few years to save time and labour.

Various Types of Nails (Fig 5.1)

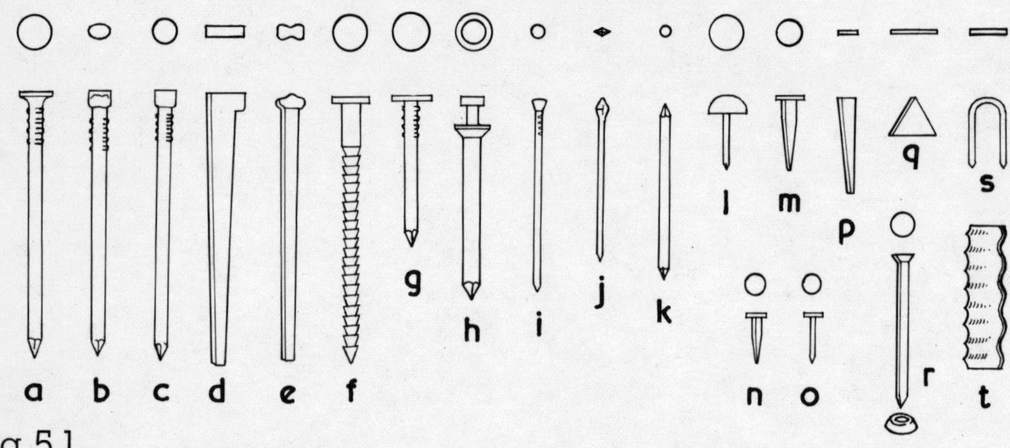

Fig 5.1

(a) Round wire or French nail. As it has a large unattractive head it is used where strength is needed rather than neatness, as in general carpentry. Also obtainable galvanised. Sizes 20mm to 150mm (¾in to 6in).
(b) Oval wire nail. Slimmer than the French nail and not so strong. Less likely to split the wood provided the head lines up along the grain and not across it. Sizes 12mm to 150mm (½in to 6in).
(c) Lost-head nail. The head can be punched below the surface and the hole filled. Used in joinery work. Sizes 12mm to 150mm (½in to 6in).
(d) Cut floor brad: If used in line with the grain it is unlikely to split the wood, even near the end of a board. Employed in flooring and carpentry. Sizes 12mm to 75mm (½in to 3in).
(e) Cut clasp nail. Very strong fixing and difficult to remove once driven home. Use in line with the grain. Employed in general carpentry, particularly roofing. Sizes 20mm to 200mm (¾in to 8in).
(f) Annular nail. Used for fixing plywood and similar boards. The barbed stem makes it almost impossible to extract. Sizes 20mm to 75mm (¾in to 3in).
(g) Clout nail. Used for nailing down roofing felt and sometimes in upholstery. Can be obtained galvanised. Sizes 12mm to 50mm (½in to 2in).
(h) Duplex nail. Although designed for nailing shuttering together for concrete work, it is useful for any temporary work where the nails are eventually withdrawn. The upper head protrudes for easy withdrawal. Sizes 25mm to 100mm (1in to 4in).
(i) Panel pin. Used for cabinet work and joinery; the head can easily be punched home and the hole filled. Smaller sizes are handy for fixing mouldings. Sizes 12mm to 50mm (½in to 2in).

(j) Hardboard pin. Has a sherardised finish which matches the colour of the hardboard. The head can be punched home and filled. Sizes 10mm to 38mm ($\frac{3}{8}$in to $1\frac{1}{2}$in).
(k) Wire dowel nail. For making hidden and end-to-end joints. It is driven into one piece and the other piece hammered on to it. Can be made in the workshop by cutting off the end of a round wire nail and filing the end to a point.
(l) Chair nail. Used in upholstery to cover the tacks which hold down the fabric – the tack is fixed first and the chair nail is inserted alongside it so that the dome covers the head of the tack. Available in antique, bronze, chrome, and copper finishes. Sizes (of head) 3mm to 12mm ($\frac{1}{8}$in to $\frac{1}{2}$in).
(m) Cut tack. Used in upholstery; there is also an 'Improved' type which has a larger head and is generally stouter. Sizes 10mm to 25mm ($\frac{3}{8}$in to 1in).
(n) Cut gimp pin. For fixing gimp or braid. Sizes 6mm and 10mm ($\frac{1}{4}$in and $\frac{3}{8}$in).
(o) Wire gimp pin. As (n) above.
(p) Sprig. A head-less brad for fixing glass in wooden frames or fastening down linoleum. Sizes 12mm to 20mm ($\frac{1}{2}$in to $\frac{3}{4}$in).
(q) Picture-framing triangles. Made of mild steel, they can be used for holding in the backs of pictures. Sizes (length of side) 10mm to 20mm ($\frac{3}{8}$in to $\frac{3}{4}$in).
(r) Square boatnail and rove. Made of solid copper, the nail is driven through a pre-bored hole and the rove is fitted over the end; the end is then cut off to protrude about 6mm ($\frac{1}{4}$in). A rove punch is fitted over the rove and tapped to drive it home; the protruding end is then burred over.
(s) Staple. Used to fix wire netting, upholstery springs, etc. Obtainable galvanised. Also in various shapes and sizes for use with staple guns. Sizes 10mm to 20mm ($\frac{3}{8}$in to $\frac{3}{4}$in).
(t) Corrugated fastener, also called a 'Wriggle nail'. For fastening light frameworks; the design tends to pull the parts together. Sizes 6mm to 22mm deep ($\frac{1}{4}$in to $\frac{7}{8}$in); 22mm to 32mm long ($\frac{7}{8}$in to $1\frac{1}{4}$in).

Various Types of Wood Screws and Hooks (Fig 5.2)

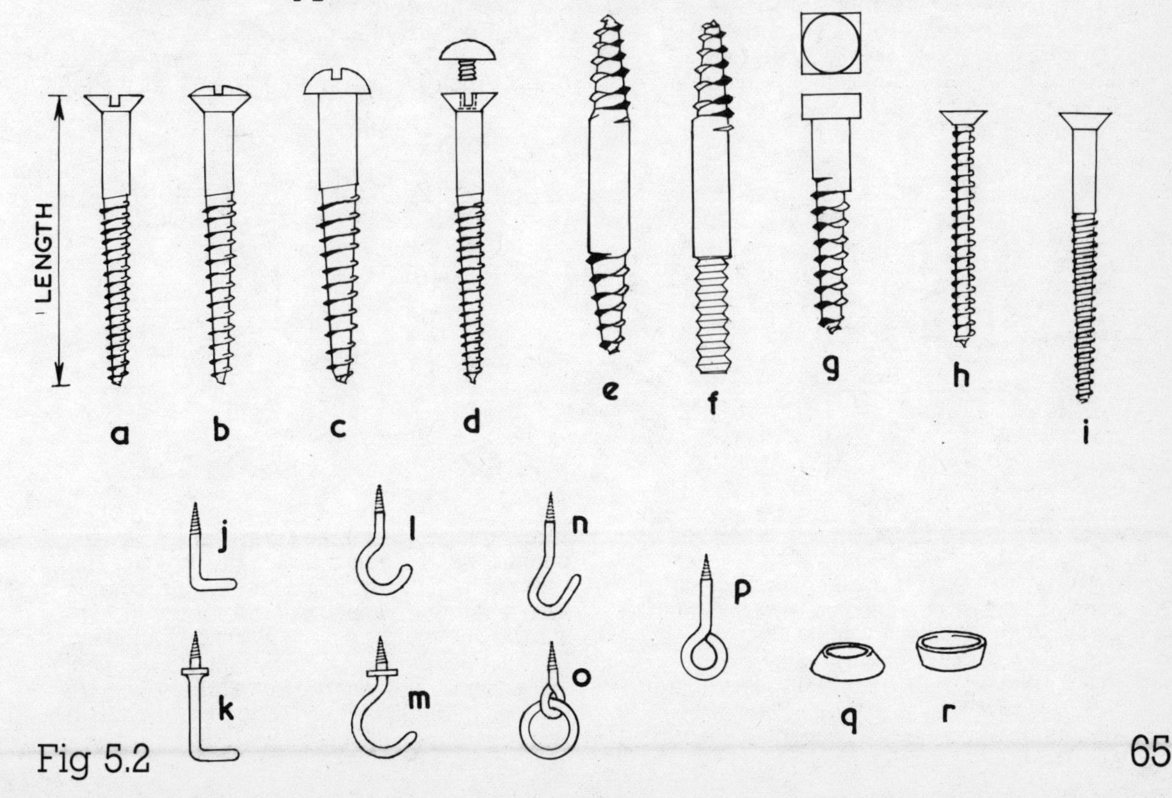

Fig 5.2

(a) Countersunk, flat-head. Used for general woodwork, fastening hinges and other hardware whose holes are also countersunk. Available in steel, solid brass, brass-plated, chromium-plated, nickel-plated, and japanned finishes. Sizes 6mm to 150mm (¼in to 6in).
(b) Raised or mushroom head. Used to fix hardware in situations where a neat appearance is desired. The holes must be countersunk. Available chromium or nickel-plated. Sizes 8mm to 50mm (5/16in to 2in).
(c) Round head. Used to fix hardware whose holes are not countersunk – the screw-head stands above the surface. Available in same finishes as (a). Sizes 6mm to 90mm (¼in to 3½in).
(d) Dome-head. For fixing bath panels, splash-backs, and mirrors. The screw is driven in the conventional way and the dome is then screwed into the end to hide it. Chromium-plated finish only. Sizes 20mm to 50mm (¾in to 2in).
(e) Dowel screw. Used on Tee-joints or end-to-end fixings. It is screwed into a pre-bored hole on one piece with a pair of pliers: the pre-bored hole on the second piece is fitted over the free end of the screw and wound on. Steel only. Sizes 20mm to 65mm (¾in to 2½in).
(f) Hand-rail screw or bolt. Used for end-to-end, or mitred corner, joining of hand-rails or similar pieces of wood; see Fig 5.3. Sizes 22mm to 90mm (⅞in to 3½in).

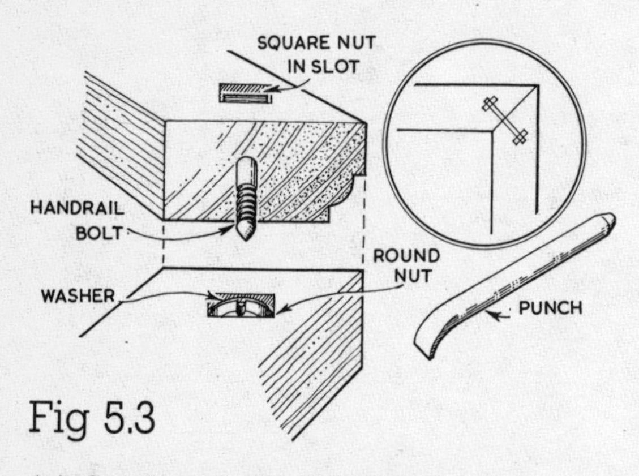

Fig 5.3

(g) Coach screw. For fastenings in heavy constructional work, such as workbenches. Sizes 25mm to 405mm (1in to 16in) long, by 6mm to 25mm (¼in to 1in) diameter.
(h) Chipboard screw. Specially developed for fastenings in particle boards. The core is slimmer than that of the conventional screw and is threaded throughout its length. Available with slotted or Phillip's head. Sizes 10mm to 50mm (⅜in to 2in).
(i) 'Supadriv' screw developed by Nettlefolds. This has a slimmer shank than the conventional screw, plus a self-centreing point and special thread which enables it to be driven more quickly. Pozidriv head only; the Mastascrew is identical but has a slotted head. Sizes as (a).
(j) Square plain screw-hook; (k) square shouldered screw-hook; (l) open-eye screw-hook; (m) plain cup-hook; (n) cranked-eye screw-hook; (o) screw ring; (p) closed eye screw-hook; (q) screw-cup; (r) internal screw-cup. Both (q) and (r) are available in metal or plastic.

Points to note when using screws
1. Screws are identified by their gauge numbers, which relate to the diameter of the shank. Gauge numbers remain the same regardless of the length; for example a 50mm (2in) × 10 gauge screw has the same diameter head and shank as a 25mm (1in) × 10 gauge. When ordering quote length, gauge, and type (eg steel countersunk, or japanned round-head, as the case may be).
2. It is necessary to drill two holes for each screw: see Fig 5.4. First drill the pilot hole (or 'thread' hole) which is slightly smaller than the

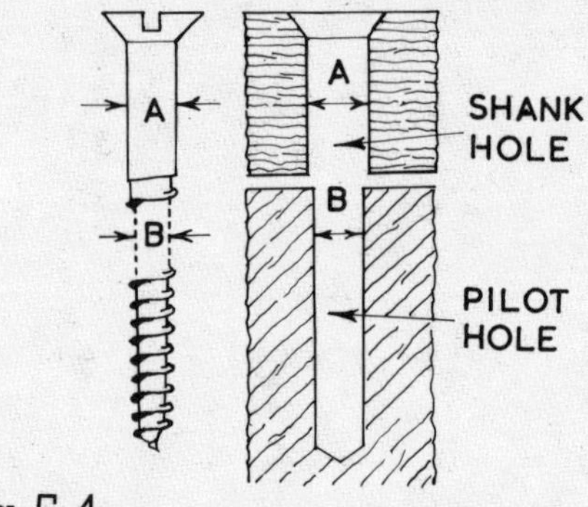

Fig 5.4

screw gauge so that the screw threads bite into the wood. Then drill the shank hole (or 'clearance' hole) which is the same diameter as the shank. If using countersunk-head screws, the end of the shank hole will have to be countersunk with the appropriate bit. The following table gives recommended sizes; in softwood the pilot holes can be a trifle smaller, and for very small screws a bradawl can be used to start them.

Screw clearance and pilot holes

gauge	clearance mm	clearance in	pilot mm	pilot in
0	1.5	1/16		
1 and 2	2	5/64		
3	2.5	3/32	1.5	1/16
4	3	7/64	1.5	1/16
5	3	1/8	2.5	3/32
6	3.5	9/64	2.5	3/32
7	4	5/32	3	7/64
8	4.5	11/64	3	1/8
9	5	3/16	3	1/8
10	5	13/64	3.5	9/64
12	5.5	7/32	3.5	9/64

3. If using solid brass screws, drive in an identical size and gauge mild steel screw first and then withdraw it. This will enable you to drive in the brass screw afterwards easily and with less risk of it breaking off due to too much torsion being applied.
4. It is good practice to rub a piece of candle or beeswax on the threads before driving the screw. Not only will it go in more easily but it will also be easier to withdraw at a later date if it becomes necessary. Do not use oil or soft wax as either could seep through to the surface and mark it.
5. Two types of screw heads have been developed recently – the Phillips and the Pozidriv. Both are shown in Fig 5.5; the Posidriv type need screwdrivers with special tips, of which there are three sizes. The purpose of the Pozidriv socket is to allow the screw to remain on the end of the screwdriver when working in awkward situations, such as corners.

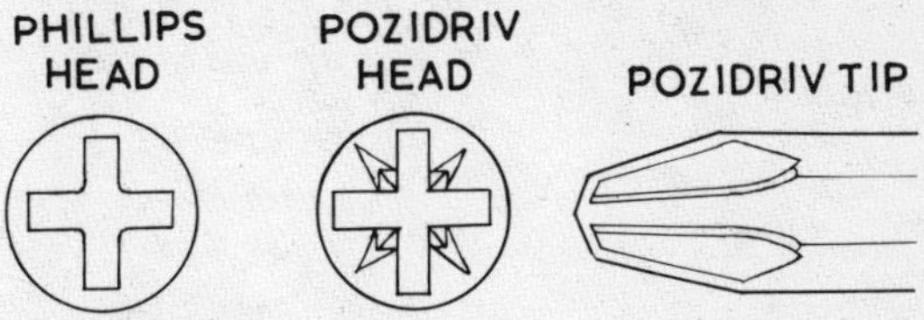

PHILLIPS HEAD

POZIDRIV HEAD

POZIDRIV TIP

Fig 5.5

Screw Materials, Finishes, and Uses

Finish	**Appearance**	**Suitable applications**
Steel Bright zinc plate	Bright attractive protective coating	All dry interior applications and where a paint finish is applied, indoor or outdoor.
Sheradised (zinc)	Dull grey protective coating. May turn brown unless painted	Most exterior fasteners for buildings. A good surface for painting.
Nickel plate	Bright reflective finish – may tarnish	Dry interior fasteners, eg shelves, heaters.
Chromium plate	Attractive bright reflective finish	Fairly dry interior work. Kitchens, most domestic appliances.
Brass plate (electro-brass)	Reflective bright yellow finish	Cupboards and furniture for matching against brass. Dry interior work only.
Bronze metal antique	Dark brown finish	For interior use with oxidised copper fittings.

Finish	Appearance	Suitable applications
Dark Florentine bronze	Near black finish	For interior use with oxidised copper fittings.
Antique copper bronze	Uniform bronze colour	For interior use with copper, bronze and matching timber finishes.
Black japanned	Overall black enamel finish	General interior use; re-painting necessary outdoors for protection.
Berlin blacked	Overall black enamel finish duller than japanned	General interior use; re-painting necessary outdoors for protection.
Steel Blued and oiled	Dark blue/black oxide coating, protective lubricating oil finish	Temporary protection only and requires painting in most applications.
Brass	Uniform bright yellow. Does not rust	All timber fastenings, brass hinges and door furniture.
Chromium plate	Brilliant reflective finish	With all chromium plated domestic goods, eg dome-head mirror screws.
Silicon bronze	Uniform dark brown colour	All exterior timber fastenings including boat building screws. Screws for copper and bronze components.
Aluminium alloy (anodised and lubricated with lanolin)	Matt silver-grey finish.	All fasteners for aluminium articles eg door furniture, bathroom fittings.
Stainless steel	Bright attractive finish	All construction applications where long term durability and freedom from rust staining is essential. May be used with aluminium components.

Timber Connectors (Fig 5.6)

Type A Has projecting teeth on both sides. Designed to give efficient joints without special equipment. Suitable for all types of timber construction – particularly frames made from small-sized timbers. Ideal for small roof trusses for domestic purposes.

A connector must be placed between each pair of timbers (see detail). To determine the number required for each joint, add together the number of pieces of timber to be joined

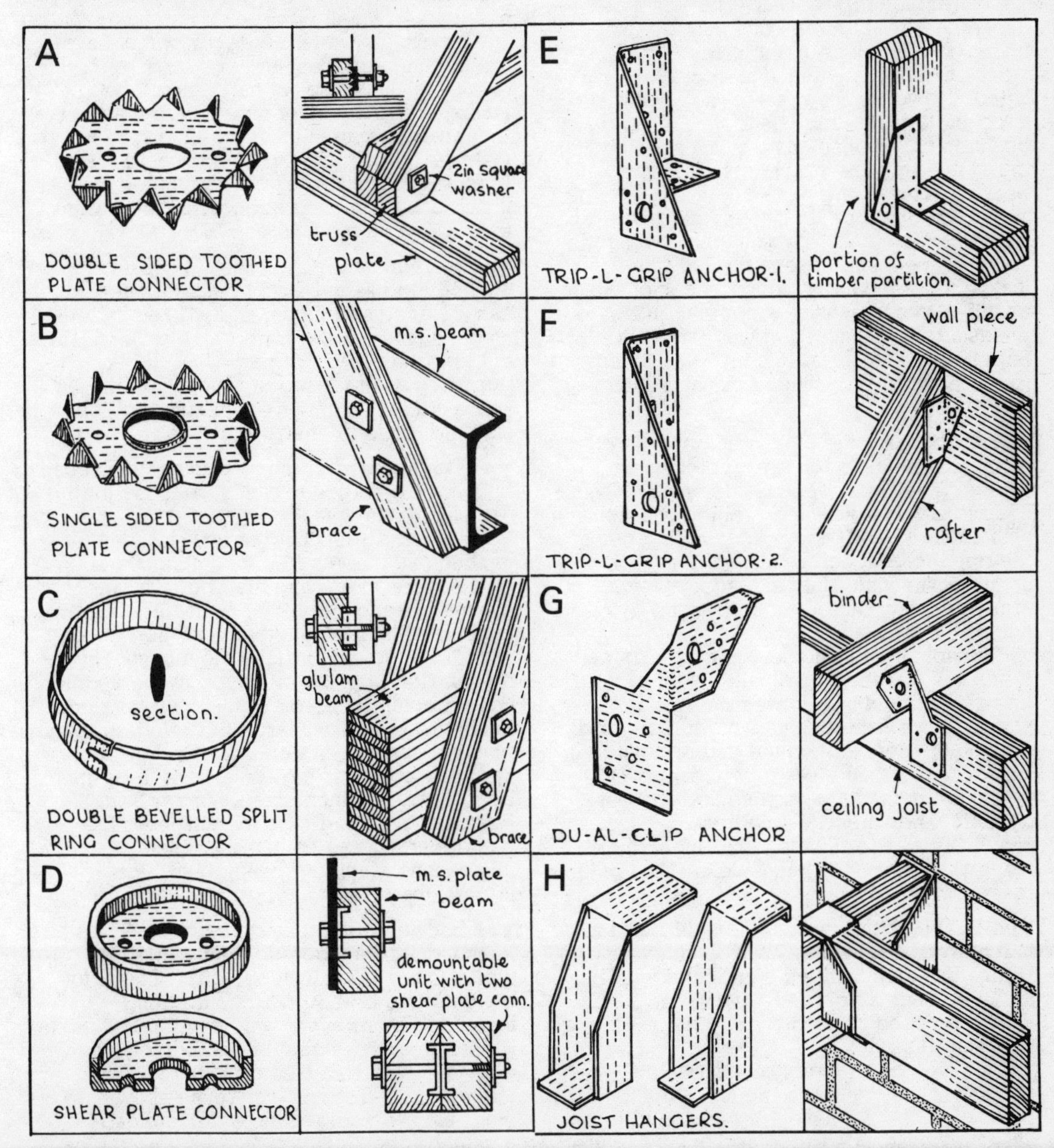

Fig 5.6

and deduct one. Always use 50mm (2in) square washers behind the bolt-head and the nut. Note, too, that the teeth must be completely embedded in the timber for full effectiveness. To ensure this, use a long bolt and a long spanner in the first instance, and then replace the original long bolt by one of the correct length. Where larger joints are concerned two or more bolts may be necessary. Supplied in four sizes: 40mm (1½in), 50mm (2in), and 75mm (3in).

Type B Designed for wood-to-metal or wood-to-concrete joints, and has teeth projecting on one side only. It also has a small raised collar round the bolt-hole which increases the bearing value of the plate.

Can be used for structures which have to be demountable. In this case, use two single-sided connectors between the timbers instead of one double-sided connector. Also useful in roof trusses where metal gusset plates are used instead of wooden ones. Supplied in five sizes: 40mm (1½in), 50mm (2in), 65mm (2½in), 75mm (3in) and 95mm (3¾in).

Type C Probably the most efficient type of connector. Suitable for any type of structure whether heavily loaded or otherwise. Consists of a circular band of steel, split at one point with a tongue-and-groove joint. Both faces of the ring are bevelled as shown in the sectional drawing. Note that special equipment is required for cutting the groove into which the ring fits.

The split in the ring serves two purposes. It ensures that the ring fits tightly on to the timber core, and also makes the ring flexible so that under load it comes into full bearing, both on the core and on the timber outside it. Unlike the toothed type, structures assembled with split rings can be dismantled without damage. They are available in two sizes: 65mm (2½in) and 100mm (4in), and can be used with 12mm (½in) and 19mm (¾in) bolts respectively.

Type D The counterpart of the split-ring for use in wood-to-metal or wood-to-concrete joints. Also useful where a structure is to be made demountable, where two shear plates should be used back to back in place of a split ring (see detail).

This type has a high load-carrying capacity. Note that the small holes in the plate allow it to be nailed in position before assembly; also, special equipment is required to cut the recesses. Available in two sizes: 65mm (2⅝in) and 100mm (4in).

Type E There are three types of *Trip-l-grip* framing anchors available, each being obtainable left- and right-handed. The first two types are shown, and all three types are 125mm (4⅞in) high, and made from 18 gauge sherardised steel.

The two shown in the top drawings have three fixing surfaces, and 11 gauge by 32mm (1¼in) galvanised clout nails should be used for fixing. Each anchor has a large hole in the triangular face to allow for the fixing of sheet material to the timber framing. Can be used for many purposes, eg partitions (see illustration), trimming in floors, fixing purlins to trusses in roof work, etc.

Type F This is the third type of *Trip-l-grip* anchor and has only two fixing surfaces. It has a sheradised finish, and is fixed with the clout nails already referred to. It is obtainable either right- or left-handed. Used for such purposes as the fixing of rafters to wall pieces (see illustration), trimming in floors, stair strings to trimmers, etc.

Type G These are framing anchors which can be used for purposes similar to those for the *Trip-l-grip* anchors.

They provide nailing on two surfaces for jointing two timbers of a minimum 50mm (2in) on the face, where one member crosses or is trimmed to another. Made from 18 gauge cadmium-plated mild steel, and then fixed with 11 gauge sherardised clout nails. The one illustrated is the only type available and can be obtained either right-or left-handed. Each anchor has two large holes to permit the fixing of surface materials to framing, while the hook is for tacking the anchor in position before nailing. Anchors are 90mm (3½in) high, and are used for such purposes as fixing binders to a ceiling joist (see illustration), studding, ceiling joists to undersides of beams or trusses, etc.

Type H There are many types of manufactured hangers for joists, and two typical ones are shown here. The first is for building into brickwork, thus avoiding inserting timber into a wall; and the second is for hanging on a beam or another joist to dispense with complicated joints like tusk tenons, housed joints, etc. Those shown are made from 10 gauge mild steel and can be obtained for all joist sizes.

CHAPTER SIX

Upholstery materials, foams, and springing

UPHOLSTERY methods have been revolutionised by the advent of foam cushioning which, with the addition of resilient webbing and specialised forms of metal springing, has made upholstering a comparatively straightforward job. Regulations governing the flammability of foam cushioning are soon to be introduced, but the working techniques are unlikely to be altered.

Foam Upholstery

Polyether foam is produced on highly sophisticated equipment by reacting various chemicals together. The result is a flexible cellular material which 'breathes', and is light and very resilient. The key to using it correctly is to choose the correct density. This is generally expressed as the weight in kilograms per cubic metre.

Another important feature is thickness. Here you must think of the base on which the foam is to be used. On the simplest form of base – a rigid board – the foam will obviously have to provide all the comfort and resilience, so the thickest cushions will be required. Firm grades need to be at least 90mm (3½in) thick, while softer grades usually need a minimum of 120mm (4¾in) when used for seating.

On many forms of sprung or elastic-webbing supports, however, these thicknesses can be reduced. Firm grades need only be 70 or 80mm (2¾ or 3¼in) thick, and softer grades 100mm (4in), provided the frame rails are not in direct contact with the cushion. If necessary, avoid such contact with the cushion by padding or modifying the base. Hessian webbing, slatted bases, and plastic 'shell' chairs should be treated as solid bases.

Laminating Foam varies not only in density but also in softness – and denser does not always mean harder. Where thickness becomes a problem in relation to design, different hardnesses can be laminated together. A 120mm (4¾in) cushion, for instance, can be reduced to 100mm (4in) by laminating 70mm (2¾in) of a soft grade with 30mm (1¼in) of a firmer grade. Such combinations can also be used with convertible furniture for sleeping and sitting; the soft grade provides surface comfort in the lightly-loaded sleeping position, and the firmer grade prevents undue compression during use as a seat.

The wide range of different grades can be fabricated to give many combinations and overcome several upholstery problems. Cushions can be domed to prevent the effect of cover-stretch; cushion sides can be stiffened to give crisp cover lines and maintain shapes; arm pads can be designed to prevent 'bottoming' from the point of the elbow; head-rests can be made very soft but with firmer edges. Supersoft grades can be utilised as a wrapping, or for a complete cushion, when a very soft, plump look is required.

Cutting and covering Though thick slabs of foam are not easy to cut neatly, you should be able to achieve a satisfactory result with a fine-toothed hacksaw blade or a really sharp long cook's knife. But the best tool for the job is an electric carving knife, which will give a professional-looking finish.

Always cut the foam slightly oversize, but make the fabric covers to exact finished dimensions. This will put the foam permanently under slight compression, ensuring clean lines and minimising wrinkles. For example, a mattress should be about 20mm (¾in) oversize in length and about 15mm (⅝in) in width, while most cushions need about 5mm (3/16in) in both length and width.

Heavy fabrics will not give crisp lines when used on softer grades of foam which should therefore be covered with light-weight materials. In particular, avoid foam-backed fabrics, which tend to grip the foam cushion and thus make fitting difficult.

Use a proper upholstery adhesive for bonding foam to itself or to other surfaces – two excellent ones are *Dunlop Thixofix,* and *Copydex.* For sticking large cushions to solid bases, spread the adhesive round the edges of both surfaces in a band about 40mm (1⅝in) wide. Where two large sheets of foam are to be stuck together, reinforce the outer bands of adhesive with criss-cross strips applied at random over the area.

Special Applications

Load-bearing in seating In Fig 6.1(1) you can see how various grades are used to get maximum support plus comfort on a chair with a rigid seating base. The front edge of the cushion support is the vital point to get right. If possible you should use a strip of 'chipfoam' (a reconstituted type), about 50mm (2in) thick at A; its density should be about 65kg, which is the softest grade for chipfoam. *Dunlopillo* make a range of seven grades from 65kg to 230kg. The wedge-shaped piece shown at B should be a medium-density foam, about 31kg per cubic metre. Two-thirds of the body-weight rests on the seat cushion C, and this should be about 32kg per cubic metre; the back cushion, D, however has a much lighter load to carry, and its density could be about 18kg per cubic metre. A lumbar support E is advisable, too; this should always be a little harder than the higher part of the back, and a density of about 31kg per cubic metre is recommended.

Cutting squares and curves Methods are shown in Fig 6.1(2). The edge of a bench and a steel straight-edge can be used as guides when making vertical or angled cuts, as at A. To cut circles or other curved shapes, you will need two templets of hardboard or stiff cardboard. Sandwich the foam between them, secure the whole thing with a length of wire, and cut round the templets, B.

Buttoning For buttoned cushions or chair backs use a layer of soft foam, 30mm (1⅛in) thick, over the appropriate firmer grade. In the case of a bedhead as in (3) a 40mm (1½in) thick soft layer stuck to the hardboard or plywood back is all that is needed, as shown. By the way, latex foam is unsuitable for buttoning.

Padded backs and seats Chamfer the edges of the foam and glue the chamfered sides to the base as at C, (4): this will form the shape shown at D. Curved supports for the back and head can be created by employing the flexibility of the material. Glued together as flat slabs, pieces of foam will form the shape E when fixed into position as a frame and webbing, or on a solid panel, as in (5).

Rounded edges Apply adhesive to the edges of the cushion, allow it to become tacky, and then pinch the edges together; see (6).

Shaped units These should be accurately cut from a paper or card templet, carefully made from the shape of the frame or base supporting them. The window seat F and the boat mattress G in (7) are examples.

Domed shapes To make deep-domed chair cushions, use two pieces of foam, each being half the finished thickness, and sandwich between them a piece 30mm (1³⁄₁₆in) thick and 90mm (3½in) smaller all round. Glue the outer pieces around the edges and the material will be pulled into a domed shape by the fabric covering, (8).

Securing cushions Cushions can be permanently fixed to a solid base by applying a 40mm (1⅝in) band of adhesive around the edges. If you want to be able to remove the cushion at any time, glue tape to the edges and tack the tape to the base H ready for the fabric covering. Tape can also be used to form hinges I and J, and rounded edges K and L; (9) shows the methods for this.

Upholstering arms (10) shows how to deal with a top load-bearing area; a pad of high-density foam may be used with a softer wrap-round. (11) illustrates an alternative method using lamination, as in the seat for the smaller arm type. The overlap should always be taken over the edges to protect the cover from undue wear.

Covering firm-based units These are shown in (12) and are self-explanatory. Where non-breathing material such as PVC or hide is to be used as a cover, vents are essential to permit the passage of air. Drilling holes 20mm (¾in) in diameter, spaced at 150mm (6in) centres, is a satisfactory method of ventilation. On hard bases, an underpad for doming can, by positioning and thickness, give a variety of styles, as in (13).

Repairs These are illustrated in (14). To repair holes, cut the end of a piece of offcut foam roughly to shape with scissors. Glue it into the hole, leaving the spare foam projecting until the glue is dry, then cut it off flush with a sharp knife or a fine saw. To repair tears, hold the tear open, apply glue, keep it open until the glue is dry and then press together.

Making your own bed If you are making your own base for a foam mattress it is extremely important to provide proper ventilation so that the mattress can breathe. A slatted base should have a minimum of 20mm (¾in) between the slats, and a rigid board base should have 20mm (¾in) diameter holes drilled at 150mm (6in) centres. With any type of rigid base there should ideally be a 50mm (2in) layer of profile-cut foam (the type used for camping mattresses, which has indentations on the underside giving an egg-box effect) upholstered on to the base, profiled side down, as in (15)M. This helps the air to circulate properly under the mattress and also to prevent any possibility of condensation forming on the underside. Any type of fabric can be used to cover the base as long as it is air-permeable.

For a rigid base you need a thick mattress – the minimum recommended thickness is 120mm (4¾in), and the minimum density 28kg per cubic metre. If a softer feel is preferred, this can be achieved by laminating a layer of soft foam to the top surface of the mattress.

The mattress for a convertible bed/seating unit is shown in (16). If the mattress is to be used for seating as well as sleeping, it is preferable to make the outer 40mm (1⅝in) of each edge from a firmer grade of foam N. This will help it to keep its shape.

A loose back-rest is an easy way of turning a bed into a settee for daytime use (17). For this to be comfortable, the rest P should reduce the width of the mattress to about 500mm (19¾in), and be firm enough to offer good support to the back.

Standard grades of foam plastic

Density – kg per cubic metre	*Main uses*
14.0 to 16.0	Head rests, soft backs, medium/soft backs
17.0 to 18.5	Medium/soft backs
21.0 to 23.0	General firm padding (back/arms)
25.0 to 27.0	Seat cushions/arms
27.0 to 29.5	Mattresses, cushion cores, backs
30.5 to 32.5	Matresses, soft cushions, backs, cores
18.0 to 20.5	Super-soft foam for pillows
20.0 to 24.0	Super-soft headrests, thick back cushions, pillows
23.0 to 27.0	Very soft backs
27.0 to 32.0	Soft seat wraps

(Information and illustrations supplied by Dunlopillo Ltd)

Resilient Rubber Webbing

This type of webbing offers a means of springing for chairs and settees of most kinds, divan beds, caravan seats and beds, bunks, and so on. Frequently it can be fitted as an alternative to existing springing when re-upholstering is required, but generally it is used to best advantage in new work, the frame being designed to resist the inward pull of the webbing. All that this involves is the use of wood thick enough not to bend easily, or the fitting of a frame composed of horizontal members as at (A), Fig 6.2, and in the case of long items, the provision of an intermediate rail (C). The latter should be dished at its top edge to allow for the 'give' in the webbing. When a soft flexible edge at the front of a seat is essential, the webbing should pass from side to side and the front rail be hollowed at the top edge as at (B). One last point is that the inner edge of the frame should be rounded over (D) as this avoids chafing the webbing.

Webbing in general use is made in widths of 19mm, 29mm, 38mm, 51mm and 57mm (¾in,

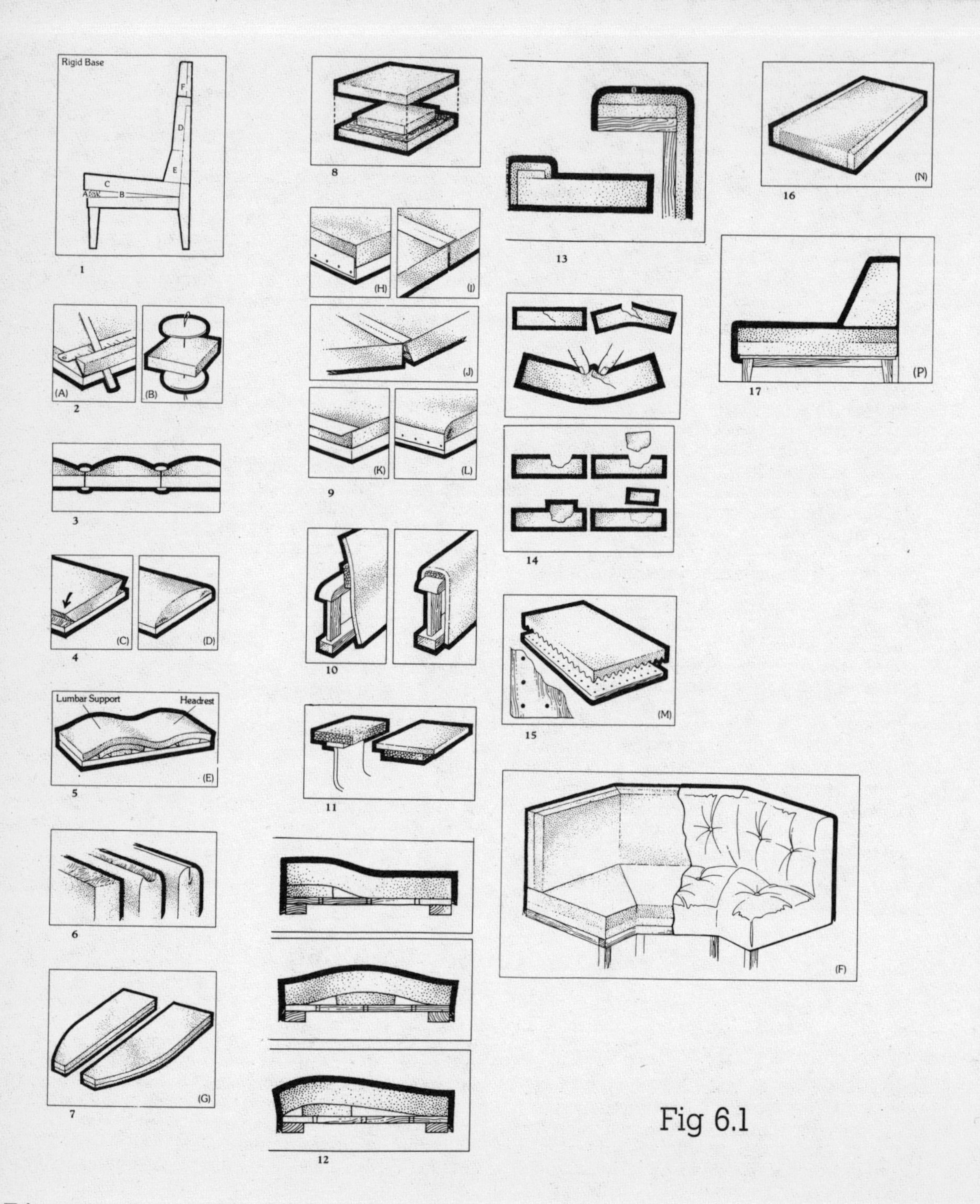
Rigid Base
F
D
E
C
A
B
1
(A)
(B)
2
3
(C)
(D)
4
Lumbar Support
Headrest
(E)
5
6
(G)
7
8
(H)
(I)
(J)
(K)
(L)
9
10
11
12
13
14
(M)
15
(N)
16
(P)
17
(F)

Fig 6.1

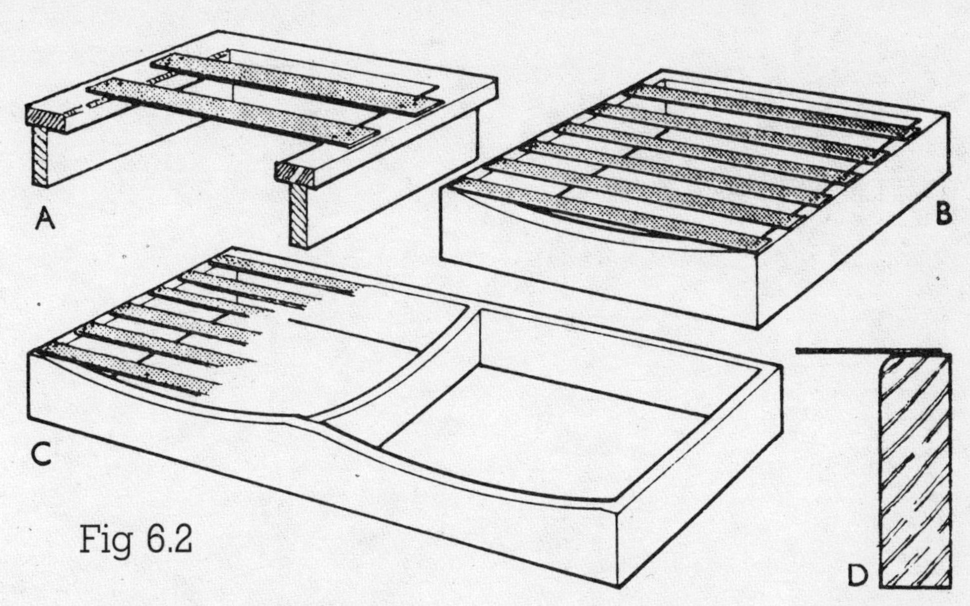

Fig 6.2

1⅛in, 1½in, 2in, and 2¼in). Of these the first two are recommended for arms and backs, and the other three seats and divan beds. The 57mm (2¼in) width is seldom needed for the general run of chairs.

Method of fixing – tacks For most work 16mm (⅝in) improved tacks are best, and a hardwood such as beech, elm, or oak is advisable for the frame as softwood does not give a good holding for tacks. The number of tacks recommended is shown at (A), Fig 6.3, and it will be seen that they should be set in from 6mm to 10mm (¼in to ⅜in) from the end. No doubling over of the webbing is necessary. We have found that when three tacks are used a slight staggering helps in that it avoids splitting the wood along the grain, see (A), Fig 6.3.

The simplest method of fixing is to tack down one end, mark with pencil the length, put a second mark 25mm to 32mm (1in to 1¼in) inwards for each 254mm (10in) of span (C), Fig 6.3, and stretch the webbing until this second mark is opposite the first position, then tack it, the surplus being cut off.

End clips These offer a rather neater method of fixing, but require the provision of a sloping groove in the frame rails. The clips are simply pushed into the grooves. Clip fixing is simple. The end of the webbing is pushed into the open clip (D), and the latter squeezed flat in vice or cramp (E). Note that the rounded side of the clip is downwards when fixing in all cases. A slope of 10 degrees to 15 degrees is needed for the groove, and it should be 4mm wide by 15mm deep (5/32in wide by 9/16in deep). Working the groove depends upon the facilities available. A circular saw (G) is the simplest way, either saw or table being set at the required angle. If the spindle moulder is used (H) a sloping jig is needed. Another means of working is the portable router (I), the wood contained between a pair of sloping fences, and the whole held in the bench vice. Alternatively the router can be reversed beneath a table, and a sloping false fence fitted to the fence proper (J). For those who have hand tools only the plough or grooving plane can be used (K), the wood held between tapered fences. A single tapered fence can be used if it is screwed to the inside of the work.

Metal tubular frame and angle iron fixing Tubular frames need a series of 2mm (3/32in) holes drilled centrally along the top, the ends of special 'A' wire clips fitting into them. Stages in fixing the clips are shown in (L to R). Holes to receive the wire staples are punched in the webbing, and the former slipped through a plate and into the inner holes in the webbing (L). The end of the latter is folded around the wire clip, and a second plate placed above (M). Finally the staple ends are bent down over the plate (N). The clip is shown in position at (O).

Sometimes the webbing can be passed

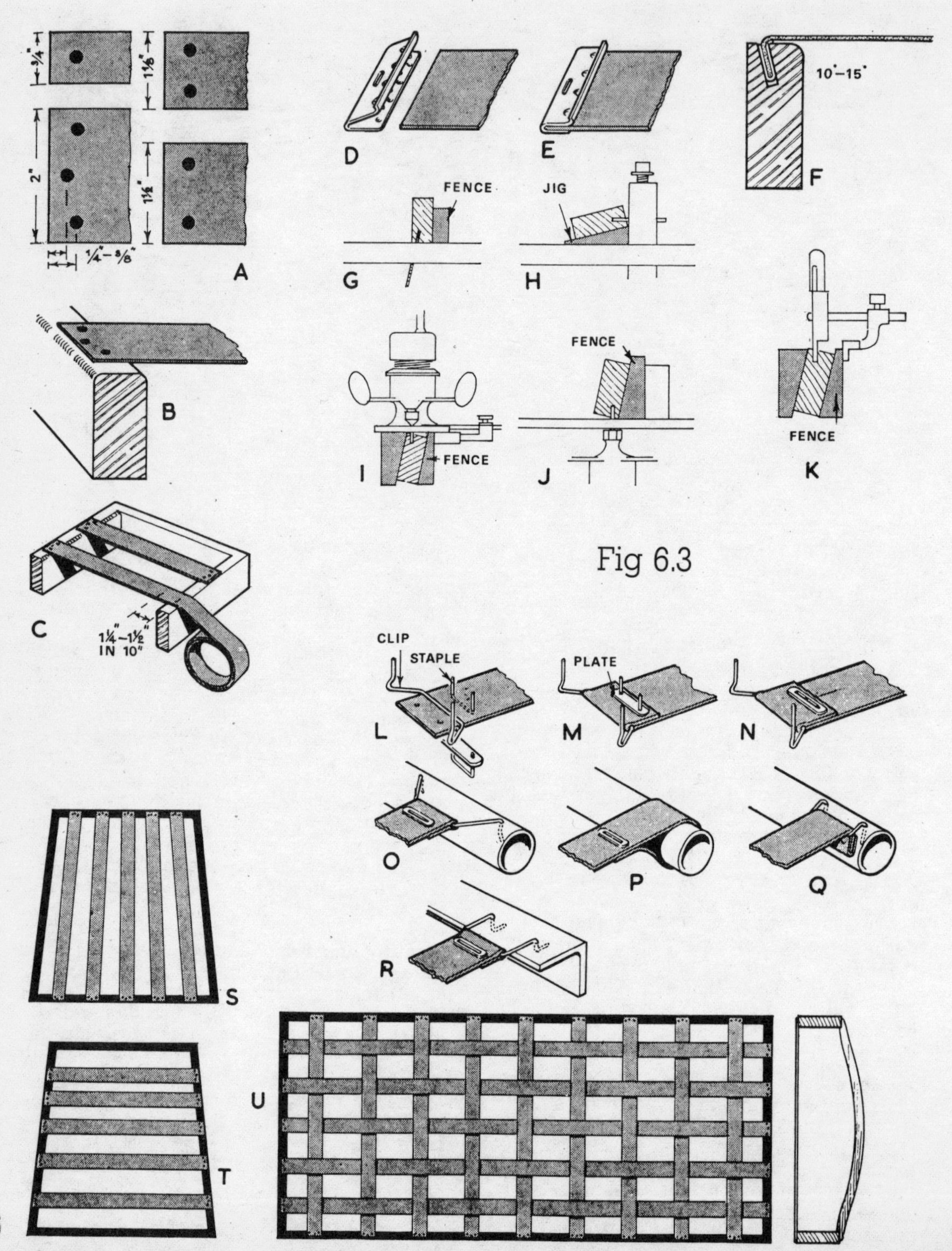

3/4"
1⅛"
2"
1½"
¼"–⅜"
A
B
C
1¼"–1½"
IN 10"
D
E
10°–15°
F
FENCE
G
JIG
H
I
FENCE
J
FENCE
K
FENCE
CLIP
STAPLE
L
PLATE
M
N
O
P
Q
R
S
T
U

Fig 6.3

right round the tube and again held with staple and pair of plates as at (P). If preferred the flat clip shown at (D) and (E) can be used in conjunction with the 'E' wire clip as at (Q).

In the case of angle irons the special 'B' clip can be used as at (R), these passing through holes in the top of the angle. Alternatively the webbing may be passed right round the angle and held with clips.

Direction of webbing in chairs depends upon design. Generally the spaces between the webs should not be greater than the webbing widths, but it may vary according to position. At (S), Fig 6.3, for instance, the strands pass from front to back and converge. When running from side to side (T) it makes a stronger seat if the webs are fixed closer together towards the back, as this area takes a greater proportion of weight.

In the case of a divan bed the arrangement at (U) is usual for a single bed. The chart below gives recommended arrangements:

Note that a centre cross strut is needed to prevent the sides from bending in. It should be curved downwards as shown to the right (U). If preferred it can be of metal.

Bed width	*Strand arrangement*	*Quantity*
600mm (2ft)	9 across width, 3 along length	10.05m (33ft)
760mm (2ft 6in)	9 across width, 4 along length	12.80m (42ft)
915mm (3ft)	9 across width, 5 along length	15.85m (52ft)
1066mm (3ft 6in)	9 across width, 6 along length	18.59m (61ft)

Other Forms of Upholstery Springing

Figs 6.4 and 6.5 show various types which can be used to support either seat or back loose foam cushions.

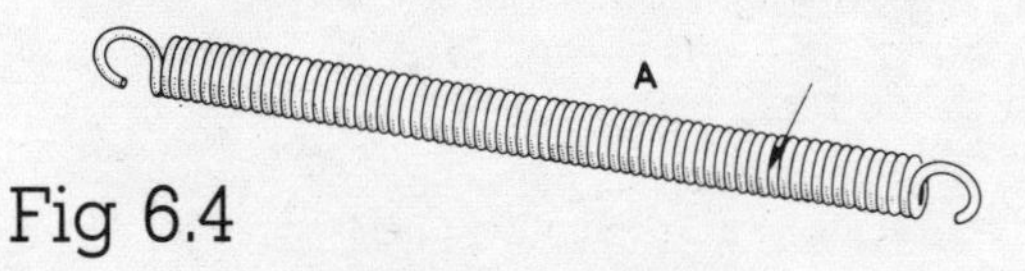

Fig 6.4

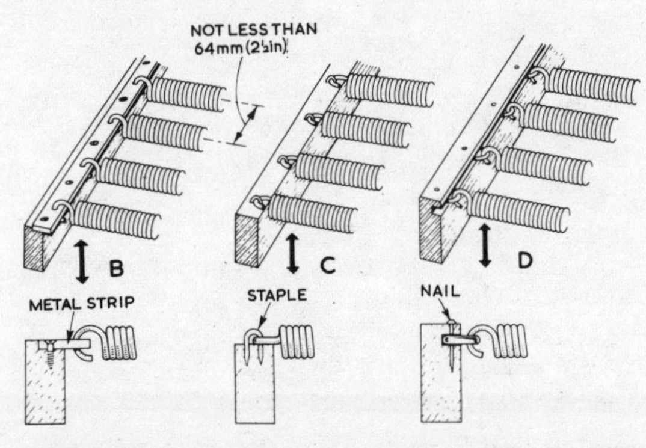

(a) Tension spring Sometimes called a 'cable spring'. Obtainable in cut lengths and supplied with a plastic sleeve to prevent soiling of the cushions. Allow about 38mm-50mm (1½in-2in) for tensioning: eg for a span of 460mm (18in) use a 406mm (16in) spring.

(b) Metal-lath fixing The laths can be obtained ready-drilled and cut to length.

(c) Staple-and-hook fixing The ends of the spring are bent out to form hooks.

(d) Shows the recommended method There are no protruding metal parts to rub the cushion. Rings are inserted into a groove and held by panel pins (with the heads punched flush): the ends of the spring engage through the rings.

Fig 6.5 Serpentine or 'zig-zag' springing This is particularly suitable for the seats of dining chairs. Method of fixing is shown at (A).

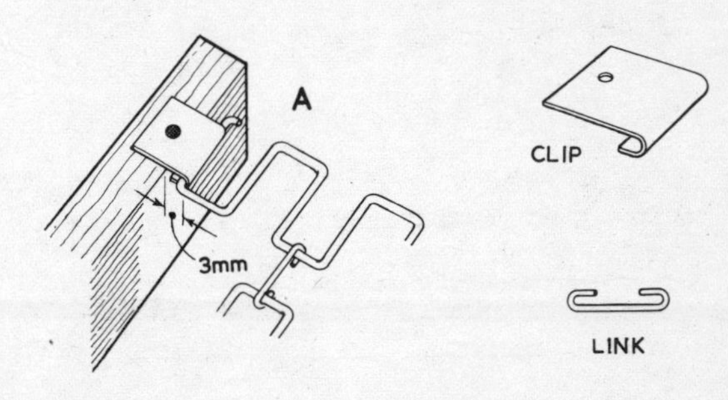

Fig 6.5

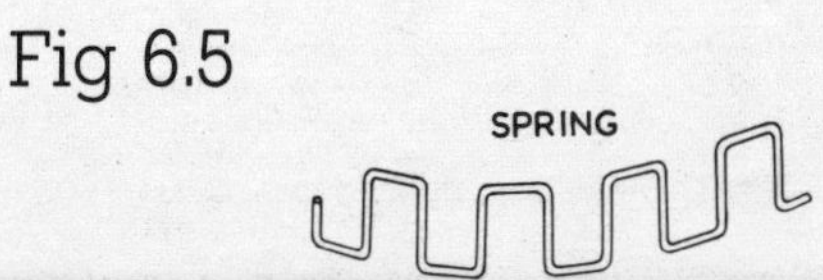

Fig 6.6 Double-cone upholstery spring Available in heights from 102mm (4in) to 254mm (10in) in 25mm (1in) increments. These are fixed by lashing to webbing.

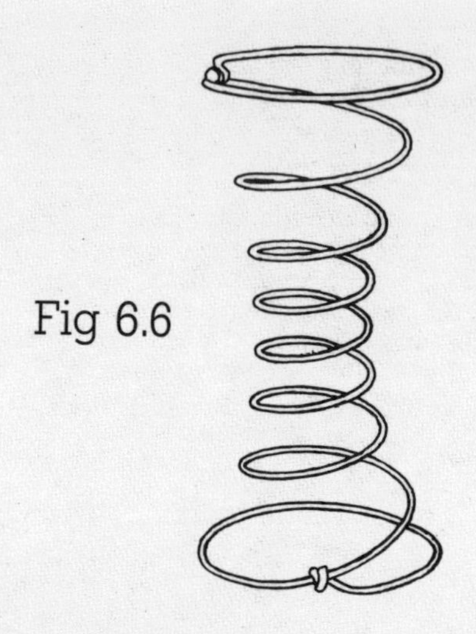
Fig 6.6

Upholstery Sundries

Upholsterers' needles Fig 6.7 (A) curved mattress needle with round point, from 51mm to 152mm (2in to 6in); (B) upholsterer's curved needle, from 51mm to 152mm (2in to 6in); (C) skewer, 90mm and 102mm (3½in and 4in); (D) packing needle, 102mm to 204mm (4in to 8in): (E) upholsterer's straight needle, round points both ends, 204mm to 356mm (8in to 14in); (F) ditto, but one round point and one bayonet point, 204mm to 305mm (8in to 12in); (G) mattress needle, 152mm to 305mm (6in to 12in); (G) mattress needle, 152mm to 305mm (6in to 12in); (H) regulator, 204mm to 254mm (8in and 10in).

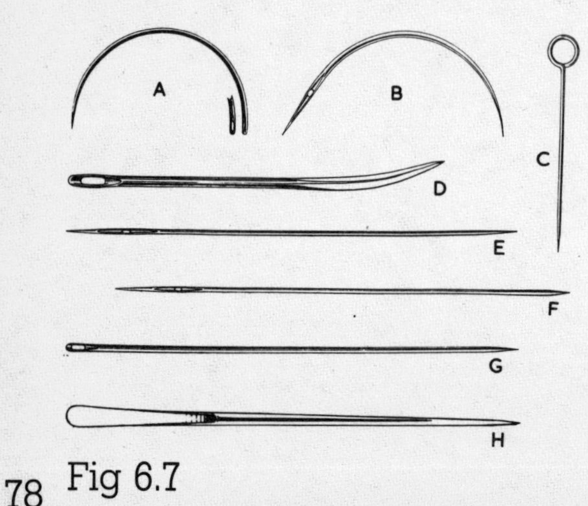

Fig 6.7

Upholstery sundries

Webbing 51mm (2in) jute: webbing, black and white super grade 51mm (2in) – both in 16m (18yd) rolls.

Piping cord three grades, No 2 Thick, No 3 Medium, No 4 Thin. In 0.9kg (2lb) cops (a cop is a reel).

Sisal in 2ply and 3ply (for lashing springs) in standard or super quality. In 0.9kg (2lb) cops.

Hessian a loosely woven jute cloth used to cover springs and loose stuffing.

Scrim similar to hessian but with a more open weave, and with flat threads instead of round. Used to cover the first stuffing.

Calico a lightweight bleached cotton fabric. Used to cover stuffed upholstery prior to applying the final cover, and can also be cut into strips for fixing foam to a frame.

Flexibead a ready-covered plastic beading which can be bent to shape and nailed in place. In several colours.

Bonded chipfoam made in sheets from 2mm (1/12in) thickness upwards. It consists of waste polyether chips mixed with a polyurethane resin, and is either extruded for thick grades, or rotary-cut for thinner grades. It is ideal as a base layer over which a softer material can be laid.

Polyester fibrefill A cushion-filling material made of either *Terylene* or *Dacron*. It can be bought as bonded batting, in which the sheets are lightly bonded on each side, or as unbonded batting in which the fibrefill is folded into layers which have to be contained between cheese-cloth.

Fig 6.8 (A) cut tack; (B) cut gimp pin; (C) wire gimp pin; (D) dome-head antique nail; (E) fabric or leather-covered stud; (F) snape-type button with fabric-covered head – it can be used instead of the string-fastened button.

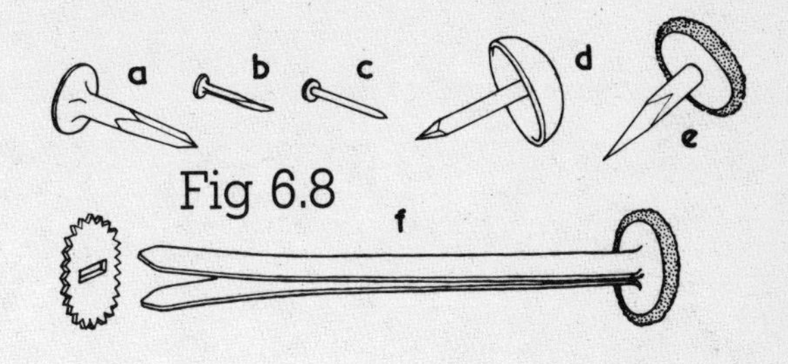

Fig 6.8

CHAPTER SEVEN

Traditional and modern adhesives; veneering

ADHESIVES used in woodworking can be divided into three groups:

(a) Adhesives which set by cooling The most common and important of these is animal glue. Other varieties which are not often found in the small workshop fall into a group commonly known as the 'hot melts'. These can only be applied using purpose-built equipment (although this includes the 'glue guns' now available retail).

(b) Adhesives which set by loss of moisture The most widely used is polyvinyl acetate (PVA).

(c) Adhesives which set by chemical reaction This large group includes urea formaldehyde (UF); phenol-formaldehyde (PF); resorcinol-formaldehyde (RF); and cross-linking polyvinyl acetate (as distinct from the PVA under B). UF is the most important, although a weather-and-boil-proof specification may call for RE instead.

All the adhesives in groups (b) and (c) are what are known as 'synthetic resins'. The word 'synthetic' in this context means that the material is manufactured by a chemical process which does not occur in nature.

The adhesives in group (b) are thermoplastic; those in group (c) are thermosetting.

In thermoplastic materials the setting process can be reversed: the set adhesive can be re-softened by heating and wetting – so adhesives in this classification should not be used where hot or wet conditions may prevail.

Thermosetting materials behave differently. Once the chemical reaction whch sets them has taken place, and the adhesive (which started as a liquid) has become a solid, the process cannot be reversed.

Animal glues The familiar Scotch glue comes from the bones and hides of cattle; used hot, it is particularly useful for veneering as it can easily be re-melted by applying heat with a warm iron and a damp cloth.

The glue itself is heated before use in a pot suspended in hot water, which should not be allowed to boil. If it is ready for use it will run off the brush in a steady stream without any lumps. The other advantages in choosing Scotch glue are that it is strong and durable in dry conditions, it can be machined or cleaned off without blunting cutters, and it is non-staining (although the glue line may be noticeable when using light woods such as holly or sycamore). It is both cheap and easy to use and its initial tackiness makes it invaluable for jobs such as putting in rubbed corner blocks. It has a long shelf life and a good pot life, but should not be re-heated too often or it weakens. Its main disadvantage is that it has to be used quickly before it starts to cool, and so may not be the best choice for a complicated job. Ideally, the wood should be warmed, too, so that the glue is not chilled on contact. It should never be used for outdoor work, as its resistance to moisture is poor. Its place has been taken largely by the white PVA adhesives.

PVA adhesives In these, polyvinyl acetate is emulsified, using water as the carrier.

There are at least three distinct families of PVA adhesives. In addition to the usual 'one-shot' which is not water-resistant, there are also one-pack and two-pack sorts which are. Of the two water-resistant PVA's only the one-pack is generally available.

The advantages of PVA adhesives include very low cost of manufacture; they are clean, have fast setting times (typically a structure can be handled in 30 minutes), need no solvent (noxious or otherwise), and are usually ready for use. In addition, they will stick virtually all woods, and are very suitable for caul and press veneering. Indeed, they will stick anything cellulosic, which may be interpreted as any timber-based materials. These include, somewhat surprisingly, many of the plastic-surfaced laminates: namely, those which are made of paper layers, and in which a paper surface is largely exposed on the back. The snag in this last application is that considerable pressure is required for a sound joint, and the process is therefore limited to factory use.

An obvious drawback is that PVA adhesives are not gap-filling. Less apparent is their unsuitability for use in load-bearing structures such as fabricated beams and stressed panels. If subject to sustained loadings, joints are very likely to fail through 'creep'.

Some adhesives bond mechanically, by locking in to the surface, and some bond chemically, by actually combining with it; PVA adhesives probably do both in varying degrees.

UF (urea formaldehyde) Nowadays the big users of UF adhesives are plywood and particle-board makers, while production woodworkers use them also for veneering, laminating, and assembly work generally. UF adhesives are, however, available in small packs suitable for home-workshop use. They are made in liquid or powder form; while the former may be more convenient to use – no pre-mixing is needed – it has a very short pot life. The powder will last up to two years or so without deterioration.

The UF adhesives comprise a resin and hardener. For those users who are able to identify their special needs accurately enough, there is a large assortment of hardeners which will suitably modify the characteristics of a mix. Most of us, however, will find little to complain of in the standard hardeners supplied in the standard packs. UF resins are reasonably capable of gap-filling; they also resist damp, infestation, and rot. In ordinary conditions, working time is about 10 to 20 minutes, and at least two hours cramping will be required before handling strength develops; maximum strength will not be reached for several days – and not at all if the timber is cold and damp. Materials should therefore be stored in warm, dry conditions.

A point to bear in mind is the risk of stains resulting from chemical reaction if any ferrous metal (such as steel) comes into contact with the adhesive before it sets.

RF (resorcinol formaldehyde) These were developed to provide durability in tough outdoor conditions and boatbuilders in particular find them very useful. They are good for finger-jointing, and structural engineers use them for laminated beams of the kind incorporated in modernistic buildings. In addition, they are perfectly capable of making durable bonds with certain non-wood materials – brick, concrete, cork, expanded polystyrene, and leather among them. Hardener and resin are pre-mixed, and then spread on to both surfaces; unmixed, the shelf life of the glue is about twelve months.

Impact adhesives Most adhesives are applied in the time-honoured way – a quantity is spread, surfaces are pressed together, and in the appropriate time the joint is made. Impact adhesives have very different characteristics, as with them a rapidly evaporating solvent carries polychloroprene neoprene in suspension. The liquid is spread evenly on the surfaces to be joined; they are left to become touch-dry, and then brought into contact. With most varieties, slip is almost impossible, so the items must be perfectly aligned before they touch; second thoughts or a crisis of confidence are both fatal.

The initial delay is necessary because this kind of adhesive is intended for use with non-porous surfaces. The solvent must be allowed time to evaporate after it has done its job in allowing the stuff to be spread. Although impact adhesives perform their role – notably in sticking plastic laminates on to kitchen surfaces, and in securing hardboard, stone, concrete and other materials – they are far from being universal cure-alls.

Their major drawback lies in the solvents used. These are flammable (although not dangerously so, provided care is taken) and -- with the exception of those in certain new formulations – they should not be inhaled.

It is as well with this family of adhesives to check the sensitivity of the materials to be joined. Although the adhesives are mechanical in action rather than chemical, they will (for example) rapidly demolish styrene foams of the kind used for ceiling tiles; in cases of doubt, the manufacturer should be consulted. Further, they can stick to metals (although special primers may be necessary for optimum strength); an unexpected warning is needed with copper or copper alloys – which includes all brasses. These react adversely with the adhesive, which leads to rapid failure of the joint.

Solvent impact adhesives perform well in the presence of water; they are also flexible, and are therefore suitable for use with leathers and leathercloths. With these and other fabrics, it is advisable to check first that the material is not sensitive. If it is not, the apparent difficulty of using an instant-stick adhesive for, say a leather desk lining, which needs to be stretched and coaxed into place, can be overcome by using the adhesive wet. This is not really approved of by the makers - - and it is essential that the under-surface is absorbent enough to take up the solvent. Sustained pressure is needed while the joint is being made.

Finally, while impact adhesives will certainly stick wood parts together, they are not suitable for the purpose and are not likely to be satisfactory – except perhaps for minor tasks such as applying edge-banding.

Epoxy resins These adhesives provide the answers to many problems of adhesion; while some of them are specially tailored to meet precise industrial applications, there are general-purpose types available to the home woodworker which are suitable for fabricating strong, loaded-bearing structures. Although the synthetic resins are physically capable of handling almost any sticking job, in practice their cost makes it expensive for woodworkers to use them in quantity.

Because the bonding action is chemical, clean surfaces are required – but happily this also means that only the minimum quantity of the adhesive should be used for a joint; there should be no thick film, and there need be no wastage. There is no point in deliberately roughening the surfaces – light abrasion is quite enough – but cleanliness is essential.

Glass is among the impressive array of dissimilar materials that can be bonded satisfactorily with epoxies; fabrics generally are not as they are flexible, while the epoxies are, if not brittle, at least stiff.

Most workers seem to be able to cope with another difficulty – the accurate judging of small quantities of resin and hardener when using them from the standard two-part kits. These, incidentally, have an indefinite and very long shelf life, provided resin and hardener do not come into contact. There is a need to apply suitable cramps and some form of heat while the joint is being made; the former problem is usually relatively easy to solve, and the latter can often be met by placing the job in a domestic oven or on central-heating radiators. Cold bonding without heat is possible but can be slow and may possibly result in less than maximum strength.

Cyanoacrylates and anaerobic adhesives These are more widely known as 'super glues', and have possibly suffered from over-enthusiastic promotion. They are expensive, and there are limits to the area of surface with which they can cope. Moreover, they are not intended for wood or porous materials, but for plastic and rubber components. They are, of course, known for the fact that they will also stick to the human skin and can stick fingers together.

The loosely related anaerobic adhesives are brittle, too, and in many applications the joints they make have a limited life – particularly when exposed to damp. Their usefulness lies principally in such tasks as locking bolts into nuts or tapped holes.

Hot-melt glues Another modern development is the 'hot-melt' glue gun, and here again there is a risk that advertising promotion may obscure its real merits by exaggerated claims. Its advantages of quick, clean working are evident to anyone who has watched a demonstration, but with a typical open working time of 40 seconds or less it takes a swift hand to assemble any but the simplest structure satisfactorily. Matters are not helped by the fact that joint strength will suffer if surfaces are moved or adjusted after contact is made.

These appliances and the glues they use are well suited to 'spot' applications, and are at their best in such tasks as fixing wood to concrete and brick without the need for drilling, fastening a whole range of plastic materials and fabrics, and securing electrical trunking and cables to walls. They are also gap-filling, which adds considerably to their general usefulness for DIY jobs.

Two Methods of Hand-Veneering

Method 1 This was first publicised some years ago by *UniBond,*but it works well with a number of other PVA (white) glues, too, but not necessarily all of them. It involves making use of the thermoplastic properties of the adhesive.

1. Joint the veneer if necessary. Plane the edges of the two pieces on a shooting board,

holding the veneers flat with a batten, or gripping them between two slightly curved battens secured at each end with a wood screw, passing the assembly over the planer. The joints must be firmly pulled and held together with veneering-tape or gummed brown paper tape. Do not use a pressure-sensitive tape such as *Sellotape*, or masking-tape. Cut them very slightly oversize, then tape up the extreme ends to reduce splitting.

2. Prepare a container of glue size, made up of one part of PVA to five parts of water. Stored in a plastic pot with a snap or screw lid, this will keep well. The size is brushed on to the back of both the veneer and the groundwork – do not make them too wet or the veneer will buckle badly. Allow to dry overnight. Next day, sand very lightly to remove any nibs. Clean the brush with warm water and detergent.

3. Coat the veneer and groundwork with the adhesive – this time a mixture of five parts of PVA to one of water. PVA should always be decanted from a metal container into a plastic one to prevent staining from rust; it is strange that some manufacturers still supply it in metal cans. Again allow to dry overnight and lightly sand smooth on the following day.

4. Place the veneer in position on the groundwork and hold it there with a few strips of gummed tape, meanwhile heating up a domestic iron to the setting marked 'wool'. Then iron the veneer on. For a single sheet, iron outwards from the centre; for a jointed piece, move the iron as much as possible towards the joint – ironing away from the joint may cause it to open. Do not neglect the edges. Always iron through a piece of clean paper; drawing- or brown- wrapping paper is suitable. Avoid printed paper as the ink may be transferred to the veneer.

As has been pointed out above, pressure-sensitive tape should not be used as the iron will melt it and a horrible sticky mess will result.

5. Obviously the groundwork will stay warm for some time. This keeps the glue tacky, during which time the veneer may rise in places, particularly near the edges. A rubber-covered roller about 150mm (6in) long (such as photographers use) can be worked over the surface until it is cool. The old-fashioned non-electric 'sad' or 'flat' iron is ideal for the job as it presses and chills at the same time; it can be kept cool by standing it on a concrete or tiled floor between applications. Alternatively, you can use a metal plane whose cutter has been well withdrawn.

6. When the glue has set, test for good contact by tapping the surface lightly with the finger-nails. Any places sounding hollow can be ironed over and chilled again. Then trim off the surplus veneer, moisten the tape with warm water and peel it off. When everything is dry, gently sand and polish.

Method 2 involves using *Glu-film*. This a thermoplastic adhesive film, sold as a paper-backed roll; it will bond a veneer to its groundwork under the heat of a normal domestic electric iron. (Photographers will find it similar in use to the dry-mounting tissue with which photographic prints were secured to their mounts). It is available in rolls 36in wide. The method of use is both simple and straightforward.

1. Cut a piece from the roll, a little larger than the groundwork. Place it in position with the glue against the groundwork and the paper uppermost. Meanwhile switch on a domestic electric iron to its lowest setting.
2. Smooth over with the warm iron and allow to cool.
3. Peel off the backing sheet, keeping it intact.
4. Position the veneer, if necessary holding it lightly in place with a few strips of gummed paper.
5. Lay on the backing sheet which has just been removed and slowly iron over the veneer, going well over the surface a number of times and dwelling on each area for about three seconds to be sure of a good melt. There is little danger of destroying the adhesive, but overheating can scorch the veneer which will release too much moisture and cause cracks; a few drops of water can be sprinkled on to the veneer to prevent this. Again, work outwards from the centre and make sure the edges are not neglected.
6. In jointed work, as with the PVA method, you need to make sure the joints are a good fit and held well together with gummed paper or professional veneering-tape. Once more, always iron towards the joints.
7. If the joints were cut by knife directly on the groundwork, a second heating allows the removal of the waste piece trapped underneath before finally smoothing down.

The advantages are obvious, as there is no smell, no boiling over of glue, no sticky hands, no water, and no wet rags. *Glu-film* will equally well secure fabrics, leathercloth, baize, and linings, and it is a very clean method of attaching the backing canvas for tambour doors. Iron-on edging veneer can be easily made by ironing *Glu-film* on to a piece of veneer and then cutting it into strips. The edges of chipboard require two thicknesses, most conveniently one on the edge and one on the veneer.

The joint is waterproof and heat-resisting and it is not affected by moisture.

Glue-film is only obtainable in the UK from The Art Veneer Co Ltd., Industrial Estate, Mildenhall, Suffolk IP28 7AY. The firm's catalogue gives a shelf life of three to four years, but under dry conditions there seems to be virtually no limit. Seven-to-eight-year-old stock still works perfectly.

Chart showing adhesives for various materials:

	MATERIAL \ GLUE	ACRYLICS	BUTYL RUBBER	EPOXY	NEOPRENE RUBBER	NITRILE PHENOLIC	NITRILE RUBBER	PHENOL FORMALDEHYDE	POLYESTER UNSATURATED	POLYSULPHIDE	POLYURETHANE	POLYVINYL ACETATE	RESORCINOL FORMALDEHYDE	STYRENE BUTADIENE RUBBER	UREA FORMALDEHYDE	VYNL COPOLYMER
	TIMBERS	3	2	2	2		2	1	2	2	3	1	1	2	1	2
	GLASS AND CERAMICS	2		1		3	3		1	2	2					3
	METALS	2		1	2	1	2	3	1	2	2			2		2
	FABRICS AND PAPERS	3	2	3	2	3	1	2	2	3	2	1	3	1	3	1
RUBBER FOAMS	POLYURETHANE	3		3	2		2		2		2			3		
RUBBER FOAMS	POLYSTYRENE			3	3		1				3	2	3		2	
RUBBER FOAMS	POLYVINYL CHLORIDE		1	3	1	3	1		3		3			1		
RUBBER FOAMS	NATURAL RUBBER			2	1	2	1				2					3
RUBBER FOAMS	NEOPRENE			2	1	3										
PLASTICS	ACRYLICS	1		2	3		2						2			
PLASTICS	NYLON			2		1	2				2		1			
PLASTICS	POLYESTER			2	3		1				3					3
PLASTICS	POLYETHYLENE						1									
PLASTICS	POLYPROPYLENE						1			1						
PLASTICS	POLYSTYRENE			3			3		2	3						
PLASTICS	PLASTICIZED P.V.C.				3	2	1									
PLASTICS	RIGID P.V.C.	2	3	3	2	3	2		3	1	3			2		3

Most suitable shown by 1; good by 2; fair by 3. Squares left blank denote unsuitability. Where two materials are to be bonded the adhesive with the highest common rating should be used.

CHAPTER EIGHT

Polishes and stains

ALTHOUGH modern plastic lacquers have made polishing much easier than it was in the old days, there are still some questions that need to be considered such as: the compatibility of stains with polishes applied over them, the best stains to use, characteristics of various finishes, details of ancillary materials, and the methods of polishing restored or antique furniture. All of these are dealt with in this chapter.

Staining

Staining is a key operation in wood finishing and must be approached with care. There are two reasons for caution. The stain colour is largely what is seen and it must be pleasant and appropriate. The vital point, however, is that while stain is fairly easy to apply, it is very difficult indeed to remove or even lighten. There is no bleach or chemical or any combination of these, however strong, which will remove wood stain – at least none has so far been discovered. Some have a slight effect, not justifying the effort involved. For complete removal, one is forced to use tool methods even to the extent of taking the job apart, getting the pieces on to a bench and bringing them again to the white, with hand plane, scraper, and glasspaper. It requires only one salutary lesson such as this to impress that the effect of staining must be investigated beforehand on scrap, and applied to the work with precision. Incidentally anyone who can devise a formula for the easy removal of stain is on the way to making real money.

We might wish to stain wood for various reasons. Perhaps to match up with some other item. Some woods have no visible figure until stain is applied. This is absorbed more by the spring wood than the autumn wood so giving the desired contrast. On the poorer timbers staining can have the effect of brightening the surface, or imitating more expensive woods, so making the article more pleasing to the eye. The general rule is that the better the timber the less stain, if any, is required.

It has to be appreciated that it is not possible to stain wood lighter than it already is and that the response from different woods is unlikely to be the same. A stain might suit on the grain but, if not weakened, would turn end grain black. Mahogany stain is not meant for mahogany. It is intended to make white wood look like mahogany.

There are plenty of excellent stains available in can or packet form. In addition, however, the polisher must be able to make up his own stains and colours. A large part of the work is in matching and restoring. In some respects he has to be like an artist able to select and mix in the right proportion and strength, and with due regard and allowance for what is to follow. He therefore required basic materials, which he can select and prepare as his judgement and experience dictates.

Aniline dyes – those obtained from coal tar – have supplanted the vegetable dyes originally used by polishers. These were usually in powder form and obtained from the root, bark, or fruit, of various plants. They are at least of historical interest and so we have listed the ones more commonly used. These were the days when Spanish mahogany was king and rich red was the craze, obtained on inferior mahoganies – all the others – by using the dyes as stains or tinting agents.

Now, we see wood stained – sometimes effectively – with practically everything, from thinned boot polish to blow lamps, and ammonia steeped in thick black tobacco to dissolved old-fashioned gramophone records. However, for anyone who does woodwork for fun, or even for money, it is adequate to have the five stains we have listed. From these, one can make water and spirit stains which will suit the majority of cases.

These stains are best prepared in (strong) bottles. The water soluble stains – vandyke crystals, bismarck brown, and ebony crystals –

are best simmered for a few minutes to extract all the colour – two ounces to the pint – then filtered into separate containers. The spirit stains, spirit black and bismarck brown – this dissolves in both spirit and water – should be dissolved two ounces to the pint of spirit. The bottles should be labelled and the labels covered with Sellotape.

All of these colours are rather crude. It is a question of mixing and diluting the water stains to suit. The same with the spirit stains. Bichro is best used on its own.

For example, an oak spirit stain can be made from one third black and two thirds red diluted to suit. The amount of dilution will depend on the depth of colour required and the absorbency of the wood. Every case is different and in every case a trial run is required. Experienced polishers use a touch of the stain on the back of the hand for a quick check. Once the formula is established the work can proceed with confidence.

The staining operation is one that must be done at speed. The idea is to complete the surface in hand before any part of it is dry. If the job is laid out as described before there will be no trouble. If assembled, plan how it can be tackled progressively. The stain can be applied with a sponge. This will overcharge the surface which can then be wiped out quickly, and excess mopped up, with a dry rag. Have a brush handy for corners.

Water and spirit stain are both grain raisers so damp down and, when dry, smooth the raised grain. This is a good plan with any stain and at the same time can give a final check on the all important tool finish.

Green, yellow, and bright red water and spirit stain can be useful on occasions. So also can earth pigments. Those listed in the table below will meet all requirements.

Always make up stain in daylight, especially when matching something else. It is difficult to reproduce a stain, so make up more than enough for the job. Water stain benefits from a degreasing agent which could be a small nut of washing soda or a dash of ammonia to the pint.

Table showing the five stains

Stain	*Solvent*	*Colour*
Vandyke Crystals	water	cold brown
Ebony Crystals	water	black
Bichromate of Potash	water	darkens oaks and mahoganies
Bismarck Brown	spirit or water	crude red
Spirit Black	spirit	black

Table showing original vegetable dyes

Dyes	*Form*	*Solvent*	*Colour*
Dragon's Blood	powder	spirit or water	dark red
Red Sanders	powder	spirit or turpentine	dark red
Alkanet Root	powder	spirit or linseed	rich red
Madder Root	powder	water or spirit	bright red
Logwood	liquid	water	dark purple

Table showing pigments

Colour	*Pigments*
Light brown	Burnt Umber and Yellow Ochre
Medium brown	Burnt Umber
Dark brown	Burnt Umber and Lamp Black
Light red	Venetian Red and Yellow Ochre
Medium red	Venetian Red
Dark red	Venetian Red and Lamp Black
Black	Lamp Black

Stains for Exterior Use

Stains are used to restore colour loss of exposed wood or to change its colour. They must possess external durability and they are usually incorporated in a water repellent-

Quick reference chart showing details of the principal external wood finishes

Finish	Initial Treatment	Appearance of Wood	Maintenance Procedure	Maintenance Period of Surface Finish	Maintenance Cost
Tar oils	Pressure, hot and cold tank steeping	Grain visible. Brown to black in colour, fading slightly with age	Brush down to remove surface dirt and apply by brush	5-10 years only if original colour is to be renewed; otherwise no maintenance is required	Nil to Low
	Brushing	do	do	3-5 years	Low
Water-borne Preservatives	Pressure	Grain visible. Greenish in colour fading with age	Brush down to remove surface dirt	None, unless stained, painted or varnished as below	Nil, unless stains, varnishes or paints are used. See below
	Diffusion plus paint	Grain and natural colour obscured	Clean and repaint	5 years	Medium to High
Organic solvents	Steeping, dipping brushing	Grain visible Coloured as desired	Brush down and reapply	4-5 years	Low
Water Repellents	One or two brush coats of clear material or, preferably, dip applied	Grain and natural colour visible, becoming darker and rougher textured	Clean and apply sufficient tinted material	4-5 years	Low
Stains	do	Grain visible. Colour as desired	do	do	do
Clear Varnish	Four coats (minimum)	Grain and natural colour unchanged if adequately maintained	Clean and stain bleached areas, and apply two more coats	3 years or when breakdown begins	High
Paint	Knotting, prime, under and finish coats	Grain and natural colour obscured	Clean and apply undercoat and top coat; or remove and repeat initial treatment	5 years	Medium

preservative/resin formulation in an organic solvent. Stains at present available fall into two groups, those that fade or wash off and those which darken. The first type can be used as an initial treatment and renewed when necessary. The second should not be applied too frequently, and it should be used only as a touch-up treatment to timber originally treated with a clear water repellent preservative, when the timber colour has begun to bleach out.

Maintenance periods with water repellents and stains are very much a matter of individual taste as the finish has no definite life but shows a steady deterioration. A typical, and recommended procedure is to give an initial dip treatment with a clear water repellent and every three to four years clean off dirt with a rag dipped in clear water repellent and treat with a lightly tinted formulation to maintain good appearance.

Clear varnishes The most attractive initial appearance for external timber is obtained by use of a clear varnish, although its durability under the action of the weather is limited. It is therefore necessary to apply many initial coats of a good quality external varnish (at least four are essential) some of which should be applied to the timber before erection. Maintenance must be carried out as soon as signs of break-down occur which with four initial coats, is at least every three years.

Maintain by cleaning down with water and a light abrasive, touching up any bleached areas with a light stain and the application of two further coats of varnish.

Paint If you use paint, follow the manufacturers' recommendations closely. Before painting, surfaces should be clean and dry, knots or resinous areas should be treated with shellac knotting, a proprietary sealer, or a self-knotting or aluminium primer.

Treat exterior woodwork with a white lead, oil-based primer. Aluminium primers are also particularly useful as vapour barriers and are effective if applied to all sides of a dry piece of wood. If used on external surfaces only, they may promote blistering. The main types of external paint in use are oil based and 'synthetic'. Both can give satisfactory performance but oil-based paints tend to be softer and more dirt retentive. Emulsion paints and emulsion primers for external use are also available but are probably less durable than oil or synthetic paints.

Paint, if properly applied, should last at least six years. Maintain by cleaning thoroughly with slight abrasion of the surface, followed by drying and application of undercoat and surface coat of the same brand as the original. Maintenance is often carried out with the object of changing the colour, sometimes before the original colour scheme has had a full period of weathering. In this case it is important to avoid too thick a paint film which will tend to fail by flaking. Thick paint films require the more elaborate maintenance process of prior removal of old paint by scraping, burning off or stripping, followed by the use of a complete paint system.

Compatibility in Wood Finishing

A bewildering variety of stains and finishes is available to the polisher. You are faced, not only with the problem of choosing one to suit the particular job in hand, but also of knowing what will go on what without subsequent difficulties arising – especially so in refinishing. You could play safe and make a practice of always stripping to the white, but this is not always necessary, or even desirable. We may wish to preserve shading, or bleaching, or other signs of ageing, which would be destroyed by stripping; or we may merely wish to touch the job up without starting again from the beginning.

Bonding We have to consider first that one type of finish may take satisfactorily to another, but the bond may be so weak that in due course it cracks or peels. A simple case is a floor lacquer applied to new lino tiles. These tiles have a makers' seal which must be removed first. This can be done with an agent specially designed for the purpose, after which the lacquer will engage and hold the surface properly.

Or take the case of lacquering a parquet floor, previously waxed. If the surface is not cleaned thoroughly one of two things will happen, depending on the type of finish. The film may harden normally, but soon crack and be picked off in quite large pieces; or, alternatively, it may never harden properly. In the first case the lacquer might be a polyurethane, which hardens chemically, even over wax. The other would be one which hardens mainly by evaporation or oxidation. Such films harden from the outside in. The surface seals over and excludes air. The air in the timber is sealed off with the wax. The interior of the film is thus sandwiched, and hardening slowed or inhibited altogether.

A situation can arise where bonding is inadequate one way but satisfactory the other. For example, most cellulose finishes bond well to shellac because the medium is also a solvent for shellac. However, the meths medium in shellac does not affect the cellulose so that the films are merely stuck together. It is possible to apply french polish to cellulose for minor repairs, if this is cleaned and flatted, so long as no oil is used, but if even a trace of oil is used the film may never harden. Another such case would be water stain on wood already oil stained. The new stain would be completely rejected, but the system would work well in reverse.

Then again there are finishes which react slowly or even violently with one another. In general a hard film should not be applied over a softer one. Hardness and elasticity are qualities generally present in inverse proportion. If the timber moves with change of temperature or humidity, a shear stress can be set up between the films which can result in checking or crazing. Some finishes refuse to go together at all. Cellulose – or rather the medium in it – will attack finishes based on linseed or similar oils, causing roughening or lifting.

With at least two hundred varnishes, all different in some way, on the market, it is vitually impossible for anyone to know just what will be happy with what. When in doubt, the sensible thing is to adopt a workmanlike approach which will ensure success. The first thing is to apply a spot of the thinners or solvent of the new finish to the existing one. If there is no reaction then we can assume that it will at least go on. We have next to ensure that the film will harden. A small cleaned test area is again required, checking after the normal curing time. It is undesirable also to put a hard film on top of one which is softer so an additional check would be to identify the old film.

Identification This can be a rather difficult business. One would require the deductive skill of a Sherlock Holmes, not to mention having a couple of analytical chemists handy, complete with their laboratory. There are subtle differences between finishes and we have known people who claimed that they could sort them out visually. This is all very well for the experienced eye when they are new, but the longer they are in use the more alike they seem to become.

The surest tests are with the appropriate solvents. Meths rubbed on for a few minutes will start to strip french polish but will not affect the others. Acetone or cellulose thinners will strip oil type finishes, french polish, and cellulose quickly, but not the others. A stripper will quickly soften these and polyurethane, but will not affect polyester.

Scraping tests can be helpful performed with a very sharp tool. French polishes will scrape off in little shavings. Cellulose fractures off in whitish dust. Polyurethanes come off in dust like the film. Polyesters need very firm pressure to scrape off a similar kind of dust. Visual examination and physical tests can each give a clue and, in total, these can at least classify the finish which is all that we require. Even the approximate age of the item is a clue in itself.

The order of hardness is french polish, oil types, cellulose – these are quite close – polyurethane, then polyester.

I have compiled the tables below to act as a general guide. However the best 'finish' anyone can have is common sense. The thing is to use the same material and even the same brand if this will meet requirements. It would be silly, for example, to put any other kind of finish on oiled teak than teak oil.

Will the finish in the vertical column bond well on that in the base?

Oil	–	Yes	No	Yes	Yes	No
French polish	Yes	–	No	No	No	No
Cellulose	No	Yes	–	No	No	No
Polyurethane	Yes	Yes	Yes	–	Yes	No
Polyester	No	No	No	No	–	No
Wax	Yes	Yes	Yes	Yes	Yes	–
	Oil	F.polish	Cellulose	Polyurethane	Polyester	Wax

Will the stain in the vertical column take well over that in the base column?

Water	–	Yes	No	No
Chemical	Yes	–	No	No
Spirit	Yes	Yes	–	Yes
Naphtha	Yes	Yes	No	–
	Water	Chemical	Spirit	Naphtha

Note. On the assumption that, as is normal, spirit stain contains the usual shellac binder.

Extract from Thomas Sheraton's instructions on polishing For inside work, polishers used beeswax applied with a cork 'where it would be improper to use (linseed) oil. The cork is rubbed hard on the wax to spread it over the wood, and then they (the polishers) take fine brick dust and sift it through a stocking on the wood, and with a cloth the dust is rubbed till it clears away all the clammings (stickiness) which the wax leaves on the surface. At other times they polish with soft wax, which is a mixture of turpentine and bees-wax, which renders it soft, and facilitates the work of polishing. Into this a little red oil (alkanet oil, qv) may occasionally be put, to help the colour of the wood. This kind of polishing requires no brick dust; for the mixture being soft, a cloth of itself, will be sufficient to rub it off with. The general mode of polishing plain cabinet work is however, with oil and brick dust; in which case, the oil is either plain linseed or stained with alkanet root . . . If the wood be hard, the oil should be left standing upon it for a week; but if soft, it may be polished in two days. The brick dust and oil should then be rubbed together, which in a little time will become a putty under the rubbing cloth, in which state it should be kept under the cloth as much as possible; for this kind of putty will infallibly secure a fine polish by continued rubbing; and the polisher should by all means avoid the application of fresh brick dust, by which the unskilful hand will frequently ruin his work instead of improving it: and to prevent the necessity of supplying himself with fresh brick dust he ought to lay on a great quantity at first, carefully sifted through a gauze stocking; and he should notice if the oil be too dry on the surface of the work before he begin, for in this case it should be re-oiled, that it may compose a sufficient quantity of the polishing substance, which should never be altered after the polishing is commenced, and which ought to continue till the wood by repeated friction becomes warm, at which time it will finish in a bright polish, and is finally to be cleared off with the bran of wheaten flour. (This must be one of the longest sentences the reader will ever encounter! To continue . . .) Chairs are generally polished with a hardish composition of wax rubbed on a polishing brush, (similar to the kind used today for shoe-cleaning) with which the grain of the wood is impregnated with the composition, and afterwards well rubbed off without any dust or bran. The composition I recommend is as follows: take bees-wax and a small quantity of turpentine in a clean earthen pan, and set it over a fire (from the point of view of fire risk, we would recommend putting it in a Pyrex jug standing in a saucepan of boiling water) till the wax unites with the turpentine, which it will do by constant stirring about; add to this a little red lead finely ground upon a stone, together with a small portion of fine Oxford ochre, to bring the whole to the colour of brisk mahogany (today we would use powder colours). Lastly, when you take it off the fire, add a little copal varnish to it, and mix it well together, then turn the whole into a bason (basin) of water, and while it is yet warm, work it into a ball, with which the brush is to be rubbed as before observed. And observe, with a ball of wax and brush kept for this purpose entirely, furniture in general may be kept in good order.' *(Cabinet Dictionary, 1803. Pages 289-90.)*

Red oil (alkanet oil) This is often referred to as a colouring agent in old-time polishes and for those who delight in authenticity, it is not difficult to make up. Alkanet is an alternative name for the Anchusa, which is grown in many British gardens. From Sheraton's *Cabinet Dictionary* we learn 'Take a quart of good linseed oil, to which put a quarter of a pound of alkanet root, as much opened with the hand as possible, that the bark of the root which tinges the oil may fly off; to this put about an ounce of dragon's blood (qv), and another of rose pink, finely pounded in a mortar (today we would use powder colours – dragon's blood is a dark red); set the whole within a moderate heat for twelve hours at least, or better if a day and a night. Then strain it through a flannel into a bottle for use. This staining oil is not properly applicable to every sort of mahogany . . . [mahogany that is] close grained and hard and wants briskness of colour, the above oil will help it much. All hard mahogany of a bad colour should be oiled with it, and should stand unpolished a time, proportioned to its quality and texture of grain; if it be laid on hard wood to be polished immediately, it is of little use; but if it stand a few days after, the oil penetrates the grain and hardens on the surface, and consequently will bear a better polish, and look brighter in colour'.

Useful Chemicals, Polishes, Stains etc

Acetic acid Can be used in the formulation of a polish reviver (qv).

Alcohol See methylated spirit.

Alcovar powder See spirit stains.

Ammonia (.880 grade) Used principally to fume oak, but if a little is added to water stain it will be more readily absorbed by the grain.

Aniline dyes Obtainable in two formulations – one soluble in water, and one soluble in methylated spirits. The two different formulations will not mix, but the colours in each one can be blended. Available in a wide range of colours.

Beaumontage Sometimes called 'cabinet stopping'. Can be bought in stick form ready for use, or can be made at home, as follows: mix equal quantities of beeswax and crushed rosin, plus a few flakes of shellac, and melt them in a shallow tin (such as a biscuit-tin lid). Stir the mixture thoroughly and add powder colour until the required shade is obtained; allow it to set. When needed, the lid can be heated and a little of the stopping applied with a pointed stick. Alternatively, if the biscuit-tin lid is tilted slightly while the mixture sets, a crude stick of wax results.

Benzene Used to remove excess oil or grease.

Bichromate of potash Sold as deep orange-coloured crystals which are dissolved in water until the solution is saturated (that is, no more crystals will dissolve); the solution can then be diluted as required. When applied to oak it gives a slightly greenish-brown hue; on mahogany a cold, deep brown; it has no effect on pine or whitewood.

Camphorated oil A mixture of four parts of olive oil and one part camphorated oil can be used to remove heat and water marks on french polished surfaces.

Carbon tetrachloride Can be used on greasy woods such as teak as a degreasing agent before gluing or polishing.

Caustic potash Can be used as a stripper for paints, varnishes, polishes etc. Normally bought as a proprietary stripper; the manufacturer's instructions must be followed exactly. Protective gloves and an eye-shield should be worn. The liquid has a tendency to darken the wood slightly.

Carnauba wax See **Wax.**

Chloride of lime Has a slight bleaching effect and imparts a greyish tone to oak which is called the 'weathered' finish.

Copperas (green) When dissolved in water this forms a pale blue solution which can be used to kill the redness of mahogany. When applied to sycamore, it gives a grey tone, thus producing 'harewood', or as it is sometimes called, 'grey wood'.

Crocus powder A very fine metallic abrasive powder which can be used to cut back a bright, polished surface to dull it.

Dragon's blood A dark red gum from the Dragon tree, a tropical palm. Formerly used as a colouring dye for polishes, it is now difficult to obtain although some printing-block makers may still have it as it is used as an acid-resist in block-making.

Emery powder An abrasive corundum powder which can be used to rub down varnished work, or mixed to a paste with a light lubricating oil (or neat's foot oil) and applied to a strop for sharpening purposes.

Flake white A white pigment powder which can be mixed into white french polish to lighten it in colour. Can also be mixed into Scotch glue to turn it white for use on light woods.

French chalk A finely powdered white chalk which can be used to fill the grain on wood to be polished.

French polish Types and colours
1 Basic french polish: mid-brown in colour.
2 Button polish. The name comes from the button-shape of the shellac. Orange colour.
3 Heavy button polish. A button polish with additional shellac to give it a fuller body. Deep orange colour.
4 Transparent button polish. Made from de-waxed shellac; gives a harder finish than standard button polish. Light brown colour.
5 Dark garnet polish. Made from a dark-coloured shellac: suitable for antiques.
6 Transparent polish. Made from de-waxed dark shellac; it gives a harder surface than 5 Light brown in colour.
7 Brush polish. Has a special additive which slows down the drying time and allows brush application. Medium brown colour.
8 Pale brush polish. As (7), but made with

pale shellac to give a lighter colour.
9 White brush polish. A white polish specially prepared for brush application. Light straw colour.
10 White polish. Made from bleached shellac; it is virtually colourless and gives a comparatively soft surface.
11 Hard white polish. As (10), but with an additive to give a harder surface.
12 Transparent white polish. Made from a bleached and de-waxed shellac, it is colourless and gives a very hard surface.
13 Coloured polishes – red, black, and green. The latter is used to kill the red colour of mahogany.
14 Outside polishes. For exterior use, made in pale and dark-brown colours.

Glue size This is a type of animal glue which is supplied in the form of crystals which look like brown sugar. It can be used to seal the pores of softwood before polishing or varnishing, or as a preliminary sealer before veneering with an animal glue. In the case of polishing, etc, the softwood should be stained first (water-based stains only), then the size is applied, and papered down. The size should be dissolved in warm water until no stickiness is felt when rubbed between the fingers.

Gold size A quick-drying varnish normally used for applying gold paint or gold leaf. When a few drops are added to ordinary linseed oil putty it makes a very hard, rock-like putty which is used for glazed doors.

Gum benzoin This resembles pieces of a white nut but is actually a resin and sometimes arrives stuck to pieces of twig etc; the whiter it is, the better the quality. Crush it and put it in a wide-mouthed jar (such as a used coffee jar) and just cover it with methylated spirit. Keep it stoppered for a week or so, and shake it from time to time; finally strain it and re-bottle it. Can be used as a glaze on french polish.

Hydrogen peroxide Can be used as a bleach; 100 vol quality is normally employed, diluted with two parts of water.

Knotting A special solution of shellac which can be applied to knots, resin-pockets, etc to stop the resin bleeding through a polished or painted surface.

Linseed oil Derived from the flax plant and obtainable either raw, or boiled. It is used in french polishing, or can be a finish on its own; it can also be added to paints, varnishes etc to thin them down without the loss of bodying properties. Putty is a mixture of whiting and linseed oil. Both types dry on exposure to the air by taking up oxygen: boiled oil dries faster and is less sticky.

Methylated spirit This is a type of alcohol distilled from wood, and (for sale to the public) has pyridine and methyl violet dye added to it to make it unpalatable and also easily identifiable. It is used to make french polish, and also in the actual polishing process itself. Spirit stains consist of powder colours dissolved in alcohol.

Naphtha Used in making coloured naphtha stains which penetrate the wood deeply and dry very quickly without raising the grain. They also contain white spirit, and should only be diluted with naphtha thinners.

Oil stains These are based on white spirit, and can therefore be thinned with it: by the same token, if any polished or varnished finish containing white spirit is used over them, the stain may bleed into the finish. Some of the darker coloured stains have a bituminous-based dye in them and sometimes this rises to the surface and precipitates out. This will prevent any subsequent polish from adhering or 'keying in' properly, and to avoid this happening the stain should be allowed to become touch-dry and is then rubbed with a clean rag.

Oxalic acid This can be used as a bleach by making a saturated solution of the crystals in warm water. The surface should be rinsed off afterwards, first with vinegar (which neutralises the acid) and finally with cold water: any traces of the acid which may be left could react with subsequent polishes. The acid is poisonous and should not be allowed to contact the skin; it is best avoided in favour of one of the safer and equally effective proprietary bleaches.

Paraffin, medicinal Can be used as a lubricant for the rubber on light coloured woods when french polishing.

Permanganate of potash The crystals dissolve readily in warm water to produce a rich purple solution; this will impart a warm brown colour to anything it contacts (including fingers!). Can be used as a stain but is not really satisfactory as the colour is fugitive.

Plaster-of-Paris A fine powder which can be used as a grain filler. Must be kept in a dry place as it readily accepts moisture and then sets hard.

Powder colours These are pigments in powder form and are available in a wide choice of colours: they can be used for making water stains.

Pumice powder A white powder obtainable in various grades. The finest grade can be used (like crocus or emery powders) for cutting back bright finishes.

Resin A general term for the natural gums which exude from trees: when distilled and purified it is known as 'rosin'. Used in the formulation of varnishes, polishes, waxes etc. There are also synthetic resins used in plastic lacquers.

Rottenstone One of the finest abrasive powders. Used for cutting back bright finishes, or to achieve a 'satin' finish. Also known as 'Tripoli' powder.

Shellac This consists of the hardened secretions of the lac insects which swarm over trees in India and Thailand. The secretion is melted, stained, and purified: it is then shipped in the form of flakes, buttons, or sticks and is used as the basis for french polish and in the formulation of several varnishes. Raw shellac must be kept either in water in a glass jar, or in damp sawdust, as it will de-nature if exposed to air for any length of time.

Silex A siliceous powder used as a paste grain-filler.

Soda This is ordinary washing soda which can be used to clean grease, dirt, etc from old furniture, or as a de-greasing agent. All traces must be removed with clean water.

Spirit stains These are prepared from either *Alcovar* or spirit aniline powders dissolved in alcohol. The advantage of the *Alcovar* stains is that they are ultraviolet light-fast, while spirit aniline powders are not. All spirit stains evaporate quickly and great care and speed is needed to cover a large area evenly.

Stains See under individual headings: naphtha, oil, spirit, water.

Terebene A drying agent which can be added to linseed oil, or to varnishes, to speed up drying.

Toppings The clear solution which forms above white french polish when it has been left undisturbed for some time. It can be strained off and used as a finishing glaze on french polished work.

Tripoli powder See **Rottenstone.**

Turpentine Pure turpentine is distilled from the resin of some types of coniferous trees which grow mainly in the USA, and as it is scarce it is used mainly by artists. Turpentine substitute (or white spirit) is commercially distilled from wood chips and is employed as a thinning agent for paints and varnishes, and as the vehicle in oil stains.

Vienna chalk Used as a burnish when french polishing: the rubber is dipped into it and worked with long strokes to clear the surface. Alternatively it can be used in conjunction with a solution of 1 part sulphuric acid to 7 parts distilled water; this is wiped over a french polished surface with a piece of butter muslin. The chalk is then dusted on to it and burnished with the palm of the hand or a piece of chamois leather. Finally, the surface is wiped clean.

Waxes There are several types, the main ones being: beeswax (bleached and unbleached); carnauba; ozokerite; and paraffin. The following are the main characteristics and uses:
1 Beeswax – can be obtained bleached or unbleached. The bleached kind is used for light-coloured polishes, and the unbleached (which is a medium brown colour) for darker polishes.
2 Carnauba – a vegetable wax, light yellow in colour, which gives a brilliant, hard shine which is not, however, long-lasting. It is therefore mixed with other waxes.
3 Ozokerite – a natural earth wax which can be used mixed with beeswax; it has a 'bodying-up' effect.
4 Paraffin – a soft wax which is mixed with others to enable them to spread easily.

There are also special staining waxes which not only impart a shine and a finish but also colour as well. They are marketed by several suppliers, but you can make up your own.

French polishes

In each of the following polishes, the solution is made from 0.5 litre (1 pint) of methylated spirit, except where otherwise directed.

Black polish Dissolve 14 grams (½oz) black aniline spirit dye in 0.5 litre (1 pint) of white polish, and strain the solution before use.

Button polish Dissolve 170 grams (6oz) button shellac in the spirit.

Coloured polishes These are made by dissolving in the appropriate colour of aniline spirit dye. Use french polish for blue, brown, green, scarlet, and yellow colours: or white polish for blue, green and yellow: or orange polish for brown or scarlet. As a basis, use about 10 grams (slightly less than $\frac{1}{2}$oz) per 0.5 litre (1 pint) and adjust as necessary, although it is best to err on the weak side. The mixture should be strained before use.

Garnet polish Dissolve 170 grams (6oz) of garnet shellac in the spirit.

Orange polish Dissolve 170 grams (6oz) of orange shellac in the spirit.

Red Polish Dissolve 10 grams (just over $\frac{1}{4}$oz) brown aniline spirit dye in 0.7 litre ($1\frac{1}{2}$ pints) of the spirit and strain the solution before use.

Wax polishes

Basic wax polish Shred unbleached beeswax by means of a nutmeg grater, or peel into strips with a potato peeler, and dissolve in (preferably) pure turpentine or best quality turpentine substitute (white spirit). Stand the mixing bowl in hot water as this will help the wax to dissolve quickly: the mixture needs to be the consistency of a thin paste. A little carnauba wax can be added to harden it. This recipe gives a medium brown coloured wax polish; for a lighter colour use bleached beeswax.

Staining waxes

Although these can be made at home by adding powder colours to basic wax polish, there is a good proprietary product called *Bison Staining Wax.* This is a mixture of eleven different waxes, including synthetic waxes to increase resistance to water and wear, and it is formulated to spread easily and dry rapidly. It does not contain silicones. It can be applied to bare wood (new or stripped) or on top of finishes such as cellulose, french polish, or varnish: apply with a brush or steel wool pad (finest grade).

Colours available are: white; light oak; Georgian mahogany (warm medium); Victorian mahogany (dark); dark oak: Tudor oak. All colours can be mixed or applied over the top of each other.

Glaze See **Gum benzoin.**

Polish revivers The simplest reviver for french polish is 1 part raw linseed mixed with 1 part vinegar. Others are: equal parts raw linseed oil, vinegar, and methylated spirit; or 4 parts raw linseed oil, 12 parts vinegar, and 1 part terebene driers.

Chart showing Characteristics of Various Finishes

Type	*Recommended use*	*Application*	*Drying time*	*Wear resistance*	*Exterior durability*	*Stain & chemical resistance*	*Heat resistance*
Alkyd varnish	Int & ext	Spray/brush	3	7	8	7	7
Chlorinated rubber	Int	Spray/brush	5	7		9	5
Epoxy 1 can	Int & ext	Spray/brush	5	8	4	7	7
Epoxy 2 can	Int	Spray/brush	5	9		9	9
French polish	Int	Pad	7	5		2	1
Linseed oil	Int	Pad	2	2		4	7
Nitro-cell lacquer	Int	Spray	8	7		5	3
Polyester lacquer	Int & ext	Spray/brush	8	9	8	9	8
Polymer latex	Int & ext	Spray/brush	8	4	7	8	4
Polyurethane 2 can	Int & ext	Spray/brush	4	8	7	9	9
UF 1 can	Int	Spray/brush	6	9		7	8
UF 2 can	Int	Spray/brush	8	9		7	8
Wax	Int	Pad	3	3		2	2

Numerals indicate marks out of ten – poor 0.3; medium 4-6; good 7-8; excellent 9-10: and for drying times – very slow 0-2; slow 3-4; medium 5-7; fast 8-10

Grades of abrasive papers (from finest grade to course in each case)

Glasspaper	Garnet	Flint	Garnet Aluminium oxide Silicone carbide (wet and dry)	Emery
			400	
	9/0		320	
	8/0		280	
	7/0		240	
	6/0		220	0
00 (flour)				
0	5/0		180	
	4/0		150	
1	3/0	120	120	F
1½	2/0	100	100	
F2				1½
M2			60	2
S2				2½
2½	1½	1½	40	3
3	2	2	36	½
	2½	2½	30	4
	3	3	24	4½

CHAPTER NINE

Sharpening equipment and methods of sharpening tools

IT'S self-evident that sharpening your own tools can save you money (particularly in the case of saw-sharpening) and make work easier. Not much equipment is needed and any expense incurred in buying it will soon be saved by keeping tools in good condition so that they last longer.

Oilstones

Dealing with oilstones first, there are two different types – the natural stones, and the industrial synthetic ones. The natural stones include the following, but it must be pointed out that they are becoming scarce and are very expensive.

The Arkansas This comes from natural deposits of stone in the USA, and at best is almost pure quartz, and white in colour. It has no apparent grain, and as it is extremely hard it is used whenever a fine, keen edge is needed.

The Washita Also an American stone. It is cheaper than the Arkansas, and is a medium grade stone, being softer and coarser. It sometimes has a tendency to harden up after a little use and become useless.

Turkey Stone Unfortunately, these stones vary greatly in texture; the hardest ones can give a really good edge but softer ones can easily be grooved.

Charnwood Forest Rarely seen these days; it gives a good edge but is slow in the cut.

Artificial (synthetic) stones in general are made from carborundum, which is a factory-made compound. The stones are available in three grades of coarse, medium and fine, and are comparable with the best natural stones. For our purposes, a 'combination' stone is probably best, as one side is coarse, and the other fine. In addition, it's a good idea to have a medium grade stone as in some cases, tools have to be sharpened on the edge of the stone.

When you have got your oilstone, the first thing to do is to encase it in a wooden box, as oilstones shatter easily when dropped. Never use a vegetable oil (linseed, olive, or cooking oil) as a lubricant as they will quickly gum up the surface. A good lubricant is a mixture of two parts fine mineral oil and one part paraffin oil: employ it sparingly, and always wipe the stone clean after use. If the stone shows signs of gumming up, brush it clean with a stiff brush and petrol; in bad cases, soak it in petrol for a day or two and then brush it clean.

Always use the whole surface of the stone so that it does not become hollowed or bumpy; if this does happen, the stone will have to be re-surfaced, which is a laborious business, and calculated to make you more careful in the future!

To do it, first find a perfectly flat slab of stone, or a flat piece of marble, or a piece of good quality plate glass (which must be well supported on a flat surface, such as a pad of newspaper on the bench top). The stone is then rubbed flat in a figure-of-eight pattern but you must, of course, use a suitable grinding paste. For natural stones, silver sand and water is an effective lubricant, while silicon carbide grit (grade 60/90) does for artificial stones. You should be able to get the grit at gem craft shops, as it is used for tumble-polishing stones. When you have finished, wash the stone with soap and water and let it dry before re-oiling.

In addition to your actual oilstones, try to collect a few assorted oilstone slips, as they are invaluable for sharpening various gouges and spokeshave blades, and you can see some of the different shapes available in Fig 9.1A.

To repair a broken oilstone

Proceed as follows:

1 Bake all the oil out of the fragments by

heating them gently on a metal tray on a gas or electric hob.
2 Use an old toothbrush or something similar to scrub the fragments with ammonia or a dry-cleaning fluid. Wear gloves and protect the eyes while doing this.
3 When dry, dust the edges thickly with powdered or flake orange shellac, working it into all the recesses.
4 Re-heat the fragments to melt the shellac, re-assemble them, and cramp them together securely. Leave overnight to set.

Grindstones

While oilstones are essential for applying the final cutting edges, you will also need a grinding wheel for grinding the cutting angle, and to remove any gashes from the edge. The old-fashioned sandstone wheel which was turned by hand, and revolved through a water bath, is now practically a museum piece. There are modern versions on the market which incorporate a wheel running in a water bath and a normal grinding wheel, both powered by electricity. The advantage of a wheel constantly cooled by water is one worth having as it avoids any likelihood of drawing the temper of the tool should it overheat.

Most of us, however, will have a powered grinding wheel which runs dry – in fact, you should never attempt to run it in water as it will turn soft. Keep a bucket of water handy and dip whatever tool you are sharpening into the water at frequent intervals. A blue patch on the edge of the tool indicates that the temper has been drawn; the only remedy is to grind away the affected part (keeping the metal cool) and to start again.

Grinding wheels are usually made from aluminium oxide and are available in various grades of grain size. For our purposes a grain size from 24 to 40 is suitable for rough grinding, and a 50 to 80 size for finishing grinding; incidentally these grain sizes are often called 'grits'.

One trouble you may have to contend with is the wheel becoming 'loaded' – this often happens because tools are pressed hard against the wheel and the metal particles are forced into the grains with the result that they no longer cut; grinding a lot of mild steel on a wheel intended for tool steel is a primary cause. Another problem is 'glazing' which occurs when the metal particles are not shed as the wheel revolves. The result is a wheel which rubs instead of grinding and soon overheats.

In both cases, the cutting surfaces will have to be restored by means of a 'wheel dresser'. This is shown at Fig 9.1C, and the tool is steadied on the tool rest of the grinder while the corrugated discs are held lightly but firmly against the wheel in order to scrape away the old, and expose the new particles.

Figure 9.1B shows the salient points to look for in any grinding wheel, and it is self-explanatory; in particular, note the visor which protects your eyes from flying particles and should always be used for this purpose.

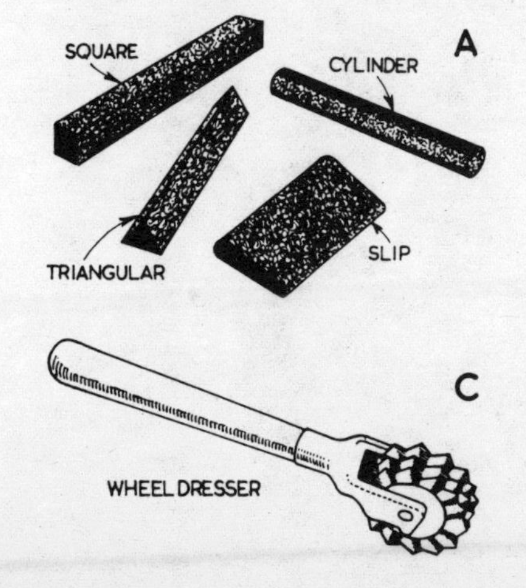

Fig 9.1

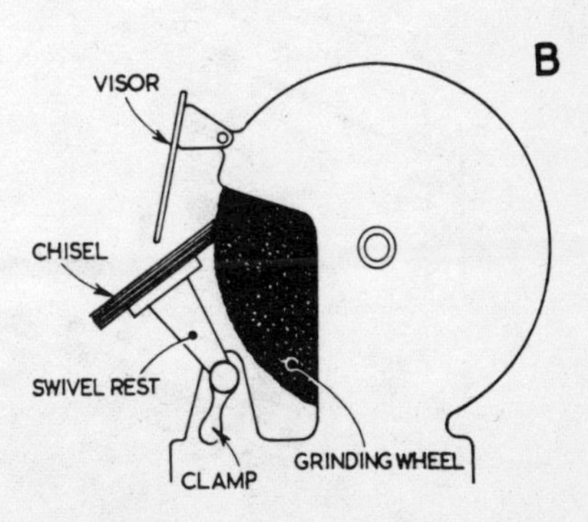

Sharpening

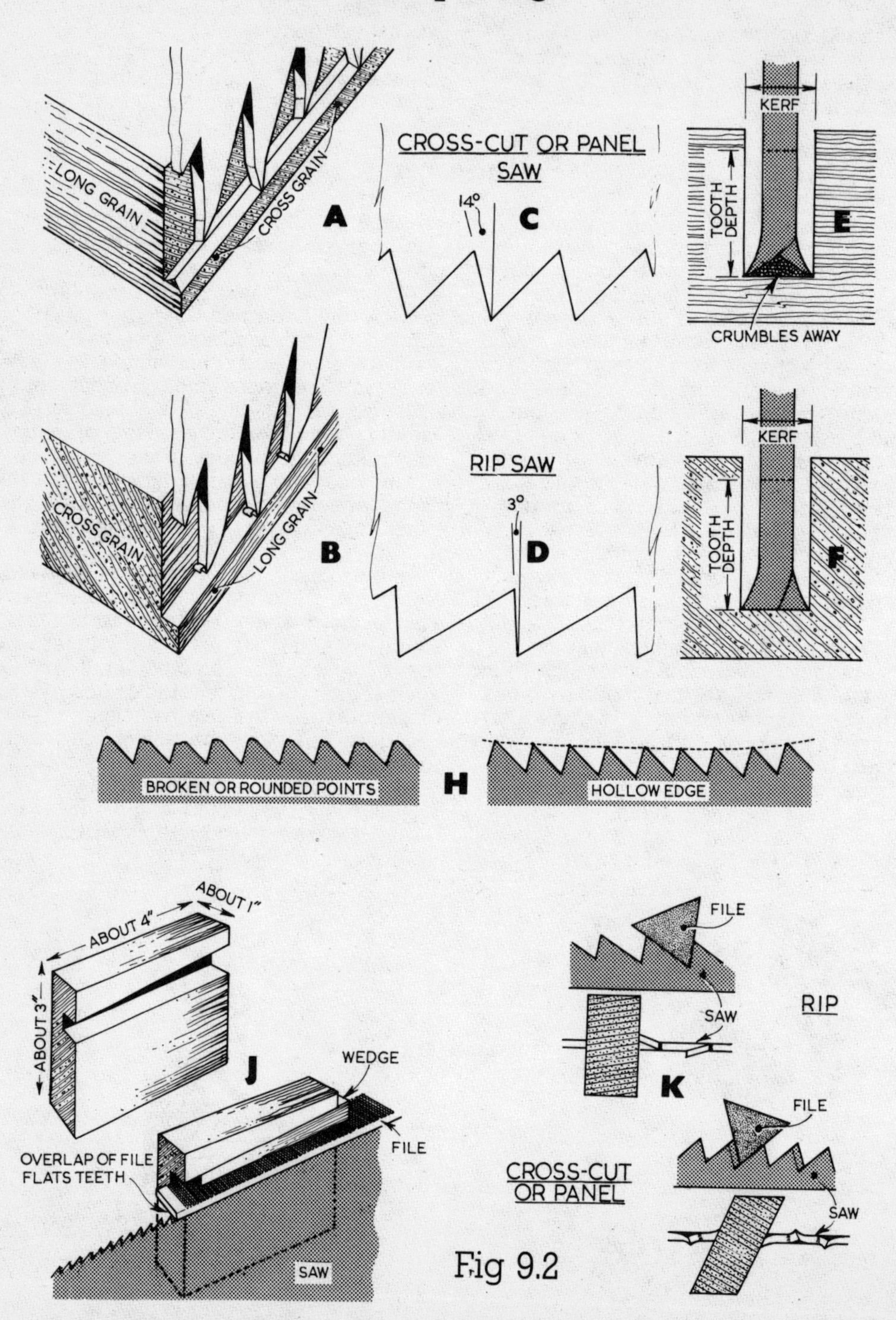

Fig 9.2

Sharpening handsaws
Don't let saw teeth get too blunt before re-sharpening them or the teeth will have to be filed so much that the saw will be ruined. But this prohibition does not apply to setting the teeth, as bending them too often will weaken them and cause them to snap off.

It is vital to understand just how saw teeth work, and the two types (cross-cut or panel saws, and rip saws) are shown at A to F, Fig 9.2. The action of a cross-cut or panel saw is similar to two knife cuts being made across the grain, about 2mm (1/16in) apart, and the wood fibres between the two cuts are so short that they crumble away (Fig 9.2A and E). On the other hand, the action of the rip saw teeth simulates that of a series of moving chisels (Fig 9.2B and F) and this is what is required for sawing along the grain.

Sharpening and shaping Before sharpening or setting, the teeth must be 'topped'. At H, Fig 9.2, two typical faults are shown – on the left, blunt or chipped teeth and, on the right, a hollow edge. The first fault can be caused by striking metal while sawing (nails in the timber, or holding the work in a vice and accidentally running the teeth across the vice jaws), or by constantly sawing through tough knots or hard glue lines. The hollow edge is almost always the result of not using the full length of the saw and confining use to the centre only.

Obviously, the saw will have to be supported in a vice while topping is being done. At J, Fig 9.2, a gadget is illustrated which is easily made and which ensures that the file is held exactly at right angles to the saw.

It must be emphasised that topping must only be done lightly, even when the teeth are grossly mis-shapen. Use a triangular file to re-shape the shallowest teeth; if necessary, the procedure may have to be repeated several times before the shape is satisfactory.

Next, the shaping of the teeth. To do this accurately the saw needs to be supported correctly. Professionals use a special saw vice but an ordinary bench vice will suffice, plus a pair of wooden strips about 230 to 250mm long by 25mm wide and about 12mm thick (9in–10in by 1in by 1/2in). Put the saw in the vice with a strip on each side of it and with the teeth protruding about 6mm (1/4in) or so. Shape the teeth with a triangular file, but make sure that the face of the file is at least twice the depth of the saw teeth, as too small a file could distort the shape; sizes recommended by *Spear and Jackson* are:

Saw points per 25mm (inch)
5(rip saw): 6: 7 to 8: 10 to 12
Length of taper-saw file
205mm (8in): 178mm (7in): 150mm (6in): 150mm (6in) (slim taper).

Holding the file properly is important and this is best achieved by placing it in the gullet between two teeth and pressing it down firmly with the left hand, the right hand holding the file handle with the thumb on top and a finger alongside. File across the saw exactly at right angles and with the file held horizontally, maintaining the same grip throughout.

In Fig 9.2 note that the angle of pitch at (C) is 14 degrees for cross-cut and panel saws; and at (D) is 3 degrees for rip saws; however, the file will automatically follow the existing angle of pitch, and this very rarely changes provided the saw is used normally.

At this juncture, all the flats on the saw teeth should have been removed and they should all have been brought to a point with the fronts and backs sloping at the correct angle; disregard bevelling the teeth at this stage as this is dealt with after the teeth have been set.

Setting the teeth This is the next step, and involves bending alternate teeth in opposite directions, but there are several points to watch for and all of them are important.

First, how much 'set' should be applied? The answer is – not too much and, in fact, rarely does it mean making a kerf more than one and a half times the thickness of the blade. A 'kerf' is a saw cut and is illustrated at Fig 9.2E; in general, most woodworkers tend to over-set the teeth and this in no way helps the saw to cut. All that happens is that unnecessary effort is expended in cutting an over-size kerf, and that wood is wasted as sawdust.

Second, should the complete depth of each tooth be bent over, or only part of it? Fig 9.3A shows that the correct procedure is to bend over only the upper half – actually, slightly less than half is best. If the whole of each tooth is bent over, the result could be distortion of the gullet at its root, possibly accompanied by cracks and teeth breaking out.

There are two ways of setting, the first one being that used by some professionals. The

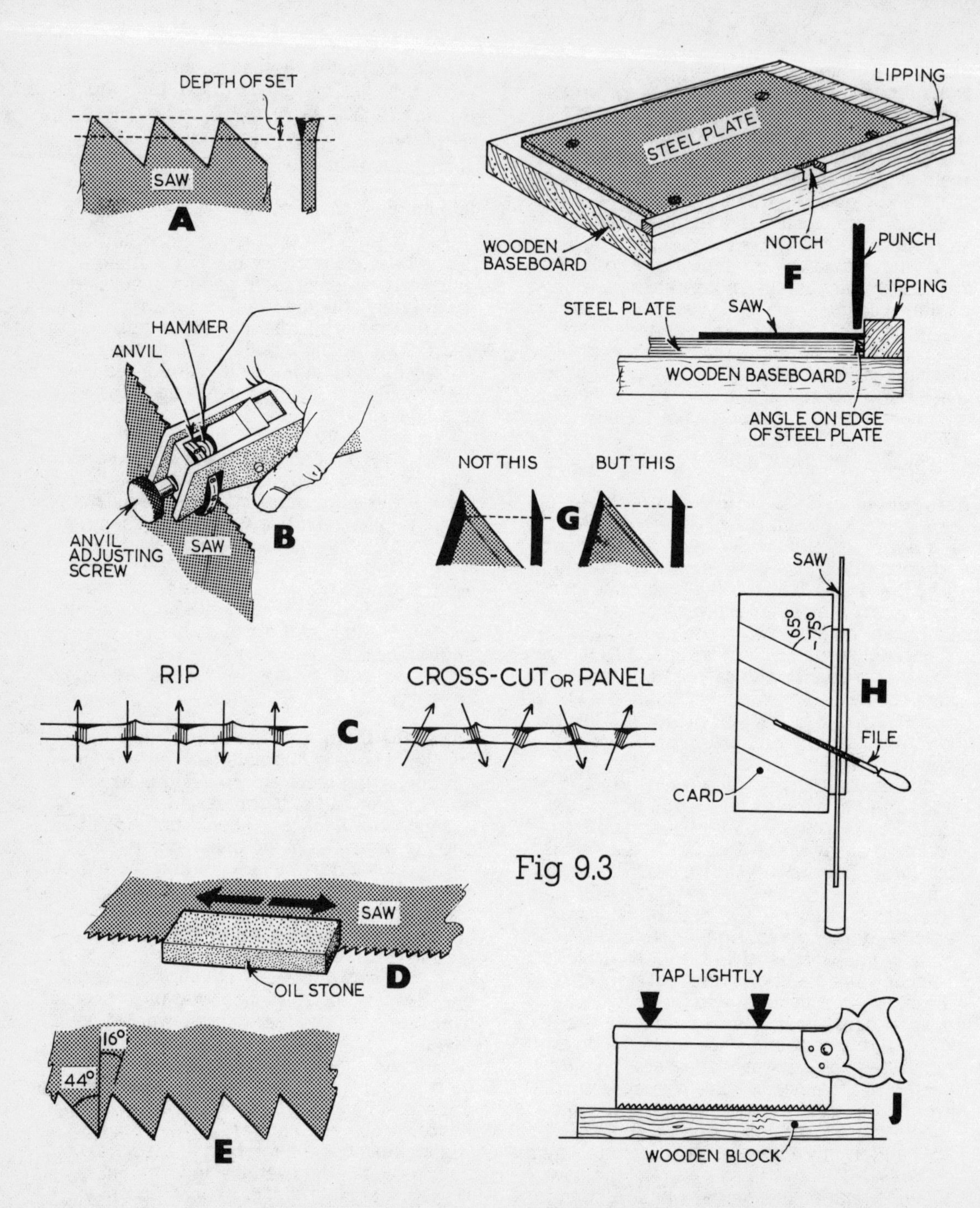

Fig 9.3

set-up is shown in Fig 9.3F, and consists of a wooden baseboard with a steel plate screwed or cramped to it. This steel plate does not have to be any exact thickness and 4mm ($^3/_{16}$in) would be quite suitable. A bevel is filed off the front edge at an angle corresponding to the amount of 'set' required; in fact, the four edges can be filed at different angles to suit the various sizes of saws being sharpened and the appropriate bevel can be chosen. Note that there is a lipping attached to the front edge, and this fulfils the important function of determining the depth of the 'set'.

The procedure is to lay the saw on the steel plate with the teeth butting against the lipping, and then use a punch to bend the teeth to the required angle, working at the point where the notch has been cut out. A 75mm (3in) nail with the point filed off to a flat makes a good punch; and needless to say, the punch should only be struck lightly with a hammer two or three times. Start at one end of the saw, setting every other tooth, and then turn the saw over and repeat the process on the teeth not treated the first time. The teeth must be set to conform with their original setting, as forcing them to the opposite sides will almost certainly break them off.

The other way to set the teeth is by using a pliers-type saw-set, which is shown in Fig 9.3B. This called the *Eclipse* Saw Set. To use the tool, place the jaws over a tooth and squeeze the handles, which cause a plunger to push the tooth over against an anvil. This anvil is adjustable to take account of the number of teeth points per 25mm (1in) – from 4 to 12 points actually; both the amount and depth of 'set' are automatically controlled by turning the anvil adjusting screw. Their latest model incorporates a magnifying eye-piece set just above the hammer, and this is an enormous help to those whose eyesight is not as good as it was.

Whichever method is chosen, once the teeth have been set the saw blade should be laid flat on the bench and an oilstone run backwards and forwards as at D, Fig 9.3. Only light pressure is needed as the aim is to reduce any teeth that are too prominent and, when one side has been dealt with, turn the saw over and do the other.

Final sharpening This is the last stage, shown at K, Fig 9.2 and C, Fig 9.3. In other words, when rip saws are sharpened, the file is held horizontally and at right angles to the saw throughout the work; while in the case of cross-cut and panel saws, the file is still held horizontally but at an angle of 65 to 75 degrees to the saw. To ensure a consistent angle throughout, it is a good idea to mark ink or pencil lines at the required angle on a piece of card which can be placed at the side of the vice, as shown in Fig 9.3H where it will serve as a handy guide. Fig 9.3G shows the result of filing at too shallow an angle, which produces a fragile tooth.

Naturally, in all cases the file is used on alternate teeth in the first pass and then the saw has to be reversed in the vice and the others dealt with. To help to see how far the teeth have been dealt with, give all the teeth a light 'topping' before starting so that they shine, and as the teeth are filed, the shine will be removed.

Back saws

So far rip, cross-cut, and panel saws have been referred to, but there is still another class to consider, namely back saws, which includes tenon and dovetail saws.

The procedure is just the same for tenon saws as it is for cross-cut saws but, as the teeth are smaller, a 125mm (5in) slim taper file should be used for those with 13 teeth points per 25mm (1in), and for 15 points per 25mm (1in), a 100mm (4in) slim taper file. Note, too, that the teeth have a 16 degree angle of pitch (Fig 9.3E) but the final sharpening angle is, like the cross-cut saw, 65 to 75 degrees.

Dovetail saws only need topping, shaping and sharpening like a rip saw; no 'set' should be put on the teeth. The sharpening angle or pitch is the same as for the tenon saw – 16 degrees.

Fig 9.3J illustrates a useful tip. After a period of use the blades of both tenon and dovetail saws may work slightly loose in the back. By standing the saw upright on a wooden block and tapping the back gently with a hammer as indicated, the blade will reset itself in the back and the sawing action will be greatly improved.

Further points that may be helpful. It's most important to do the job in a good light, and a desk-lamp strategically placed, plus a magnifying glass, will make the work much easier. It's a good idea to keep an old paintbrush and some white spirit handy; give the teeth a thorough cleaning before starting to remove any gummy deposits which may have built up as they may cause the file to be tilted at the wrong angle. White spirit is ideal for this job as it evaporates quickly and does not cause rust. When not in use, hang the saws up by their handles and give them an occasional rub over with *Vaseline* or a light machine oil (not vegetable oil such as linseed, which tends to become gummy) to keep them bright, shining, and in good working order. Never try to correct a buckled blade; either get it done professionally or buy a new saw. When hand saws are made they are specially tensioned, so that they are 'springy', and a buckled one will just sag lifelessly if you hold it out in front of you by the handle. The main cause of buckling is hitting the tip of the saw on the floor while sawing because the support for the work is too low.

Sharpening circular saws

If your circular saws are the TCT (tungsten-carbide-tipped) kind, don't attempt to sharpen them as it needs special equipment. The non-stick Teflon-S coated blades can, however, be sharpened in the normal way.

Before dealing with the actual sharpening and setting of circular saws, it is a good idea to have a look at the various kinds you are likely to meet. The four types shown in Fig 9.4 by no means exhaust the complete range of saws available, but they are the most popular.

The combination rip and cross-cut blade at (A) is intended for use in a saw bench and is more suitable for ripping than cross-cutting. The two principal features are the raker teeth and the gullets; the former is not meant to be a cutting tooth, but serves to keep the gap clear of dust and shavings as the saw rotates, while the gullets also help in the same task, and also assist in increasing the speed.

Another combination blade is shown at (B) and this one is likely to be found either in a saw bench or in a portable saw. It is happier working at ripping, but it can also cross-cut, although it gives a rough finish and is obviously labouring under difficulties. Again, it has the gullets which are a characteristic of circular rip saws, although they are not so pronounced as those in (A).

The radial-toothed cross-cut saw (C) is the best one for cross-cutting and will give you a nice clean finish, particularly on plywoods, hardboard, and the like. A peg-tooth cross-cut saw blade, such as (D), is often used in accessories which work off a power tool, and it is essentially a cross-cutting blade.

This is as good a place as any to point out that there is a fundamental difference between a portable saw, where you take the saw to the work, and a saw bench, where you take the work to the saw. As a result, the direction of rotation is opposite in each case, as illustrated at (E) and (G). The rotation in the portable saw (E) is anti-clockwise; on the saw bench (G), it is clockwise.

A consequence of this is that when you are cutting a plastic-faced board (or for that matter any board which has one show face) with a portable saw, the face should be downwards; the opposite obtains when cutting it on a saw bench, as the face is placed upwards.

Two more things to bear in mind: one should always start the motor before presenting the saw to the work; and you should adjust the depth of cut to suit the thickness of the work so that the teeth just break through the underside if you are employing a portable saw, or through the upper side on a saw bench.

The first task before beginning the actual sharpening and setting is to 'range down' the tips of the teeth, and this is done to preserve the true circularity of the saw. The procedure is shown at (H) and you will need to make up a cradle from odd scrapwood into which you can fit a broken piece of emery stone or, better still, a piece of an old grinding wheel. Whichever you use, make sure it is held very firmly in the cradle, and this can be done by tightening down the cross piece on to the emery stone. The saw is then started up and the emery stone in its cradle is advanced up to just brush the tips of the teeth until the high teeth points are removed and all the points are bright. Do not overdo it or you could spoil the shape of the saw. Note that you can only range down a saw blade mounted in a saw bench, and it is most important that the guard should be in place.

When you have done all this, make a test cut or two in a piece of scrapwood. At (L) you can see three test cuts, no 1 being satisfactory, while that at 3 means that you will need to do a little more ranging down to achieve the square-ended cut as shown at no 1. No 2 shows how a correctly set cross-cut saw should cut.

The device shown at (F) is indispensible, and is known as a saw-sharpening vice, or a 'sawhorse'. Mine is double-ended and made from odd pieces of chipboard. One end is for 203mm (8in) saws, and the other end for 153mm (6in) saws; in the case the radius of the curve is from the centre of the saw blade to a point about 6mm (¼in) from the bottom of the deepest gullet, or tooth. In my case, the radii are 80mm (3⅛in) and 67mm (2⅝in) respectively, but you will make yours to suit your saws, of course.

Secure the saw by means of a bolt through the centre hole and tighten up the wing nut; then put the whole thing in your vice. But note that you'll need a piece of packing which is

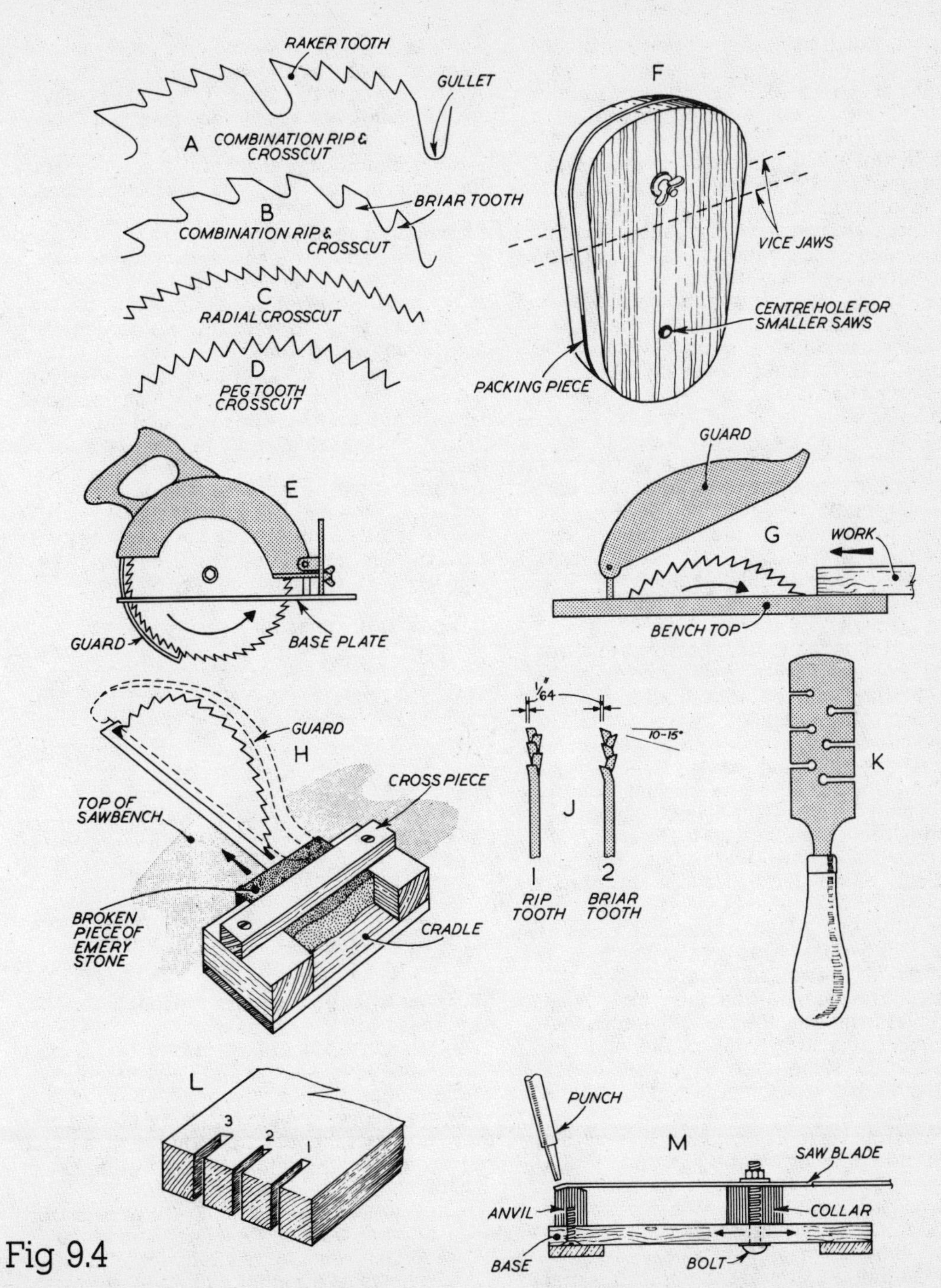

Fig 9.4

the same thickness as the saw blade at the bottom end of the saw horse (as illustrated), and a piece of cardboard will do for this.

Re-shaping the teeth is best done with a 152 or 178mm (6 or 7 in) taper saw file applied across the gullet at right angles until each tooth point which has been topped becomes a point. When dealing with a gullet tooth saw, use a 152 or 203mm (6 or 8in) millsaw flat file with round edges, which will preserve the shape of the gullets.

Unfortunately, the pliers-type saw set can only be used for the smaller sizes of circular saws, as generally the teeth are much too large. There are two ways of dealing with this problem, namely the gate saw-set (see K), and the anvil device shown at (M).

You can visualise the way the gate saw-set works from the illustration; the slots vary in width to suit the different gauges of saws. The alternative anvil method shown at (M) needs some explanation, although the principle should be clear enough. The saw blade is held down on to a collar by a nut and a bolt through the central hole in the blade. The bolt should be free to move sideways in a slot cut in the base – the length of the movement is governed by the sizes of the saw blades you are dealing with. The collar can be a piece of metal piping cut to a convenient length.

The anvil is a more difficult proposition, as it should (ideally) be machined from the solid and tapped to take the fixing screw. However, you could compromise by using a thick-walled piece of tubing with the edge filed to the setting angle; a piece of hardwood dowel jammed into the tube could provide an anchorage for the fixing screw.

At (J) you will see that the amount of set is a maximum of 0.5mm (1/64in) which should be applied by bending alternate teeth to the left and right equally. Note that the bending should only be applied to the top third of each tooth.

Final sharpening follows the same rules as outlined for handsaws, as crosscut and ripping circular saws can be regarded as equivalent to handsaws from this point of view. For a gullet tooth saw, file straight across the gullet with a second cut millsaw file; and file the teeth in the same direction as the set, making sure that you do not distort the shape of the tooth.

For crosscut teeth use a 152 or 178mm (6 or 7in) second cut taper sawfile at an angle of about 80 degrees to the face of the saw. It's best to go right round the saw at least twice so that you do not distort the shapes of the teeth by filing away too much at one pass. If you have done the job properly, the resulting trial cut should look like no 2 (L).

'Briar' shape teeth, as illustrated in (B), need an extra filing across the tops of the teeth at an angle of 10 to 15 degrees on alternate teeth, as shown at (J).

Do not worry too much if the set you have given is slightly more or less than that recommended, as the important thing is that the set should be consistent for all the teeth; the same remarks apply to the filing angles.

Sharpening bandsaws

In theory, bandsaw teeth should be set (when this becomes necessary) before they are sharpened. However, although it is best to have them set professionally, the occasional sharpening will do little harm.

Use a triangular taper-saw file, with second-cut single teeth. This type of file has rounded corners and thus leaves a rounded gullet at the root of the teeth which is less likely to crack.

The saw will need to be held in a long horizontal vice and each tooth is given one stroke of the file in exactly the same way, as bandsaw teeth have no front or back bevels. Fig 9.5 shows details of the procedure.

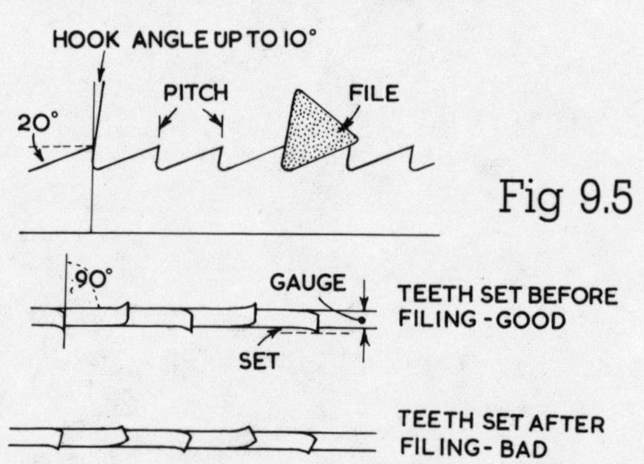

Fig 9.5

Sharpening hollow square mortise chisel and auger bit

The hollow chisel can have its cutting edges filed; in industry, sharpening is done either with a reamer or a conical grinding wheel.

There are two bevels as shown in Fig 9.6, they consist of the cutting-edge bevel, and the clearance bevel – details are shown in the illustration.

Points to note are that filing too heavily and so removing too much metal can cause the chisel to split; also, burrs which form on the outside faces as a result of filing have to be removed. The best way to do this is to rub them very lightly on an oilstone, keeping the chisel absolutely flat so that the outside face of the chisel is touched as little as possible.

Fig 9.6 also shows the areas to be filed on the auger – namely, on the insides of the scribing wings, and on the undersides of the cutting edges. It is important that the circle cut by the lips should always be larger than the square of the chisel, otherwise the latter will be overloaded.

The correct shape of a chain tooth is shown in Fig 9.6, together with the sharpened angle which can be lightly touched up with an oilstone slip from time to time.

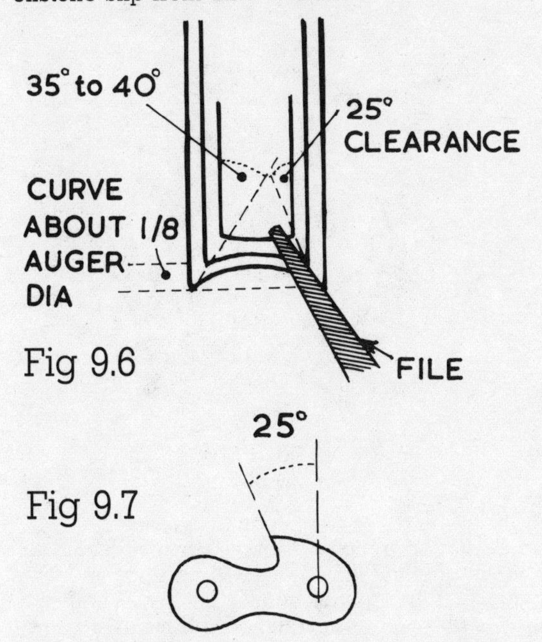

Fig 9.6

Fig 9.7

Sharpening plane irons

One important factor in discussing the angle at which plane irons should be ground is to appreciate that it is the front angle at the cutting edge which is the effective one, and (as shown in figs 9.8D and 9.8E), this depends on the 'pitch' angle at which the cutter is mounted in the plane. Fig 9.8D relates to most bench planes and Fig 9.8E to most metal planes – you can see that the cutting bevel is opposite in each case.

The grinding angle for plane cutters is always 25 degrees and this is sharpened at the cutting edge to a higher angle of approximately 28 to 30 degrees. Figs 9.8F and G show how the cutter is sharpened by hand; in F the cutter is held with the bevel flat on the stone at first, then the hands are raised slightly to give the sharpening angle.

Sliding the cutter backwards and forwards on the oilstone causes a small burr to form and this is illustrated in Fig 9.8H. Some woodworkers prefer a loose circular motion, and Fig 9.8F shows that the cutter should be held firmly. To remove the burr and thus impart a keen edge, the cutter is next turned over and laid absolutely flat on the oilstone and sharpened with small rotary motions, as in Fig 9.8G. Repeating this process will eventually cause the burr to break off, leaving a sharp edge.

Follow this procedure when sharpening either plane irons or chisels. If you want to improve the edge still further, you can strop it on a stropping board, which is simply a piece of leather glued to a handy-sized wooden block. The leather should be dressed with a paste of fine emery powder and oil (although engineers' grinding paste makes a good substitute); draw the cutter along the strop several times with the bevel downwards, and then turn the cutter over and repeat.

Although it is not essential, it is a good idea to dub off the corners of trying and smoothing plane cutters as shown in Fig 9.8J to prevent them digging in; the edge of the jack plane is even more rounded to ease its cutter through the work.

This seems the right juncture to mention the special honing guide (Fig 9.9A) made by *Eclipse* Tools. This comprises an adjustable clamp which can hold chisels and plane cutters, and which is mounted on a roller. The amount by which the tool protrudes governs the angle at which it is sharpened, and the measurements are embossed on the side of the guide. The only reservation I have about it is that the roller has to run on the surface of the oilstone, which could result in excessive wear. To combat this I remove the oilstone from its box and butt it against a wooden block which is exactly the same height; this means that the roller runs mainly on the wood and not on the oilstone. To hold the stone and block against each other I clamp them between two bench stops which yields first class results.

Sharpening chisels and gouges

Assuming that you use your chisels for a wide range of work, the grinding angle should be about 20 degrees, and the sharpening angle 30 degrees. However, if you like to use them for the purposes for which they were intended, then you will need to have different angles for each.

From Fig 9.8K, you will see that the

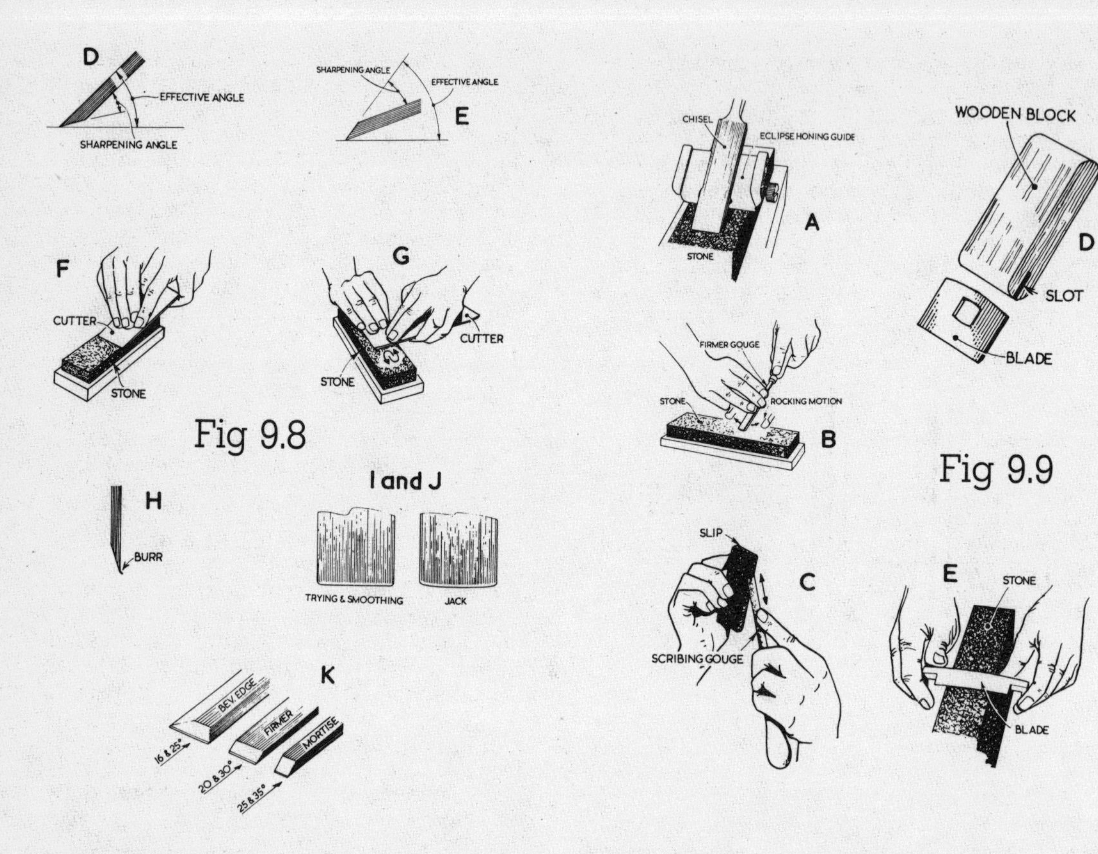

Fig 9.8

Fig 9.9

bevelled edge chisel has a grinding angle of about 16 degrees and a sharpening angle of about 25 degrees. This low angle is necessary as the chisel is meant to make slicing cuts, and not to be struck with a mallet.

The firmer chisel, however, is intended to be used with a mallet, and to cut across the grain as well as with it. So, a more acute angle is called for as a shallow one would break off or jam in the wood, and the grinding angle is therefore about 20 degrees and the sharpening angle 30 degrees.

Lastly, we come to the mortise chisel which is almost invariably used with a mallet, and which employs a chopping action to cut cross-grained stuff. Here, an even more acute angle is needed to stand up to such robust treatment and the grinding angle and the sharpening could well be 25 and 35 degrees respectively.

Both the grinding and the sharpening techniques for chisels closely follow those outlined for plane cutters, and a burr should be built up and then removed in just the same way; chisels can be honed on the same stropping board.

Sharpening the two types of gouges – firmer and scribing – demands two very different methods. Dealing with the firmer gouge first, the gouge should be positioned at right angles to the oilstone with the bevel lying flat, Fig 9.9B; rock it back and forth so that every part is treated, and finally remove any burr by sliding an oilstone slip up and down inside it. The slip will need to match the inside curvature exactly, of course.

An oilstone slip will be needed for sharpening the scribing gouge, Fig 9.9C. The curve on the slip should be slightly less than that of the gouge; remove any burr by rocking the gouge backwards and forwards on the oilstone, with the bevel held flat.

Sharpening spokeshaves

There are two kinds of spokeshave – the metal one which has a small blade, and the wooden type which has a blade with a tang at each end.

The first is dealt with just as if it was a small plane cutter and as it is so small, it's worth making a wooden holder as shown in

Fig 9.9D with a slot cut in it which accepts the blade as a push-fit.

Fig 9.9E shows the method of dealing with the other kind of blade by sharpening it on the edge of an oilstone; in both cases, any burr is removed by turning the blades over and rubbing them on the oilstone.

Sharpening a cabinet scraper

Fig 9.10 shows a set of vice jaws fitted with leather linings which not only make filing easier but also reduce the amount of unpleasant noise which can accompany the job. Arrange the set-up so that when the linings are in place, the vice jaws are naturally open a trifle more than the thickness of the scraper.

Any good quality fine (not superfine) artificial oilstone is suitable, but a small circular axe stone (Fig 9.12) is preferable. This is used with a lubricating oil such as a fine sewing-machine oil used neat, or half-and-half with paraffin; or alternatively, neat's foot oil. A burnisher will also be needed and it is advisable to get the proper type as shown in Fig 9.11. Although the edges of other tools such as chisels, gouges, etc can be used they will not give a consistently good result.

The following is the procedure;

1 Stone the four edges flat, removing any burr from previous sharpenings (Fig 9.12).
2 Set the scraper blade in the vice jaws and file the edges straight and square, removing all traces of previous edges (Fig 9.13).
3 Finish by draw-filing, still keeping the file square to the scraper (Fig 9.14).
4 Repeat the same processes with the oilstone to remove any file marks (Fig 9.15).
5 Do the same thing to the other long edge.
6 Remove any burrs by oilstoning (Fig 9.12). There should now be two long edges trued to 90 degrees in section, as in Fig 9.16.
7 Oil the burnisher lightly and burnish the faces flat (Fig 9.17).
8 Return the scraper to the vice jaws and burnish the edge with a few firm strokes at exactly 90 degrees. This produces edge sections as in Fig 9.18A.
9 Repeat the process at an angle of about 85 degrees which will produce the cutting edge shown in section in Fig 9.18B.

Fig 9.19A shows the cutting position and the angle at which the scraper should be held in use when it has been properly sharpened. In Fig 9.19B too great an angle has been given in the final burnishing, with the result that the tool cuts only when held at an awkward angle. In use, it should cut not as in Fig 9.20A or B, but as in C – with a slicing action.

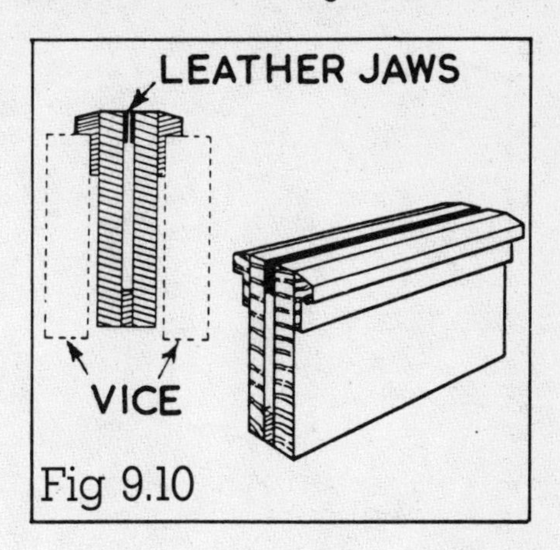

Fig 9.10

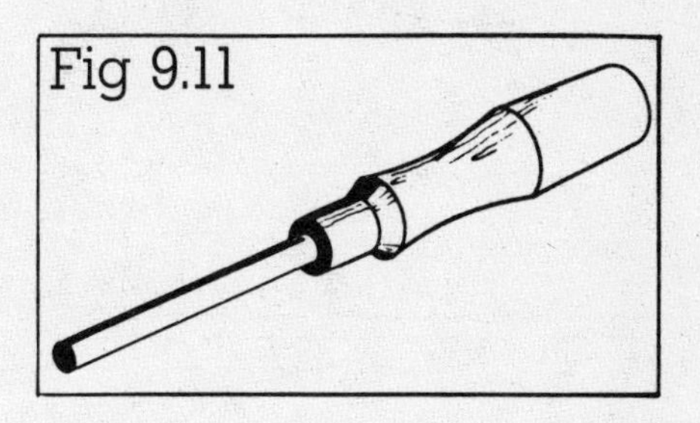
Fig 9.11

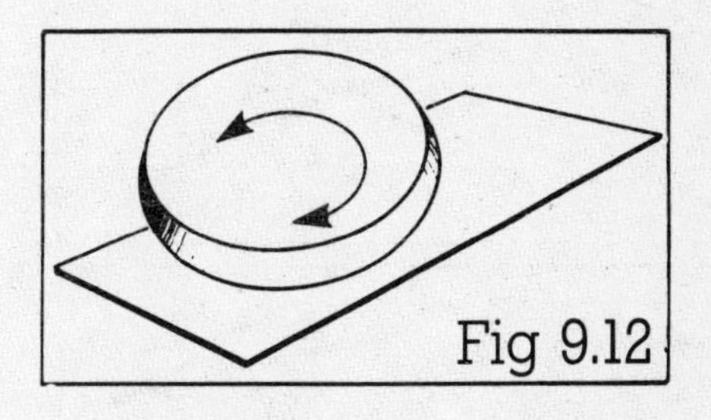
Fig 9.12

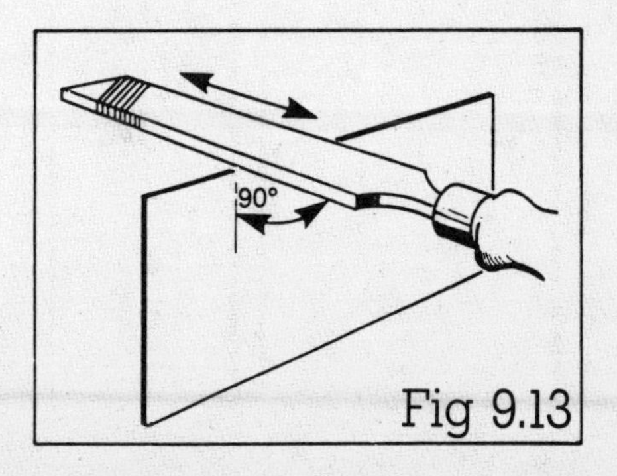

Fig 9.13

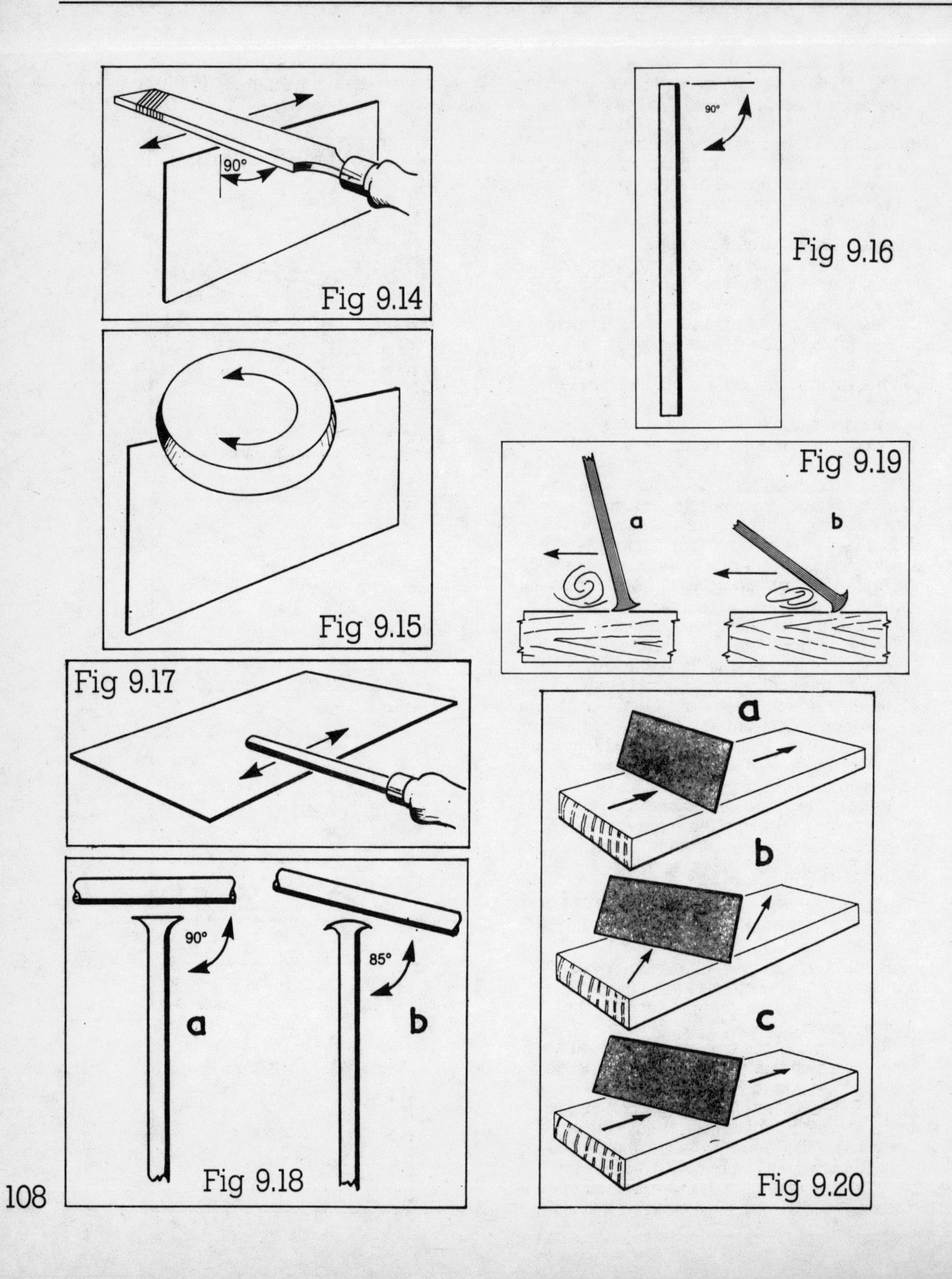

Fig 9.14

Fig 9.15

Fig 9.16

Fig 9.17

Fig 9.18

Fig 9.19

Fig 9.20

Sharpening the scraper plane blade
These tools look like large spokeshaves, the idea being that as the scraper blade is held in a wooden stock, there is no need to strain the fingers while bending it in use, nor will they get hot.

Its blade is sharpened differently from the cabinet scraper. The filing angle is not 90 degrees but 45, which necessitates using a different holding device while sharpening.

The one illustrated in Fig 9.21 makes it easy to file at 45 degrees while keeping the file horizontal. The jaws are lined with leather, and the space between is an easy fit for the blade; the jaws are closed by a bolt and wing nut – only one jaw is glued and screwed to a horizontal strip, the other being free to move. When the device is dropped into the vice the blade is held firmly at 45 degrees.

To sharpen the blade, first take off any old edges with the oilstone as shown in Fig 9.12. Next, file the bevel as in Fig 9.22. Remove any burr and marks left from filing by using the oilstone, and then remove any further burr which may remain from using the oilstone – in other words, sharpen like a plane iron, but at 45 degrees. Repeat the procedure on the opposite edge.

Now remove the blade from the jaws and lay it flat on the bench. Burnish the flat side as shown in Fig 9.17, keeping the burnisher flat (and slightly oiled). Next, hold the blade upright in the bench vice and burnish as shown in Fig 9.23. Lay the burnisher on to the blade at an angle of just over 45 degres and give a firm stroke (Fig 9.23A). Lift the burnisher to about 60 degrees and give a heavier, firm stroke (Fig 9.23B). Finally, holding the burnisher at 80 degrees, give one firmer and heavier stroke (Fig 9.23C). The edge should now be fit for use. Repeat on the opposite edge.

Insert the blade carefully into the stock, making sure that the three screws are slack and that the cutting edges are kept clear of any metal. The flat side of the blade leans forward while the bevel should be towards the adjusting screw. Stand the plane on a flat piece of wood and press the blade firmly down, holding it there by tightening the two clamping screws. In this position the tool may cut finely or not at all – the cut is obtained by turning the central screw. The more this is turned, the more the blade is bent and the thicker (but narrower) the shaving. Use the scraper plane in the same manner as the cabinet scraper – that is, parallel to the grain but with a skew or slicing cut (Fig 9.20).

When the scraper plane refuses to cut, the trouble is usually as shown in Fig 9.24. Here, the burnisher has been applied at too square an angle, with the result that (as shown at X) the actual cutting edge is not in contact with the wood.

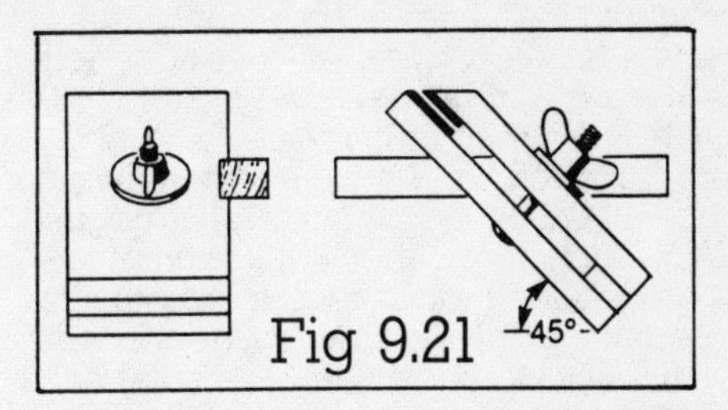

Fig 9.21

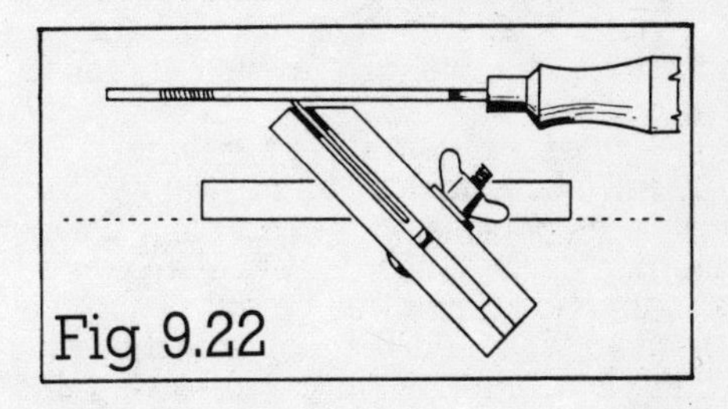
Fig 9.22

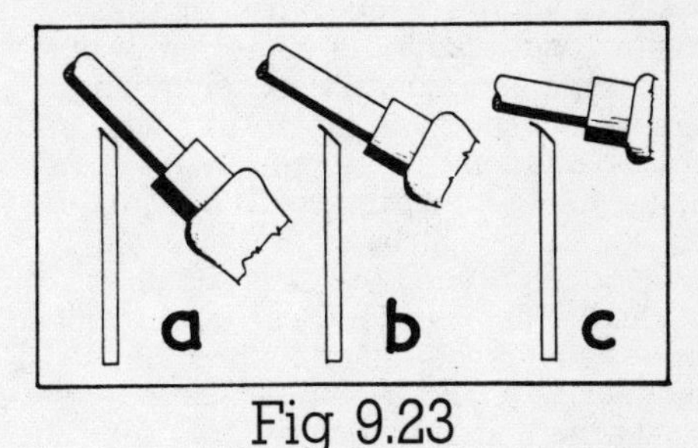

Fig 9.23

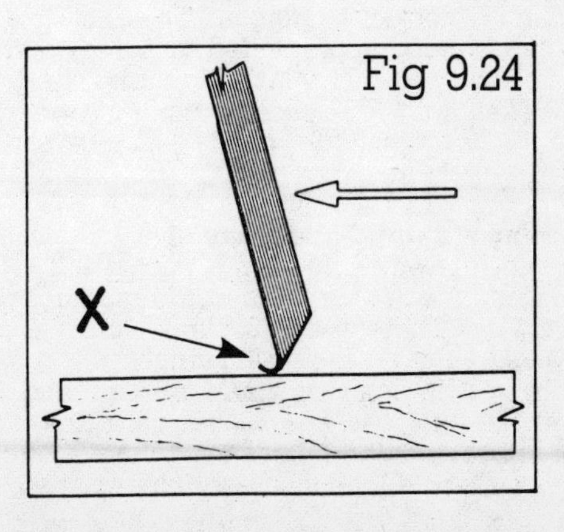

Fig 9.24

Sharpening router cutters

However excellent a router may be, it can only perform well if the cutter is in good condition. When the edge becomes dull, there are several ways to put it right, depending on the grade of cutter.

Generally speaking, it is advisable to send all cutters to a reputable sharpening firm, since accurate equipment is needed to restore them to a standard as near as possible to the original. In the case of high-speed steel cutters, however, hand-honing with a fine stone can be carried out on the inside flat edges; Fig 9.25. Only an expert should attempt to hone the outside radius, as it is easy to alter the clearance angle and ruin performance; Fig 9.26. It should be remembered that honing is purely a touching-up operation; but, if it is done regularly after each short-to-medium run of work, the cutter will give excellent results over a long period.

If the cutter is allowed to deteriorate, honing will be ineffective, and it will need to be sent to a specialist for re-grinding. Overall, the merit in having one's cutters sharpened by a firm with specialised equipment cannot be emphasised too much. So often it is thought that there is a simple short cut to solving this problem. Having said this, a re-grinding attachment is available for some hand routers, and it is sometimes possible to sharpen cutters with it. However, the correct setting-up of the apparatus is most important, and only the minimum of material should be ground off at any one time. Cutting angles must be maintained, and feedback from those attempting to use the gadgets suggests that it is not as easy as the instructions on the accompanying leaflet would indicate.

Re-sharpening of tungsten-carbide-tipped (TCT) cutters should not be attempted at all without the correct equipment. This includes special diamond-impregnated grinding-wheels which ensure correct reliefs are maintained. Fig 9.27 shows a TCT cutter ground correctly. Note the deep gullet for good clearance of swarf.

Dressing a natural stone wheel

The simplest way to true-up a worn grindstone is to use a piece of steel or iron piping about 25mm (1in) diameter and 305 to 460mm (12 to 18in) long in order to obtain sufficient purchase. The piping is cranked round and round about its axis, and should be inclined a little in both plan and elevation so that it offers a new surface all the time as it traverses the width of the stone, see Fig 9.28. It should be used dry.

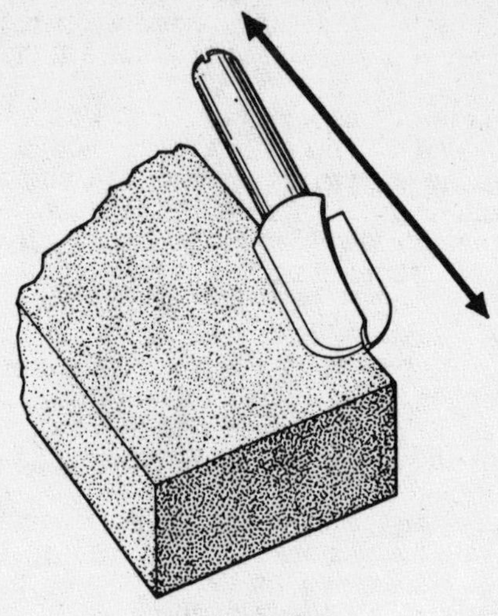

Fig 9.25

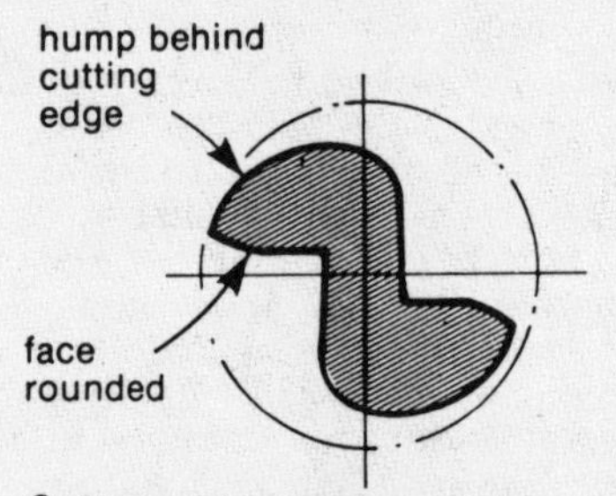

• *Sharpening: incorrect (above) and correct (below)*

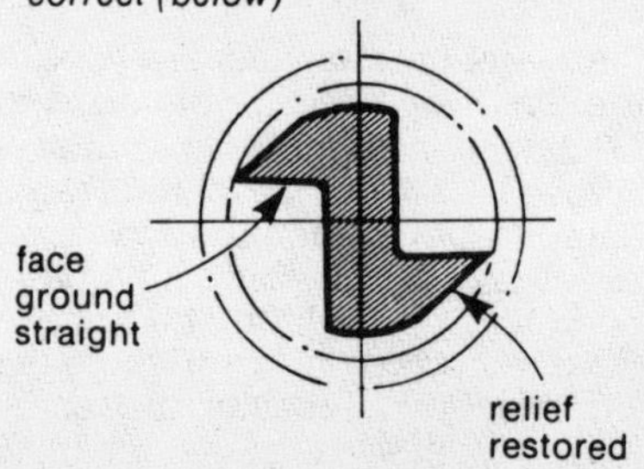

Fig 9.26

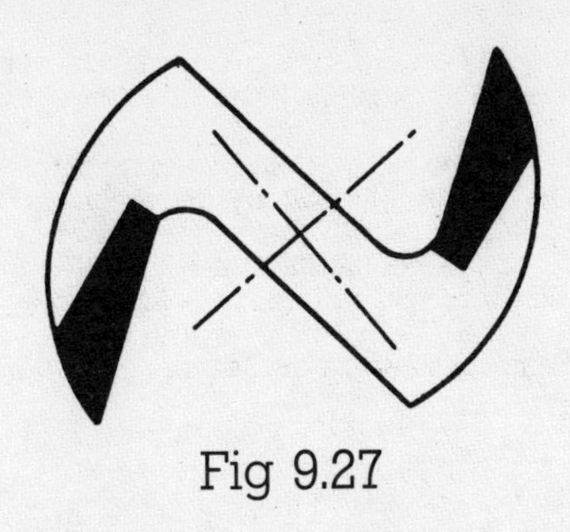

Fig 9.27

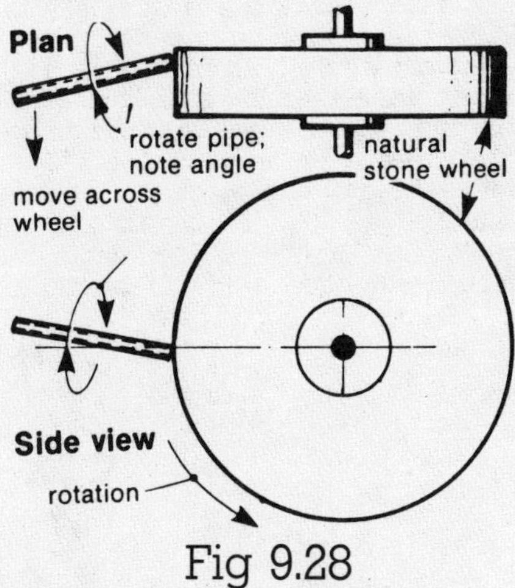

Fig 9.28

Sharpening bits

Starting with bits, the first point is that the cutters on all types are sharpened in the same way, namely, on the underside only and using a triangular file working through the throat, as shown in Fig 9.29A. Each cutter should be filed at the original angle, and by the same amount as its partner, so that the chips produced by each cutter are equal in thickness.

At this juncture note that a coarse file should never be used, but a fine-toothed one; this will enable you to remove only just as much as is necessary – it is only too easy to ruin a bit by removing too much metal.

Bits with wings or spurs need special treatment, so first look at those with spurs, which are the Jennings and solid centre types; (Fig 9.29B), where the spurs cut a circle ahead of the cutters. The spurs should be filed lightly with a flat file which has safe (i.e. plain) edges, and the filing must be confined to the inside of the spurs, as filing the outside would reduce the effective clearance for the twist diameters and thus cause binding.

Turning now to the Scotch-nose and spur-nose types, shown in Fig 9.29C, these have wings (instead of spurs) which afford additional strength to the cutters when making holes in hard or rough timber. Use a square file for this job, and sharpen the wings lightly on the inside only.

The centre bit (Fig 9.29D) has three components, these being the central point, the nicker which cuts the grain ready for the cutter, and the cutter itself. The central point will need an occasional touching up, and the nicker is always sharpened on the inside (never on the outside, for reasons already given) and its edge is slightly angled so that it does actually cut rather than scratch. Sharpen the cutters as shown, using a flat file with a safe edge.

One of the most efficient bits for use in a power tool is the flat bit shown in Fig 9.29E. There is nothing complicated in keeping this in good trim as it consists of filing the edges as shown, making sure that the original angles are retained. And, of course, the point can be sharpened from time to time using either a knife file or a flat file with a safe edge. Again, do not file the outside edges or the effective boring diameter will be reduced.

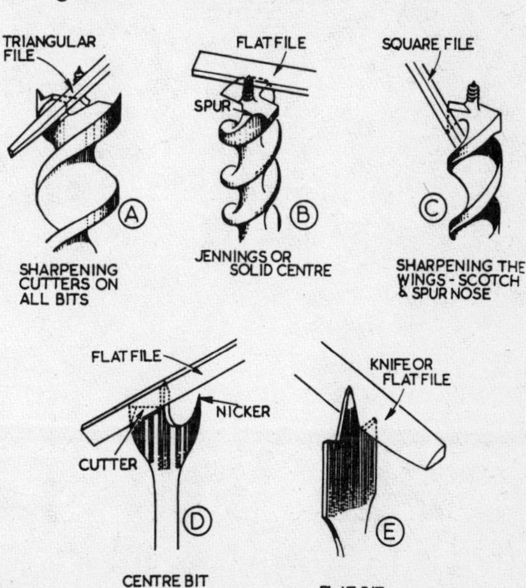

Fig 9.29

Sharpening twist drills

These are surprisingly difficult to sharpen by hand without some kind of jig. The difficulty arises from the fact that the actual cutting point of the drill is complicated, and Fig 9.30 shows the details. As can be seen, the overall angle is 118 degrees, but this is 'backed off' by 10 to 12 degrees because the cutting faces (shown shaded) are not in fact flat but slightly curved. The problem when sharpening is, of course, to give effect to this 'backing off'.

The problem has been solved by the introduction of the ingenious *Eclipse* Drill sharpener (Fig 9.30B). In principle, the drill is clamped at the correct angle in a guide so that either one or other of its cutting faces just rests on a sheet of abrasive paper supplied with the device. The whole thing is then pushed backwards and forwards a few times, so that one cutting face is sharpened, and then the drill is released and turned so that the other face receives the same treatment. 'Backing off' is accomplished automatically because the back wheels are mounted eccentrically and this imparts a motion which gives the necessary degree of backing off on the cutting face.

Fig 9.30C illustrates the sequence if the job is to be done on an ordinary grindstone. Note, first of all, that the clearance gap between the wheel and the rest should be reduced to the smallest practicable distance – 2mm (1/16in) would be ideal – as this prevents the drill from being snatched between the wheel and the rest.

Start by holding the drill with its axis at 59 degrees to the face of the wheel as shown at (1); it is a good idea to mark the various angles on a piece of card to ensure that you present the drill at the correct angle.

Hold the cutting lip horizontal at first (1), and then begin rotating the drill clockwise between your fingers; move on to the next stage (2) by reducing the angle to 55 degrees, still rotating the drill until stage (3) is reached, where the drill is backed off to approximately 49 degrees. This means that one whole rotation has been completed and the job

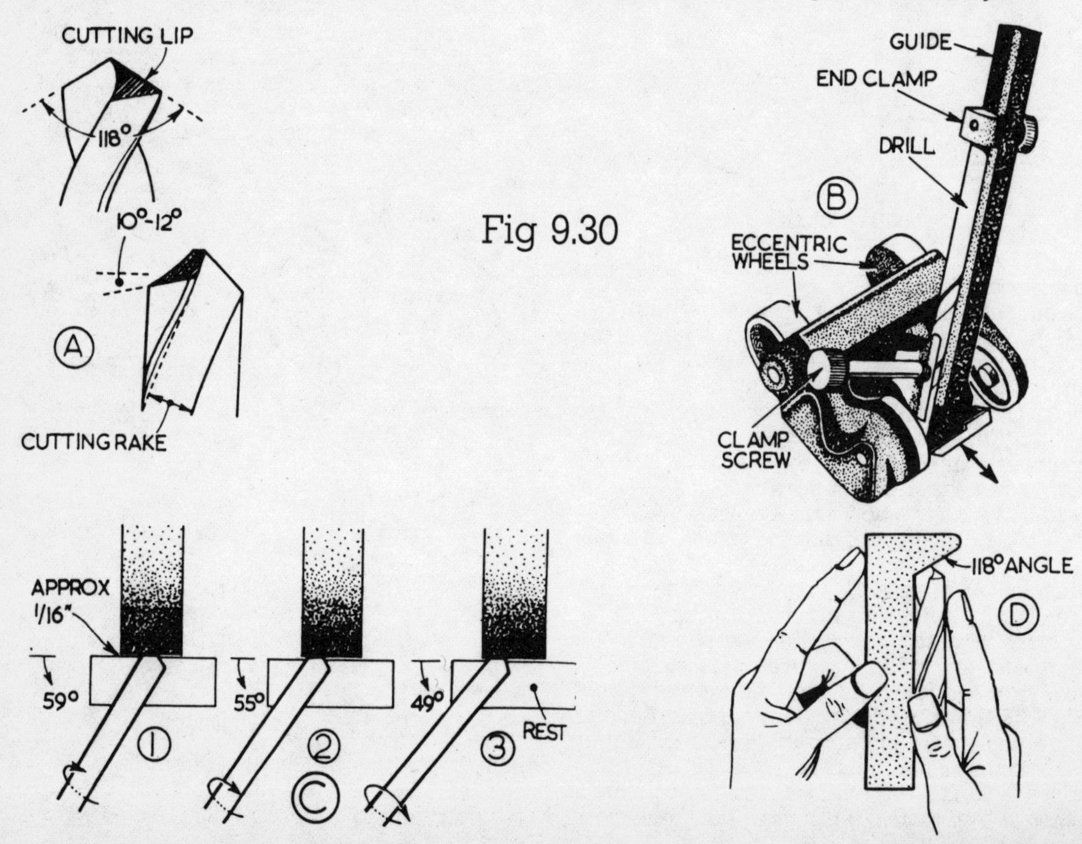

Fig 9.30

should be finished. To complicate matters, the drill should be horizontal in stage 1 and then gradually moved downwards all through the operation, using only light pressure. The resulting angle of the tip can be checked by means of the simple gauge shown in Fig 9.30D.

Fig 9.31 shows the types of surfaces used on various files

Note that a 'safe' edge is one which is left uncut or plain. Sections are given from (a) to (f), as follow; (a) square; (b) triangular; (c) round; (d) half-round; (e) mill; (f) flat (thicker than the mill). Cuts are: (g) bastard single cut; (h) second single cut; (i) smooth single cut; (j) bastard double cut; (k) bastard second cut; (l) smooth second cut. Second cuts have deeper teeth than singles.

Fig 9.31

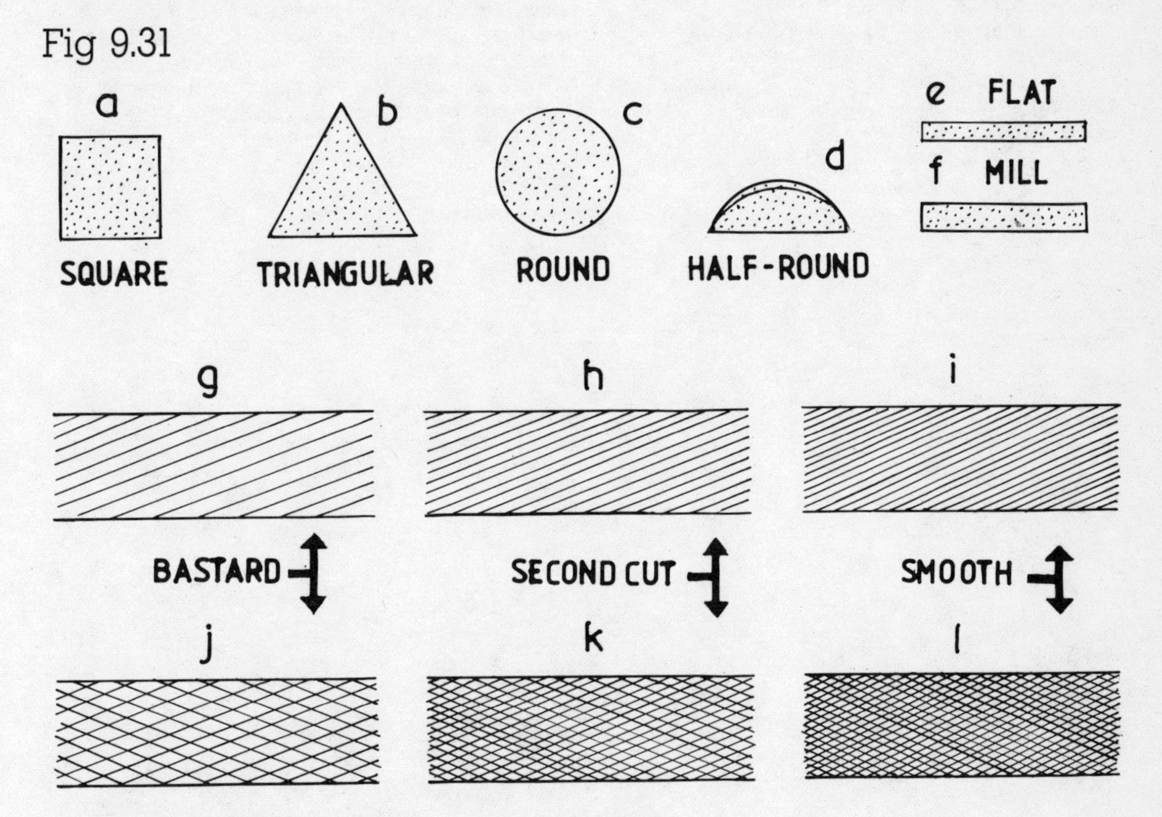

Japanese Water Stones

These have only been introduced to this country during the past few years, and the method of using them is very different from sharpening with oilstones.

The basic kit consists of two water stones; one coarse 800 grit and one fine 6,000 grit; a flattening plate; honing grit (coarse, medium and fine); chamelia oil (which is very thin); and a piece of Nagura stone. There are two types of water stones, namely 'natural' and 'man-made', and since the natural is difficult to obtain and very expensive, the following recommendations apply to man-made stones only.

Water stones can be kept totally immersed in water to which a little bleach has been added to prevent it going stagnant, and a plastic bowl makes a good receptacle. Otherwise, they can be kept in airtight plastic bags or containers: if you do this, remember to take the stones out of the containers an hour or two before you want to use them. Immerse them completely in water, leaving them until the water stands in puddles on the surface when they are lifted out – if it merely soaks into the stone and disappears, further immersion is needed. There is no need to worry about the wooden base the stone may be mounted on as the water will not harm it. Remember that coarse stones need to be soaked for a longer time than fine ones, as they take up a lot of water.

When sharpening, adopt the following procedure:

1 Apply a few drops of chamelia oil to the flattening plate and sprinkle a small amount of coarse grit on to it. The tool to be sharpened (for example, a chisel) should have its back worked up and down on the plate until all high spots are removed and the surface has a uniform degree of shine over its whole surface. Wipe the coarse grit off both the chisel and the flattening plate, and repeat the operation with the medium grit, followed by the fine grit.

2 Now rub the Nagura stone up and down the coarse water stone until a creamy paste is achieved, adding a few drops of water if necessary to prevent drying out. The back of the chisel should be worked along the coarse water stone, and the process repeated on the fine stone, once again employing the paste.

3 To sharpen the bevel, rub it along the coarse stone, having covered it with paste first, followed by the fine stone and more paste.

CHAPTER TEN

Workshop geometry and basic design

BASIC geometry is involved in even the simplest forms of woodwork, and the enthusiastic woodworker soon finds that more complicated problems have to be solved. The problems we discuss here include plotting polygons, scrolls, spirals, trefoils and quatrefoils and the calculation of compound angles. Two other subjects are dealt with, namely the plotting of the sections of the basic shapes of mouldings, and the 'Golden Mean', which will particularly help those who like to design their own pieces.

Designing

To divide a board of any width into a given number of equal parts by using a rule
Draw a line AB at right angles to the edge of the board (Fig 10.1). Place the rule diagonally across the board so that its zero end coincides with one edge: the division on the rule which corresponds with the number of parts required (in this case, thirteen) should be located on the opposite edge. The divisions can then be marked and parallel lines drawn along to intersect AB.

Bisecting an angle
Although an angle can be halved by using a protractor, it can sometimes be tricky for an angle such as 37½ degrees, where half the angle equals 18¾ degrees – a difficult number to read off accurately. The method described in Fig 10.2A does the job easily and precisely.

Suppose the angle is the one lettered as x, y, z. Then, using x as the centre and with any convenient radius, draw arcs cutting the arms of the angle at a and b. Next, reset the compasses at a smaller, suitable radius and draw arcs with a and b as centres, so that the arcs intersect at c. Then the line xc bisects the angle.

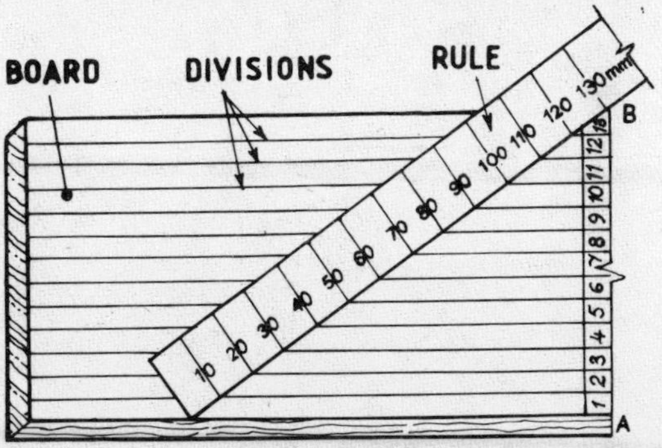

Fig 10.1

Centreing square
This is shown in Fig 10.3A and was made from offcuts of 2mm acrylic sheet, but hardboard or thin plywood would do. The first job is to mark out a cross, shown by ab and cd; sizes can be whatever is convenient, but 128mm (5in) and 64mm (2½in) would be suitable, and the distance cx could be 25mm (1in). The two pins, e and f, are inserted at equal distances from x; the rounded shape at the top is purely decorative.

To use the device, locate the pins on the circumference of the cylinder or disc and mark a line; then move it to another position and mark a second line – where the lines intersect will be the centre.

Drawing an octagon in a square
This is shown at Fig 10.2B. First of all draw the square a, b, c, d, and then put in the diagonals, ad and bc. Next put in the vertical and horizontal lines ef and gh, and using the intersection, j, of the lines as centre, draw the circle. At each point where the radiating lines cut the circle, draw a line at right angles, and this procedure will give the octagon.

Drawing an octagon around a circle
See Fig 10.2C. The method is the same as used for drawing an octagon in a square except that there is no need to draw the square.

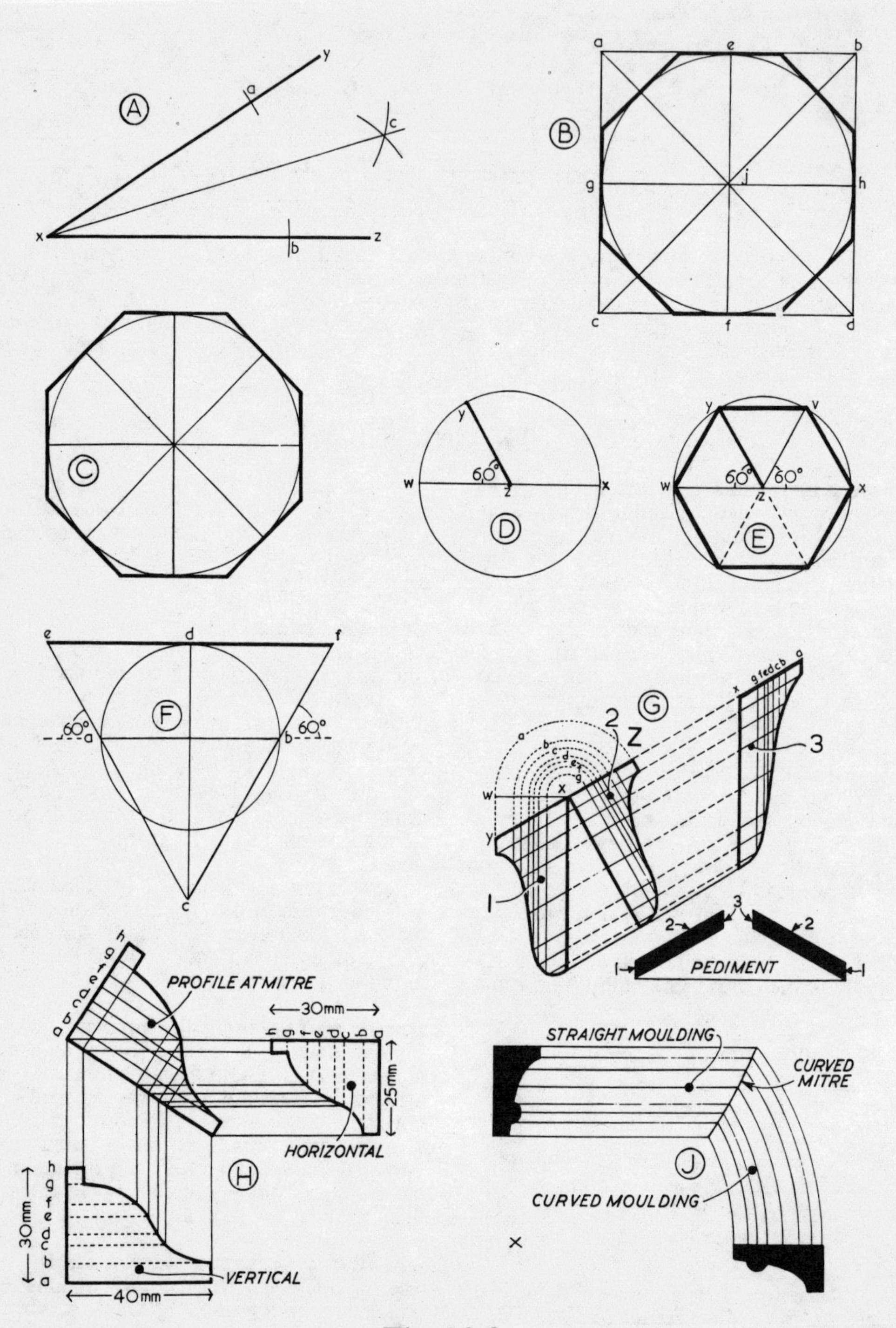
A
B
C
D
E
F
G
H
J
PROFILE AT MITRE
30mm
25mm
HORIZONTAL
VERTICAL
40mm
PEDIMENT
STRAIGHT MOULDING
CURVED MITRE
CURVED MOULDING

Fig 10.2

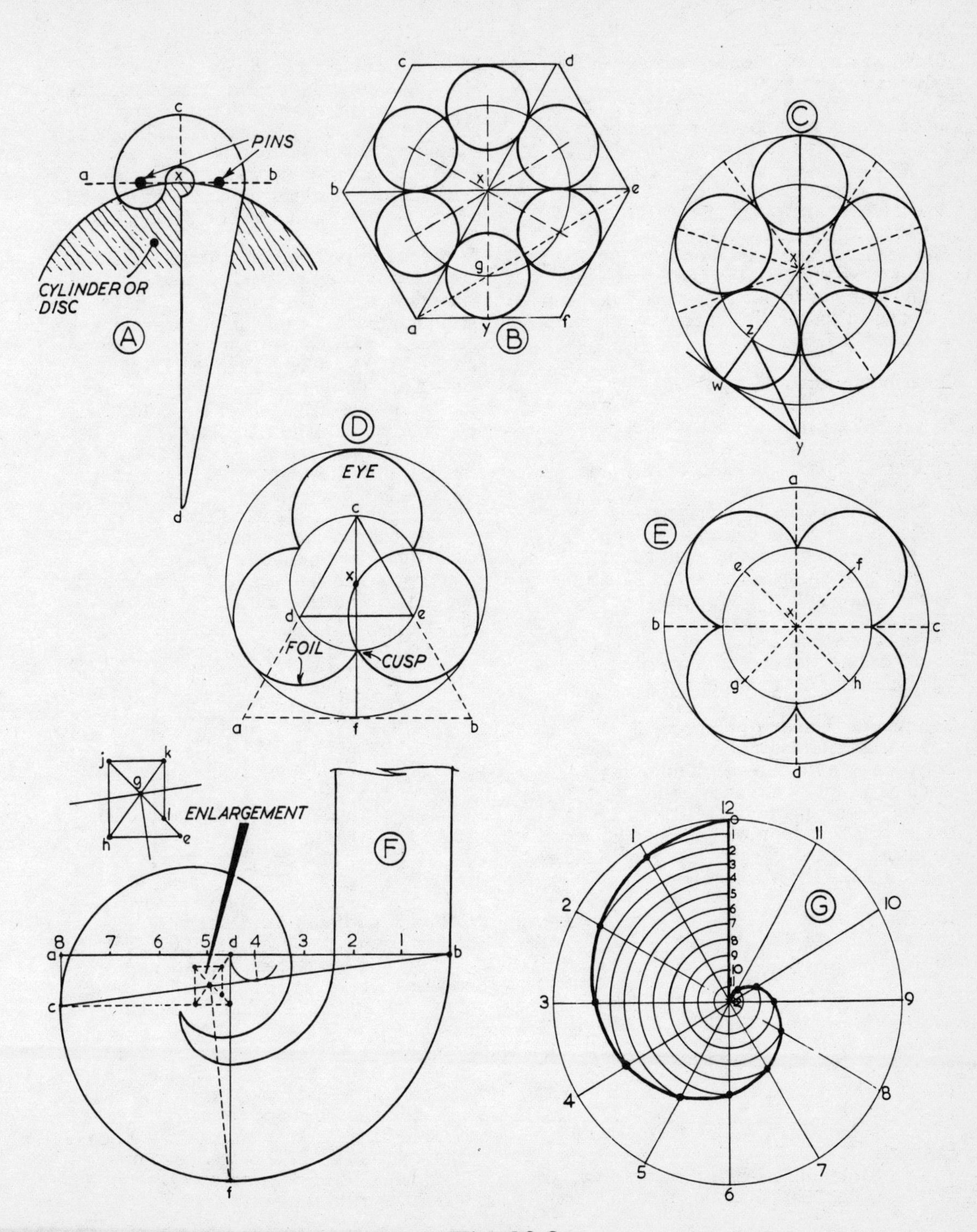

Fig 10.3

Drawing a hexagon or an octagon in a circle (alternative method)
See Fig 10.2D and E, for drawing a hexagon or an octagon in a circle using set squares only. In D, the radius yz is obtained by placing a 60 degree set square on the diameter wx and drawing a line. The following Fig 10.2E shows how the next line, vz, is marked by turning the set square over and repeating the process. The lines yz and zv can then be extended and where these lines cut the circle gives the points for the corners of the hexagon. If you substitute a 45-degree set square, the result will be an octagon.

Inscribing circles in a polygon
This is shown in Fig 10.3B, the idea being that there are the same number of circles as the polygon has sides; in the example this is six. Further, each circle must touch one side and two other circles.

Start by drawing the hexagon as already described, and then join all the diagonals ad, be, and cf. Bisect the angle daf so that the line ae cuts the perpendicular at g. Using the centre x and with xg as radius, draw another circle with centre g and radius gy. This is one of the circles required, and the radii of the others can be stepped off around the circumference of the larger circle.

Formula for drawing polygons
There is an alternative method for drawing polygons with from five to thirteen sides; it involves using the formula S = R divided by F, where S = the length of each side, R = the radius of the circle in which the polygon can be inscribed, and F = the appropriate factor from the table below.

Number of sides	Factor
5	0.851
6	1.000
7	1.152
8	1.307
9	1.462
10	1.618
11	1.774
12	1.932
13	2.090

Example
What is the length of each side of an octagon which can be inscribed in a circle of 250mm radius?
Answer: 250.000 (radius) divided by 1.307 (factor) = 191.3mm

Mitreing curved mouldings
Fig 10.2J shows the mitre between a straight piece of moulding and a curved piece of the same section. This is plotted quite easily by extending ordinates from each piece until they intersect, which willl give plotting points to be joined up. The ordinates must, of course, be the same for both pieces of moulding.

To reduce or enlarge mouldings to match a sample moulding proportionately
Draw the sample moulding as ABC in Fig 10.4, assuming that the mouldings to match it are 25mm and 50mm deep respectively. Then, through A draw a horizontal line XL of any convenient length as a base line, and through B draw the line XD, again of any convenient length. Erect the verticals JG and FK so that they are 25mm and 50mm respectively. Next, from G and K draw horizontal lines parallel to the base line XL; then from X draw a line to C, extending it to cut the line KE at E. This will give the outer points of the required mouldings. Draw ordinates from X through the salient points of the sample mouldings to plot them on the required mouldings.

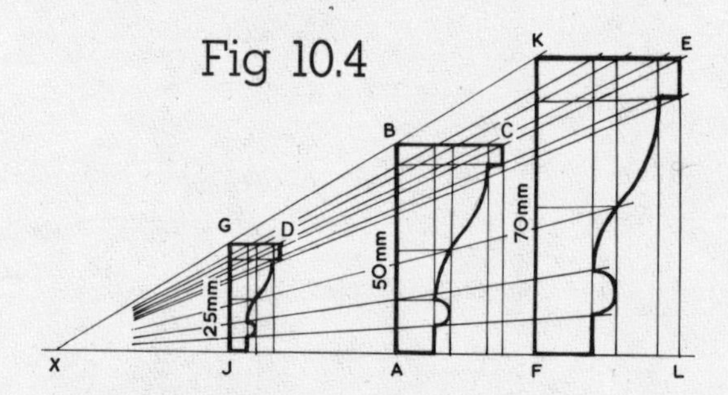

Fig 10.4

Profiles of pediment mouldings
The first example shown at Fig 10.2G refers to the profiles of the mitres on a broken pediment. Profile No 1 relates to the horizontal return moulding, No 2 to the 'raking moulding' (this is the true section), and No 3 to the return at the break.

The working method for G, H, and J is more or less the same, and any reader who has produced valley, hill, and mountain profiles from map contours should soon feel at home!

Returning to G, the first step is to draw the raking moulding (No 2) with its appropriate profile as shown; at point x, draw a perpendicular downwards. Now points have to be chosen where to draw in the 'ordinates' which are the horizontal reference lines on the sectional drawing. There can be as few or as many as is convenient, the general rule being that the more complicated the shape of the moulding, the more ordinates are likely to be needed.

Put in the ordinates on section No 2 first and from each point where an ordinate touches the profile draw a line upwards to join yz and at right angles to it; this will give a series of reference points a,b,c,d,e,f, and g. Continue by transferring these reference points over to line wx by means of compasses, describing a series of concentric arcs. From line wx, drop perpendiculars from the transferred reference points, and the intersection of each perpendicular with an ordinate will enable the profile to be plotted by joining up the points.

Moving on to profile No 3, the points a to g on profile No 2 can be marked off along the edge of a piece of card and transferred to the line xz. Perpendiculars dropped from the points will enable the profile to be plotted. Alternatively, a start can be made with profile No 1 and No 2 developed from it by reversing the process.

Mitreing mouldings of different sizes

It must be emphasised that a mitre need not necessarily be at 45 degrees; it is actually the line which bisects the angle at which two pieces meet. So, in the case of the two pieces of moulding shown in Fig 10.2H which have the same profile but differ in width, the angle of the mitre is not 45 degrees, but varies according to the relative sizes of the mouldings.

The method used is very similar to that employed for Fig 1G and does not need further explanation.

Finding the circumference of a circle

The standard method for doing this is to measure the diameter of the circle and multiply it by 3.14 (π), the result being the length of the circumference. This is not strictly accurate, as π is a recurring decimal, and while this may not matter when dealing with small circles, the inaccuracy can be significant with large ones.

The method shown in Fig 10.2F is quick and accurate. First, draw the circle and a diameter ab. Using a 60-degree set square based on the diameter, draw lines through a and b to meet at c, and extend the lines to e and f. The line joining e and f will then equal HALF the length of the circumference.

Inscribing circles in a larger circle

This is illustrated in Fig 10.3C, and the first job is to draw the large circle, with centre x. Divide the large circle into the same number of sectors as smaller circles required (in this case five); the easiest way to do this is to divide the 360 degree circle by 5, which equals 72 degrees, using a protractor to mark off five 72 degree sectors from the centre x.

Next, bisect each sector, again using a protractor, although the method shown at Fig 10.2A will be more accurate. Then, from the centre x draw the line xw and at w draw another line at right angles to it; from x draw a line to cut the one from w at y. Bisect the angle wyx just made, and point z is where the bisecting line meets xw and is the centre for the first circle.

If a circle is drawn with radius xz and its centre at x, the points where it cuts the sectors are the centres for the remaining circles.

Plotting trefoils and quatrefoils

Trefoils (Fig 10.3D) and quatrefoils (Fig 10.3E) are designs often needed by woodcarvers, especially those engaged in church work.

To draw the trefoil, make a tangent ab to the circle, and from f draw a line to x. Using a 60-degree set square, construct the equilateral triangle cde; next, with centre x and radius cx describe a circle. Where this circle cuts the sides of the triangle cab gives the points d and e, which are the centres for other arcs.

To describe the quatrefoil draw the larger circle first, and with the same centre x, draw the inner circle; the diameter of this depends upon the size of trefoils wanted. Then draw in the intersecting lines ad and bc and the intersecting lines eh and fg, which will give the centres and the cusps.

Setting out a scroll

This is one of the more complicated pieces of marking out and is illustrated in Fig 10.3F. Begin by dividing the overall width of the scroll ab into eight parts, and from a draw ac at right angles, making it the same length as one of the divisions, and joining c to b.

From point No 4 draw an arc which is tangential to bc, and where this cuts ab mark in point d. Next, draw a line downwards from d at right angles to ab, and mark in ce, parallel to ab. Use centre d to describe the arc from b to cut the extension of de at f. Now, with e as centre, draw the arc fc.

From f, draw a line to cb and at right angles to it, which will give point g; a line drawn from d through g and extended to ce will locate point h, which is the next centre. From h, draw a line upwards and vertically to find centre point j, and a line from j to line dh locates centre point k. From k, a line dropped vertically gives you a centre point l. The inner line of the scroll can be drawn parallel to the outer curve.

The Archimedean spiral

Fig 10.3G shows the solution of this interesting problem. Divide the circle into twelve sectors (use a 30 degree set square or a protractor to do this) and then divide any radius into twelve equal spaces. Starting at division 1 and working downwards, draw arcs to meet the numbered radii. Join up the points freehand to obtain the spiral.

To set out arches

It should be clear from Fig 10.5A to H where the centres for the different kinds of arches are situated, but the following notes should also help.

(a) This is an equilateral arch where the centres are at the 'springs' (the lower corners) of the arch and an equilateral triangle (shown by the dotted lines) could be inscribed.

(b) Lancet arch with a comparatively sharp apex; it is often required in Gothic designs and church work.

It is best to draw an isosceles triangle (one in which the two sloping sides are equal) and this is shown dotted; each centre is located on the base line outside the springs at a point equal to half the actual base of the arch (called the 'span') – YU, UX, XV, and VZ are all equal in length.

(c) Drop arch. Again, draw an isosceles triangle of the requisite dimensions. The centres are both inside the arch and are located so that YU, UX, XV, and VZ are all equal in length.

(d) Three-centred arch. This is a compound-curve arch, and the dotted lines (which can be at any suitable angle) along which both centres are located indicate the junction of the two curves. The centres for the upper curves can be at any points along the shorter straight line XY.

(e) Four-centred (depressed) arch. The shapes and proportions of the curves can be varied to give different patterns. Also, the angle of the dotted lines on which the centres are located can be altered, as can the positions of the centres themselves, provided they remain on the dotted lines.

(f) Straight-topped arch. Similar to E, but with the upper lines towards the apex being straight. The dotted lines on which the centres are located can be at any angle; however, the straight section must always be at right-angles as shown.

(g) Ogee arch. The centres on the lower base line can be at any suitable points, and the dotted lines on which the upper centres are located can be at any suitable angle; the centres can be at any point outside the arch to give the required apex.

(h) Depressed arch. The upper centres must always be at the intersections of the sloping dotted lines with the base line. The central, flatter, curve of the arch should have a much larger radius than that used for the smaller curves at the springs.

To reduce or enlarge a shape from one side of a sample

In Fig 10.6 ABCD is the sample shape. From a convenient point, X, draw lines to each corner of ABCD and, if the required shape is to be bigger, extend them to a convenient length. Line XA can be divided into the number of equal parts by which the sample shape is to be reduced; so by dividing XA into three equal parts to give A′, the reduced shape can be plotted from that point. To enlarge, the line XA is extended by the required number of equal parts (in this example, five) so that the enlarged shape can be plotted from A″.

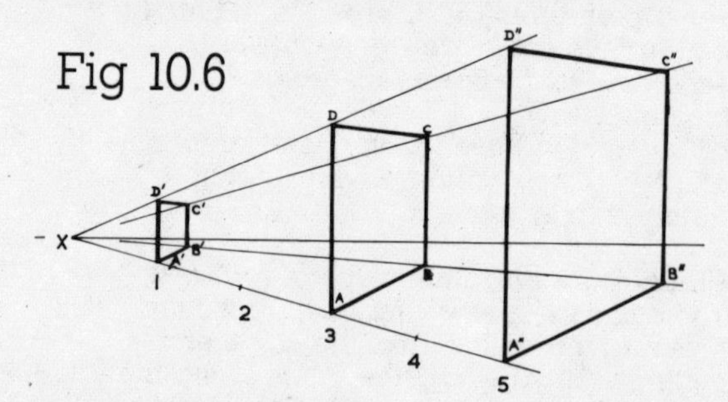

Grinding cutter profiles

To grind a cutter for any particular moulding, proceed as follows. Draw a plan view (Fig 10.7A), marking in the positions of the cutter, and the nut and bolt clearance. Next, draw the shape of the moulding required and divide its curves into any number of convenient points: in this case 0,1,2,3. Then draw a radial line XY as shown and project the points on to it; with X as centre draw arcs to project these points on to the face of the cutter as 0′1′2′3′. Then draw

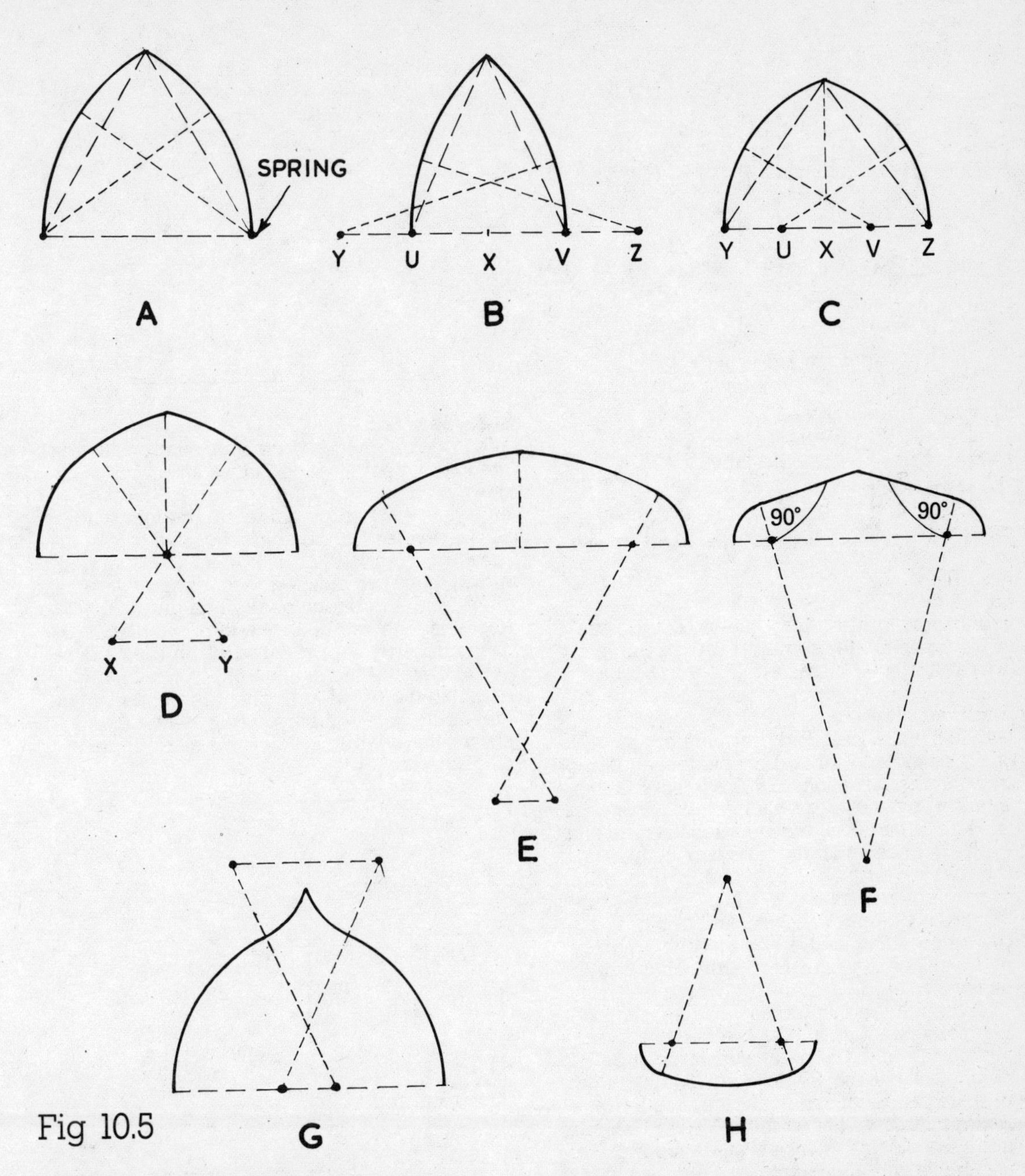

Fig 10.5

horizontal lines from this last set of points across to the true shape of the cutter – verticals drawn up from the first set of points (0,1,2,3) will intersect the horizontal lines to give the required shape which is formed by joining 0″1″2″3″. Fig 10.7B is a sketch of the finished moulding cutter.

Compound angles – inclined and splayed work

The development of inclined surfaces occurs so often in carpentry and joinery that a sound knowledge of the geometry of inclined or splayed work is essential to the craftsman following these trades. Roofing work, linings

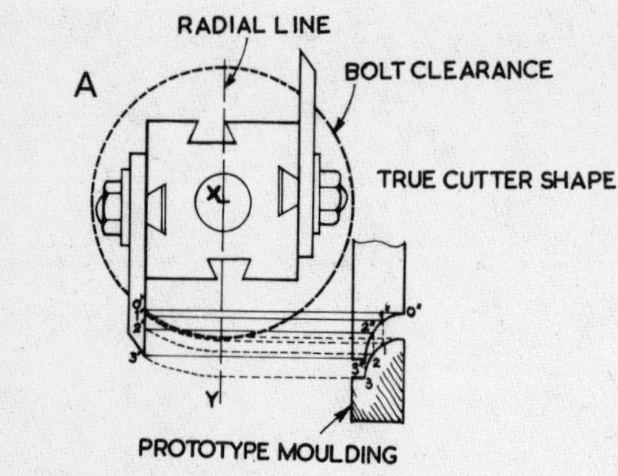

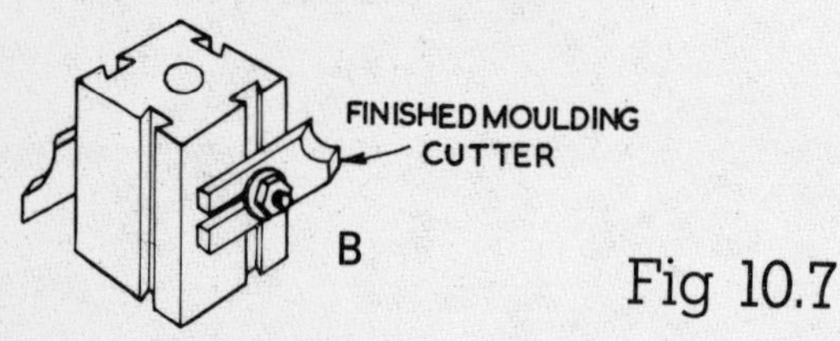

Fig 10.7

round door and window openings, and form-work for concrete are only a few examples where these problems are likely to occur.

Inclined plane

Fig 10.8 is the plan and elevation of an inclined surface a-b-c-d. Its inclination can be seen in the elevation, and the plan of the surface, a-b-c-d, can be seen below the elevation. The problem is to develop the shape of the surface. With the compass point in a, in the elevation, and radius a-b, describe the arc to give point b″ on the X-Y line. Drop a vertical line from b″ to meet horizontal lines brought over from points c and b in the plan to give c′ and b′. Then a-b′-c′-d is the true shape of the surface a-b-c-d.

Although the surface can be seen in the plan, this is not its true shape because it is inclined from the edge a-d upwards at an angle, in this case, 30 degrees. To obtain its true shape we must imagine that the surface is being laid down flat on the X-Y line. If this is done the point b in the elevation follows the arc drawn with the compasses and would come to rest at b″. Viewing this movement from above, b and c in the plan would move towards the right and come to rest immediately below point b″ to give the points b′ and c′. Notice, too, that the points b and c move outwards at right angles to the hinge line a-d.

Fig 10.8

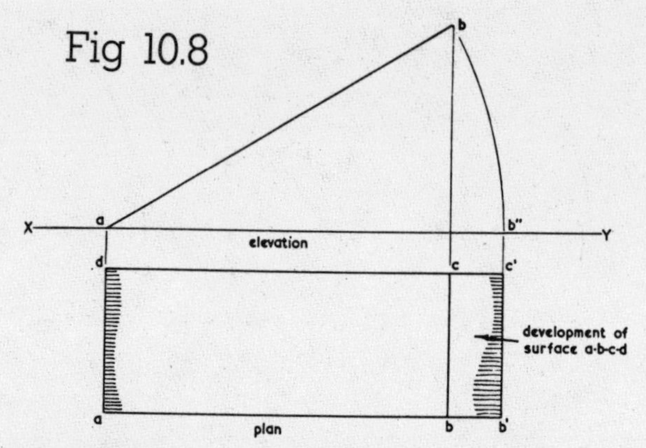

Splayed work

When developing any inclined plane with this method, all points which move sideways or downwards or, in fact, in any direction, must always move at right angles to the hinge line. This is evident in the second series of drawings (Fig 10.9). These show the plan and elevation of two inclined fascia boards to a shop front and intersect at an angle of 90 degrees. The two boards a-b-c-d and a-b-e-f are mitred together at a-b. The problems here are to develop the shapes of the two boards and also the bevel to apply to the ends so that they mitre together correctly. As the elevation shows, the boards are inclined at an angle of 60 degrees.

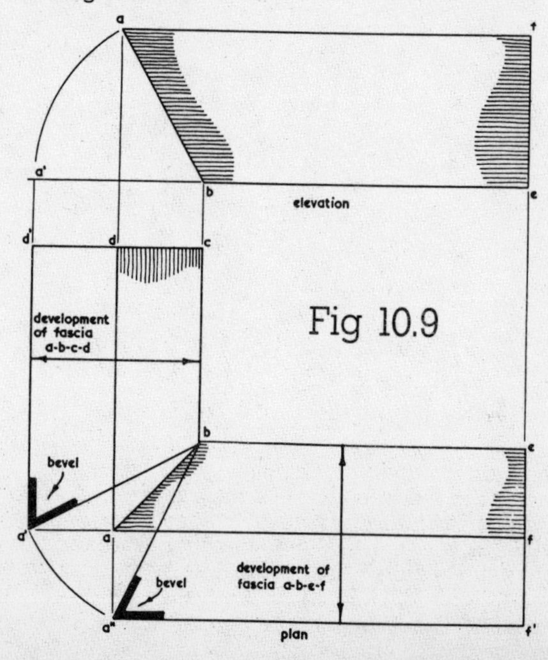

Fig 10.9

To develop the boards, place the compass point in b in the elevation, and with radius b-a describe the arc to give a′ on the horizontal line brought out from b. Drop a vertical line downwards from a′ to give points a′ and b′ in the plan. a′-b-c-d′ is the development of one of the boards. In this case b-c is the hinge line, and so points a and d must travel outwards at right angles to this line.

The width of the other board, a-b-e-f, is exactly the same width as the first, so it is quite a simple matter to draw the true shape of this surface. The bevel required (both boards require the same one) is equal to the angle of the mitred ends of developed boards.

Fig 10.10 is the plan and elevation of four sides of a box, all inclined at an angle of 60 degrees. The joints at the corners on the left-hand side of the box are butt joints, and those on the right-hand side are mitres. The problems are to develop the shapes of the sides and the bevels to make the joints at the corner. The end of the box to the left of the plan has its outside surface marked e-f-g-h, and to develop this surface the point of the compasses is placed in point f in the elevation and with radius f-a describe the arc to give point a″ on the horizontal line brought out from the base of the elevation. From a″ drop a vertical line downwards to intersect with two horizontal lines brought out from points e and h in the plan to give points e′ and h′. e′-f-g-h′ is the developed outside surface of the side.

At the opposite end of the box the corners are mitred. The outside surface in this case is b-c-k-i, seen in the plan. To develop this surface, place the compass point in i in the elevation and with radius i-b describe the arc b-b′. Drop a vertical line from b′ to give points c′ and b″ on horizontal lines brought out from points c and b in the plan. The developed surface is b″-c′-k-i. The development of the outside surface of one of the longer sides of the box is seen on the lower end of the plan.

To develop the outside surface of side a-b-i-j drop vertical lines from points a and b in the plan and with compass point in i and radius i-b″ describe an arc to give point b‴ on the vertical line drawn from b. Draw a horizontal line from b‴ to give point a′ on the vertical line dropped from point a. a′-b‴-i-j is the developed outside surface of the longer side of the box. The outside surface of the other long side is the same as the one developed.

Whether the corners are mitred or butt jointed a bevel has to be applied to the ends

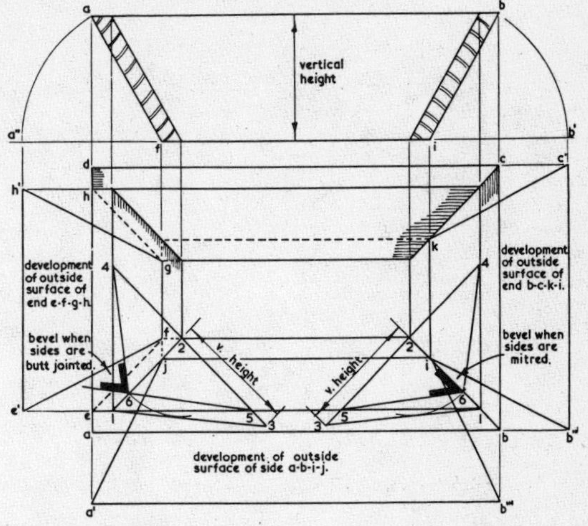

Fig 10.10

of the pieces so that each piece will fit against the surface of the adjacent piece correctly. If the corner is mitred, the ends of both pieces have to be bevelled, but if butt jointed a bevel is applied to one of the two pieces only.

Mitred corner

Let us consider the mitred corners first. To obtain the mitre bevel the dihedral angle of one of the corners must be developed. The dihedral angle is the angle made by two adjacent sides, and involves developing the shape of a triangle which will just fit on the two inside surfaces of the corner with the surface of the triangle at right angles to the corner line.

To develop the dihedral angle for the corner at b:

1 Obtain the true length of the corner 1-2 by drawing line 2-3 at right angles to 1-2. Make the length of 2-3 equal the vertical height of the box. Line 1-3 equals the true length of 1-2.
2 Extend 2-3 across to give point 4 on the inside edge of the adjacent side of the box.
3 With compass point in point 2 and the compasses open to just touch 1-3, describe an arc to give point 6 on line 1-2.
4 Join 6 to 4 and 6 to 5 with straight lines. Angle 4-6-5 is the dihedral angle of the corner. The mitre bevel is exactly half of the dihedral angle and is 2-6-5.

Butt joint

To obtain the bevel to apply to one of the ends when the joint at each corner is a butt joint, the dihedral angle is developed as before and the

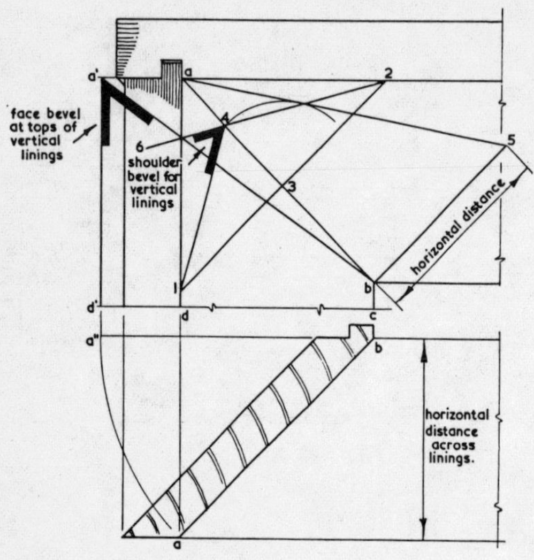

Fig 10.11

external angle set up by the dihedral is the bevel required (see corner a).

Fig 10.11 is another example where the dihedral angle has to be developed to obtain the bevel for a butt joint to piece of work with splayed sides. In this case the drawings illustrate a corner of some splayed linings round a door or window-opening. The joint shown is a tongued-and-grooved joint but the shoulder to the tongued portion is the same as a butt joint and so the same geometry applies.

The inside surface of the vertical lining is developed in a similar way as in the previous drawings. With compass point in b in the plan and radius ba, describe an arc to give point a″ on a horizontal line brought over from b. From a′ draw a vertical line upwards to intersect with horizontal lines brought over from a and d in the elevation to give points a′ and d′. a′-b-c-d′ is the developed surface and angle b-a -d′ the bevel to apply across the wide surfaces of the two vertical linings.

The dihedral angle is developed by first finding the true length of the corner a-b. Make a-b-5 a right angle and b-5 equal to the horizontal distance across the linings. a-5 is the true length of a-b. Draw 1-2 at any point so that it is at right angles to a-b. Then with compass point in 3 and the compasses open to just touch a-5, describe an arc to give 4 on a-b. Join 2 and 4 and then 1 and 4 with straight lines. Angle 1-4-2 is the dihedral angle. Angle 1-4-6 is the bevel required.

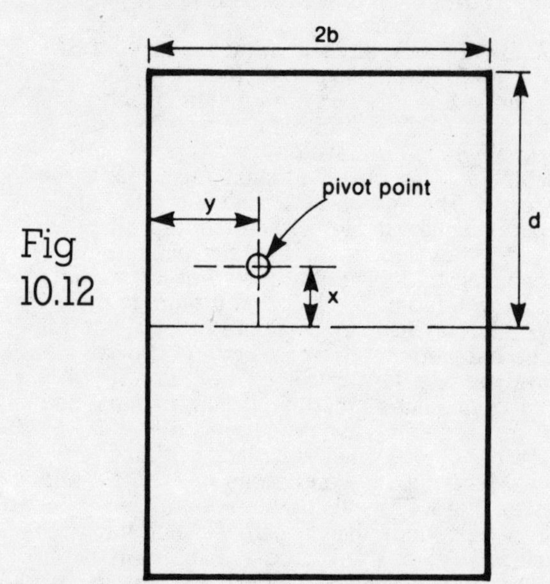

Fig 10.12

Finding the pivot point for a hinged swivelling table top; Fig 10.12.
Distance y equals (2b minus ½d) divided by 2; distance x equals b minus y.

Designing

The Golden Mean (also called variously 'The Golden Rule', 'The Golden Cut', The Golden Section', 'The Divine Proportion'). This is a method of ascertaining the most pleasing and aesthetically satisfying proportions for any artefact, particularly those connected with furniture or architecture. Its origins are lost in antiquity, but it is widely used today by industrial designers and architects (such as le Corbusier, who included the formula in his book *Vers une Architecture* (Towards a New *Architecture).*

The formula, or principle, is that the first part is to the second part as the second part is to the whole or sum of the two parts. It is shown diagrammatically in Fig 10.13A, and the method of dividing any line, no matter what length, in accordance with the formula is shown at (B). Here, the line AC is to be divided according to the Golden Mean; with centre A and radius AC draw a semicircle and extend AC to meet it at Y. At A erect a perpendicular to meet the semicircle at Z; bisect AY at X and with X as centre and XZ as radius draw an arc ZB to meet AC. Then the parts AB and BC accord with the Golden Mean.

As a rule-of-thumb method of applying the principle, we can regard it as being approximately a ratio of 5:8 (five to eight). Thus, if we have a panel 50cm wide and wish to know what length it should be according to the Golden Mean we can make the equation:

5 is to 8 as

50 is to X (which is what we want to know. By cross-multiplying, we arrive at 5X (5 × X) = 400 (8 × 50); therefore X is 80cm.

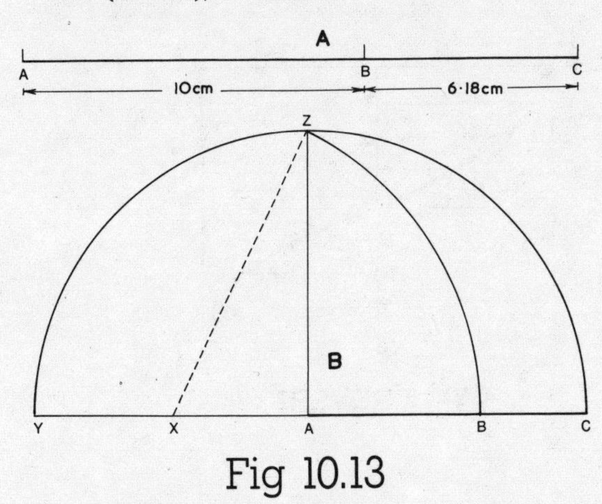

Fig 10.13

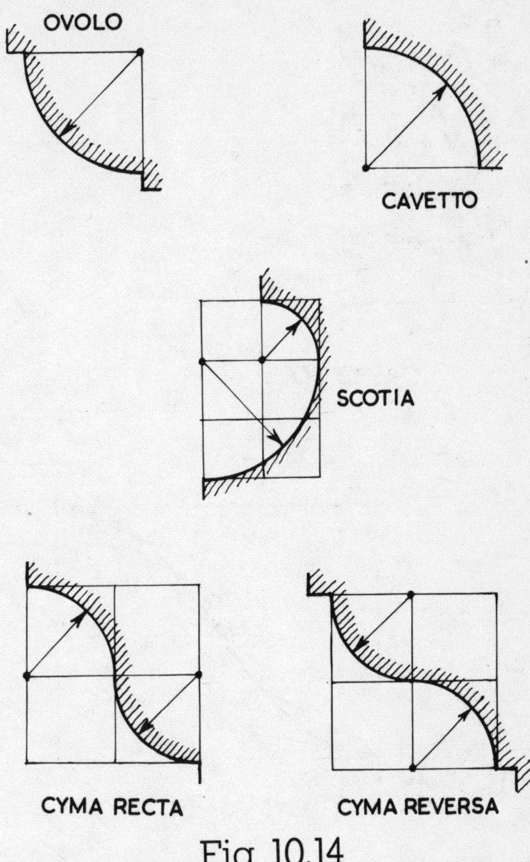

Fig 10.14

Mouldings

There are two distinct methods of plotting curves for classical mouldings – the Roman, and the Greek. They comprise the five principal basic mouldings, namely the Ovolo, the Scotia, the Cavetto, the Cyma Recta, and the Cyma Reversa (both the cymas are also known as 'ogee curves'). All are derived from classical architecture.

Dealing first with the Roman style, their mouldings were based on the square and are shown in Fig 10.14; the methods of plotting are self-explanatory.

The Greeks were enthusiatic geometricians and the profiles of their mouldings were based on conic sections, either elliptical or parabolic, Fig 10.15. The ovolo and the cavetto are mirror images of each other and the same procedure can be used for drawing both as shown. Here, each side of the rectangle ABCD is divided into four parts. Additionally, one of the shorter sides, AD, is extended to E so that AD is equal to DE. Then the point E is used as a centre for a set of radiating lines drawn through the points on the longer side DC; another set of radiating lines is centred on A and joined to the points on the shorter side CB. The intersections of these lines provide the plotting points for the curve.

Plotting the curve of the scotia mouldings is done in a similar way. A parallelogram ABCD is drawn which will contain the profile; next, its size is doubled by extending BA to F so that BA is equal to AF, and extending CD to E so that CD is equal to DE. Join E to F, mark off the halfway point G and draw the bisecting line GH. Next, divide the lines DC, AB as shown and draw in the radiating lines from G and H; the intersections of these lines provide the plotting points for the curve.

The remaining two mouldings, namely the cyma recta and the cyma reversa, are plotted similarly.

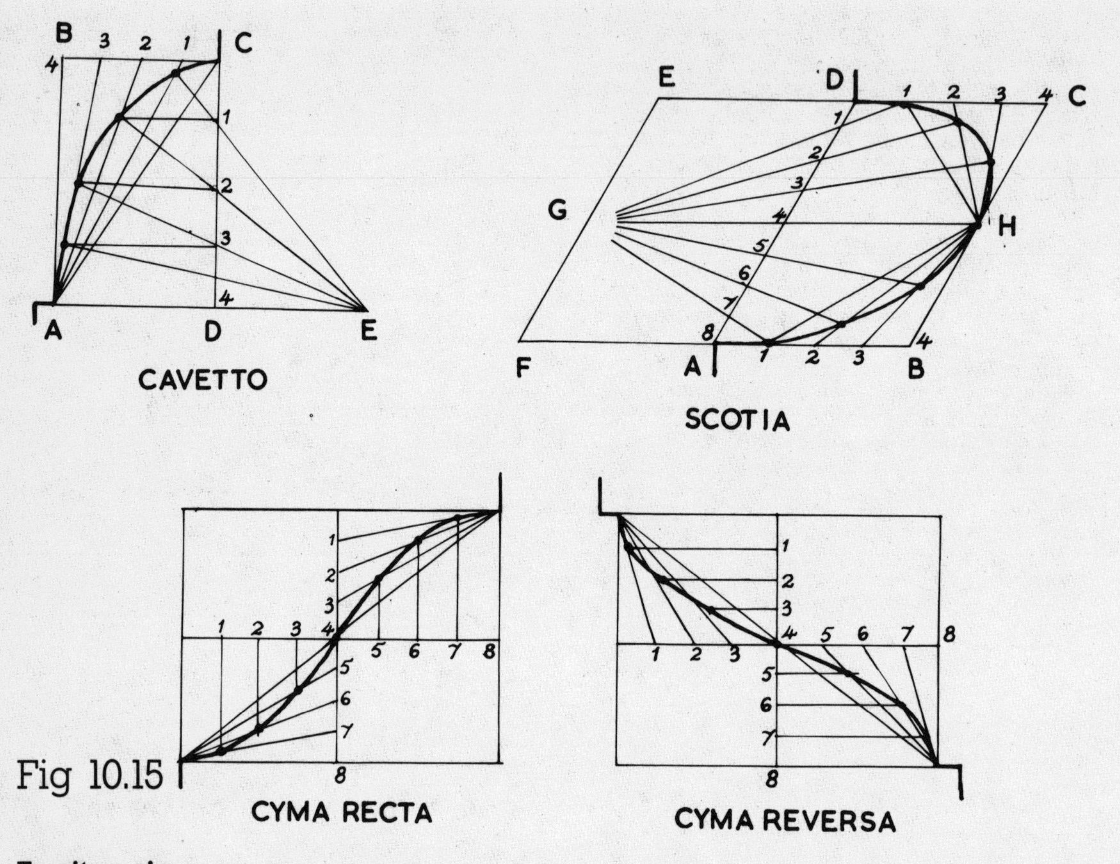

Fig 10.15

Furniture sizes

Fig 10.16 Average sizes of adult males (female sizes shown in brackets). Millimetre dimensions.

Fig 10.17 Recommended sizes for seating furniture and beds. Millimetre dimensions.

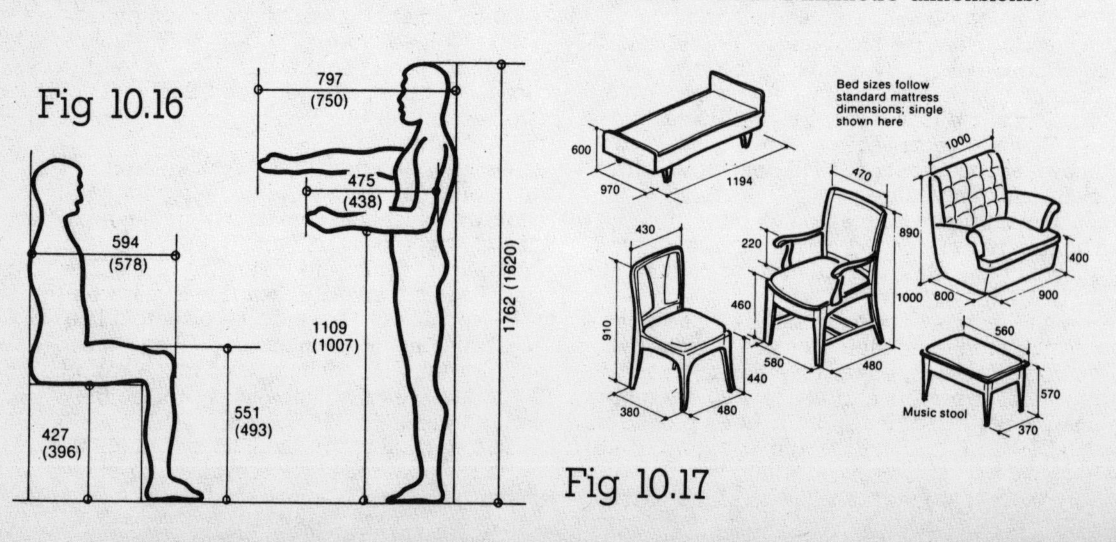

Fig 10.16

Fig 10.17

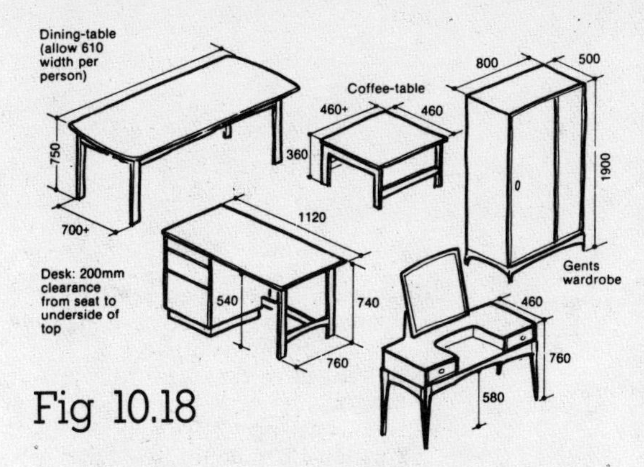

Fig 10.18 Recommended sizes for tables and case furniture. Millimetre dimensions.

Areas

Of a square — two adjacent sides multiplied together.
Of a rectangle (oblong) — one long side multiplied by one short side.
Of a circle — twice (π x radius squared): the circumference = twice (π x radius).
The Greek symbol π = 3.1416 which can be converted to $3\frac{1}{7}$ approx for those who prefer not to use decimals.
Of a cone — multiply half the slant height by the circumference of the base.
Of a right-angled triangle — multiply the height by half the length of the base. Many irregular figures can be divided into right-angled triangles for the purpose of calculating their areas.
Of a cylinder — multiply the area of the base by the height.
Of a cone — multiply one-third the area of the base by the height.

Volumes

Of any rectangular solid — multiply the length by the width by the height.
Of a cylinder (π x the radius squared) × the height.

INDEX